JUN 0 9 2022

YA
ANDERS
FLIGHT
1

Swift
The Fligh

D0901731

"With magic stemming from its vibrant language and enchanted creatures, *Swift* is a spellbinding and delightful fantasy."

— FOREWORD REVIEWS

"An exciting, richly plotted novel... R.J. Anderson adeptly weaves ancient myth with topical questions on the nature of threat and protection in a civilized society."

— BOOKTRUST

"A compelling read and beautifully crafted."

— BIRMINGHAM POST

"A soaring tale about the courage needed to question, to trust—and to fly."

— ROSAMUND HODGE,

New York Times best-selling author of *Cruel Beauty*

"In a writing style reminiscent of Brian Jacques, Anderson brings to life a world full of piskeys, faeries, and spriggans. *Swift* is a coming-of-age tale that will delight readers of all ages. She certainly delighted this booklover!"

— MORGAN L. BUSSE,
award-winning author of the Ravenwood Saga

"An inventive addition to faery lore with a classic fantasy feel. Ivy is a plucky, passionate heroine, and the immersive setting is complemented by a well-rounded cast of characters and a twisty, keeps-you-guessing plot. Charming, gripping, and masterfully told."

— JOANNA RUTH MEYER, author of *Beyond the Shadowed Earth*

"With characters that captivate and a story that intrigues, R. J. Anderson imbues our ordinary world with a sense of magic again."

— CHAWNA SCHROEDER, author of *The Vault Between Spaces*

"*Swift* is charming and beautifully written with an evocative sense of place. While it reads like a throwback to mid-century children's classics, this little book tackles big questions of tradition, prejudice, and tribal loyalty with grace and hope."

— SUZANNAH ROWNTREE, author of Watchers of Outremer

SWIFT

DISCARDED
HURON PUBLIC LIBRARY

Books by R.J. Anderson

No Ordinary Fairy Tale Series

Knife
Rebel
Arrow

Uncommon Magic Series

A Pocket Full of Murder
A Little Taste of Poison

Ultraviolet Series

Ultraviolet
Quicksilver

The Flight and Flame Trilogy

Swift
Nomad
Torch

Ingram 7/15 3/22

SWIFT

THE FLIGHT AND FLAME TRILOGY BOOK 1

R.J. ANDERSON

Swift
Copyright © 2012, 2020 by R.J. Anderson

First published in the UK by Orchard Books (a division of Hachette), London

Published by Enclave Publishing, an imprint of Third Day Books, LLC

Phoenix, Arizona, USA.
www.enclavepublishing.com

All rights reserved. No part of this publication may be reproduced, digitally stored, or transmitted in any form without written permission from Third Day Books, LLC.

This is a work of fiction. Names, characters, places, and incidents are products of the author's imagination or are used fictitiously. Any similarity to actual people, organizations, and/or events is purely coincidental.

ISBN: 978-1-62184-132-6 (hardback)
ISBN: 978-1-62184-134-0 (printed softcover)
ISBN: 978-1-62184-133-3 (ebook)

Cover design by Kirk DouPonce, www.DogEaredDesign.com
Interior design and typesetting by Jamie Foley

Printed in the United States of America.

In memory of my grandmother, Ivy-Mae Menadue
Whose legacy of love and saffron cake still endures

PROLOGUE

"You could always make it *look* as though you had wings," said Jenny, her voice echoing off the granite walls of the treasure cavern. "A little glamour, just for tonight—"

Ivy let the delicate wing-chain slide through her fingers, spilling it back into the chest. "I'm not that good with illusions. Cicely can cast better glamours than me, and she's five." She shut the lid with a snap. "Anyway, why bother? I'm not going to fool anyone."

Jenny looked pained, but did not argue. At thirteen she was already a beauty, with the sturdy bones and warm complexion that all piskeys admired. Her wings were no less striking, all gray-white ripples above and a blush of pink beneath. She didn't need jewelry to make herself look fine.

Ivy, on the other hand, had inherited her mother's pale skin and small, spindly frame. No matter what she wore, Jenny would always outshine her. But Ivy didn't care about that. She wouldn't mind if she were ugly as a spriggan, if only she'd been born with wings like Jenny's.

Or indeed, any wings at all.

Swallowing her envy, Ivy blew the dust off another chest and heaved up the lid. "What are these? Pipes?" But no, they were too shiny for that. Unusually large armbands, perhaps.

"That's armor," said Jenny in hushed tones. "It must be a hundred years old."

Ivy had heard of the ancient battles between the piskeys and their enemies, but she'd never seen armor before. Daring, she slid her arm into one of the guards and held it up to the light. But of course it looked silly on her; it had been meant for a warrior, not a skinny girl-child. She dropped it back into the chest.

"Girls, it's time." The soft voice came from Marigold, Ivy's mother. There were shadows beneath her eyes, and the wan glow of her skin barely lit the archway in which she stood. She'd been working too hard again, no doubt, helping the other women prepare for the feast. "You'll have to hurry."

"I'm done," said Jenny, touching the topaz pendant at her throat. "I was just helping Ivy a bit." She nudged the younger girl affectionately. "I'll see you later."

Marigold stepped aside to let Jenny pass, then moved to Ivy. "What's the matter?" she asked. "I thought you'd like to pick out something special to wear to your first Lighting. Do you want me to help?"

Her mother meant well, Ivy knew. But her tastes ran to the pink and glittery, and that wouldn't suit Ivy at all. "No, it's all right," she said. "I'll find something next time."

She expected Marigold to lead the way out, but instead her mother lingered, fingering Ivy's black curls. "You've grown so much these past few months," she murmured. "My little woman. Are you frightened to go above?"

"Not really," said Ivy, truthfully. She had made Jenny tell her everything she could remember about her first two Lightings, so she would know what to expect and no one could trick or scare her. It was her only defense against her brother Mica and the other piskey-boys, who would be trying all night to catch her in their pranks.

"Not afraid of anything?" asked her mother. "Not even the—" Her voice caught. "The spriggans?"

No wonder people said Ivy's mother was flighty. She was always worrying these days, even when there was nothing to fear. "They won't come," said Ivy. "Not with Aunt Betony to protect us." Betony, her father's sister, held the title of Joan the Wad—the most powerful, important piskey in the Delve. It was her responsibility to surround the Lighting with wards and glamours to keep out intruders, and Betony never did anything carelessly.

Ivy picked up the trailing end of Marigold's shawl and draped it over her mother's shoulder. "We can go now," she said. "I'm ready."

As Ivy followed her mother through the tunnels toward the surface, she was glad for the lights of her fellow piskeys heading in the same direction. Not that she was afraid of losing her way even in the dark, for Ivy knew most of the Delve's twists and turnings by now. But the tunnels were magnificent, and it would have been a shame not to see them.

Every passage carved by the piskey miners—or knockers—was unique, from the polished granite of Long Way where Ivy's family lived, to the delicate mosaics of plants and animals on the walls of Upper Rise, where she and the other children sat for lessons. But Ivy's favorite tunnel was the one they were walking through now, lined with tiles of deep blue china clay. Her father had told her once that it was the color of the sky, and when no one was watching her, Ivy would run through it with her arms outstretched and pretend that she was flying.

Which was what Jenny and the other girls would soon be

doing—spreading their wings and launching themselves up the crude but useful shaft that the humans had dug long ago, before the mine was abandoned and the piskeys moved in. The Great Shaft was the quickest route out of the mine, and if it weren't for Ivy, Marigold would have flown to the Lighting that way herself. But now the two of them could only plod through the tunnels to the surface, like the men.

Humiliation curdled in Ivy's stomach. What crime had she or her parents committed, that she'd been born wingless? Her magic might not be as strong as some piskeys', but it was good enough: she could make herself tall as a human or tiny as a mole, even turn herself invisible if she didn't mind a bit of a headache afterward. But something had gone wrong with Ivy's making while she was still unborn, and she'd come out with nothing but a pair of bony nubs between her shoulders where her wings should be. And neither Yarrow's healing potions nor the Joan's most powerful spells could change that.

Though not long ago, Ivy's mother had said something about her own wings not being right when she was young... or had that been a dream? Ivy had been struggling all day to remember, but every time she tried her head began to swim.

Perhaps she was just tired. After all, she'd been looking forward to the Lighting so much, she'd hardly slept.

"We're almost there," whispered Marigold, taking Ivy's hand. After the twisting bends of the Narrows and a climb up the Hunter's Stair, they had reached the Earthenbore, a tunnel of packed clay baked to hardness by the power of the Joan herself. Ivy had never been this close to the surface before, and her pulse quickened as she followed the other piskeys into the passage.

At the first junction they turned right and began to climb again, the tunnel narrowing and the floor rising steeply as they neared the exit. The air smelled earthy, sweet with heather and bracken and the scent of blossoming gorse—plants that until now Ivy had only ever seen cut and tied in bundles. What would it be like to walk among them, see them living and growing? It was hard to imagine, but in a moment she wouldn't have to. She would know.

"Look at her big eyes," snickered one of the younger piskey-boys, nudging his companion, and Ivy stiffened. Just like Keeve to tease her at a time like this. He'd be calling her *Creeping Ivy* next.

"Ivy's always got big eyes," said the taller boy, elbowing him back. "Shut your mouth." He glanced at Ivy and gave her a shy half-smile before ducking out the archway into the night.

And that was just like Mattock, always looking out for the younger ones. She thought of her little sister Cicely, tucked into her bed with a sleeping-spell that would keep her there until morning. Last year Ivy had been just as oblivious to the celebrations taking place above her head, but it was her time now. She would not cling to her mother, like a baby; she would step out boldly, as the others were doing. Ivy pulled her hand free of Marigold's, plunged forward...

And with a crackle of undergrowth and a last wild thump of her heart, Ivy was outside.

As she stepped out onto the surface of the world, the scrubby grass crunched beneath her feet, and a dry rustling filled her ears as the breeze—the first she had ever felt—stirred the gorse and bracken that surrounded the tunnel entrance. Underground the air was still, but here it danced around her, teasing and tugging her from every side. She turned a slow circle, trying to accustom herself to the strangeness of it. Then she looked up—and her mouth fell open in awe.

Jenny had tried to describe the sky to her, and she'd heard the droll-teller mention it in his stories. But what words could capture the grandeur of a roof that stretched out forever, too high for even the mightiest giant of legend to touch? It should have terrified Ivy to stand beneath that vast purple darkness, with the innumerable stars burning white-hot above her and the moon like a crucible of molten silver. But it only made her feel quiet and very, very small.

Then there was the landscape, just visible beyond the patches of waving bracken and bristling tufts of gorse that walled her in. It had no walls to contain it, only a few scattered outcroppings of rock. And those square shapes in the distance... could they be human dwellings? Even at piskey size—about half the height of a grown man's knee, or so the droll-teller claimed—Ivy could have walked to one of those houses.

"Come," said Marigold, taking Ivy's arm. "We mustn't keep the others waiting."

The old Engine House stood at the top of the slope, its broken chimney jutting into the sky. Even after a century of neglect its walls held strong, but the roof had crumbled long ago. Two of its windows still gaped like empty sockets, but the others were smothered in a mass of the same plant that had given Ivy her name. From a distance the ruined mine building looked desolate, even haunted.

But that was an illusion, meant to keep intruders away. In reality the place was anything but neglected, for the piskeys of the Delve had been using it as their feasting and dancing ground for decades. They'd piled rocks and soil beneath the doorway to make it easy for small people to enter, and smoothed out the precipitous drop in the floor. Now the Engine House was filled with light and festivity, as the piskeys of the Delve bustled about setting up chairs and laying the tables. On the far side of the dancing green her father Flint was tuning his fiddle, while Mica and the other piskey-boys played a game of hunt-the-spriggan around the pile of wood that would soon become their wakefire.

"I'm going to talk to Nettle," said Marigold, clutching her shawl tighter about her shoulders. "Jenny's over there; why don't you go see her?"

"I will in a minute," said Ivy, surprised. Usually Marigold stayed close to Ivy when there was a crowd, in case she felt sick or needed anything. But perhaps her mother had finally understood what Ivy had been telling her for months—that she could manage perfectly well on her own, and there was no need to fuss over her.

She watched her mother make her way to the bench where most of the older piskeys were sitting, chatting comfortably to one another. What would Marigold want with Nettle? The old woman had attended the previous Joan and managed to outlive her, and now she waited on Betony. But other than that, Ivy knew little about her.

"Boo!" yelled a voice, and Ivy let out a shriek as Keeve leaped in front of her. "Got you!" he said, grinning.

Disgusted, Ivy pushed him away and headed toward Jenny. But Keeve affected a wounded expression and fell into step beside her.

"I just wanted you to notice me, that's all," he said. "Pretty Ivy, won't you dance with me tonight?"

Ivy faltered. The wicked glint in Keeve's eye had vanished, and his expression was earnest as she'd ever seen it. "Do you... you don't really mean that, do you?" she asked.

Keeve chortled. "Got you again!" he said, and scampered off.

Ivy ground her teeth. Most piskeys loved pranking, especially the younger ones—and especially on nights like this, when the one who played the most successful pranks would win a prize. But she'd never liked trickery, and she wished her fellow piskeys would leave her out of it.

"There you are," said Mica, jogging up to her. He was growing broad and strong like their father, his black hair thick over his forehead and his eyes dark as tin ore. "Did you see the giant?" He pulled Ivy to the doorway and pointed into the distance, where a pair of baleful lights swept the landscape. "See his eyes glowing? He's looking for piskeys to eat..."

"Oh, no!" Ivy exclaimed in mock horror. "And let me guess—those flashing lights overhead? They must be wicked faeries spying on us!"

Mica scowled. "Jenny told you."

"Well," said Ivy, "it's not my fault you play the same trick every year."

Her older brother sighed. "Fine. You know what those lights are, then?"

"Human things," she replied. Not that she'd ever seen a car or an airplane, or had any idea how they worked. But everyone knew that there was nothing to fear from the Big People; most of them didn't even believe in piskeys any more.

"Keeve and I have a bet on," said Mica. "He says as soon as he becomes a hunter, he's going to disguise himself as a human and get a ride in one of those cars. I told him they'll never stop for him, but he thinks all he has to do is—"

"All gather for the Lighting!" bellowed a voice, and the conversation ended as Ivy and Mica hurried to find a seat. Mica wriggled in between Keeve and Mattock, while Jenny patted the bench beside her and leaned close as Ivy sat down.

"Wait until you see this," she whispered, nodding at the far side of the circle where the Joan stood with her consort Gossan by her side. "I still can't believe she's your *aunt.*"

Betony was a strongly built woman with hair as black as Ivy's, though longer and not so curly, and their kinship was evident in the angles of her cheekbones, her pointed chin. With grave dignity she extended her arms over the woodpile...

And flames exploded from her hands.

Ivy jerked back in shock, nearly upsetting the bench. She'd known that the Joan would light the wakefire, but she'd never expected her to do it like this. Jenny patted her shoulder in reassurance as Betony lowered her blazing palms to touch the kindling. The twigs glowed bright as molten copper, and instantly the whole heap of wood sprang alight.

"All hail!" shouted the piskeys. "Hail Joan the Wad!"

Wad was the old Cornish word for *torch*, and until now Ivy had thought it just a fancy title. But her aunt could literally conjure fire from the air. "You never told me," she said, turning reproachful eyes on Jenny.

"Of course not," replied the older girl, undaunted. "Surely you didn't want me to ruin *all* the surprises for you?"

Around them, the other piskeys were moving closer to the fire—not for warmth, but for light. This was their chance to replenish their skin's natural luminescence, which would serve them better than any lamp in the dark tunnels underground. As Ivy rose to join them a tingle ran over her body, and her lips curved in a proud smile. Now she too would glow when she returned to the Delve, and she could go anywhere she wanted.

Where was her mother? She should be here, sharing this special moment. On the other side of the wakefire, her father Flint nodded and returned Ivy's smile—but Marigold was nowhere to be seen. Was she still talking to Nettle? No, Nettle was with the Joan, pouring piskey-wine into a bowl for the next part of the ceremony.

Maybe Ivy's mother had forgotten something, and gone back underground to fetch it. Perhaps she just wanted to make sure Cicely was safely asleep. After all, she'd seen the Lighting many times before, and the fire would burn all night. Telling herself it was childish to feel hurt about it, Ivy returned to her seat.

The rest of the evening passed in a blur, one magical moment dissolving into another. Ivy ate and drank and laughed with Jenny, watched the dancers whirl and leap to the music of her father's fiddle, and basked in the light of the wakefire until her skin could hold no more. Finally she tumbled down by the old droll-teller's feet with the other children, and lay half-drowsing while he told stories.

As usual, the tales revolved around a single theme: how clever piskeys of the past had outwitted their enemies. The first story was about a foolish human miner who tried to trick the knockers out of their treasure and ended up with nothing but a sore knee—all the children laughed at that. Then came the tale of a faery who met a wandering piskey-lad and tried to lure him into marrying her, a dark and sinister tale that made Ivy hold her breath. But fortunately, the boy saw past the faery's pretty face to her cold heart and escaped.

"Yet wickedest and most deadly of all," said the droll-teller, bending close as though telling a secret, "are the spriggans."

The younger children squirmed and cast uneasy glances at the doorway as the droll-teller went on, "Like us, spriggans can change their size at will, and they love to play magical tricks. But they're the ugliest, most maggoty-pale creatures you can imagine, and all their pranks are cruel."

It wasn't the first time Ivy had heard of spriggans, but still the description made her shudder. She could picture them lurking in the darkness all around the Engine House, rag-wrapped monsters with glittering eyes and long bony fingers, waiting for the first careless piskey to pass by. And not only to frighten them, either. Her father had told her that spriggans were hungry all the time and would eat anything—or any*one*—they could catch.

"Spriggans love treasure," the droll-teller continued, "but they're too lazy to dig for it. So in the old days when we piskeys lived on the surface, the spriggans would wait until the knockers went off to work in the mine—and then they'd attack." His voice dropped to a dramatic whisper. "They'd kill the guards and the old uncles and even the youngest boy-children, and cast a spell over all the women that would make them think the spriggans were their own menfolk. Then they'd settle in to feast and gloat over their stolen treasures."

Ivy's nose wrinkled in revulsion. It was horrible to think of being eaten, but to be tricked into living with a spriggan as your husband was even worse. She was wondering how such a dreadful tale could end happily when Mattock spoke up from the back of the crowd:

"But then the knockers would come home and find the spriggans there. Wouldn't they?"

"They would, indeed," said the droll-teller. "Tired as they were, they'd pick up their hammers and their thunder-axes and fight. Most often they won, because a good knocker is braver than three spriggans put together. But even once all the spriggans had been killed, their evil spells were so strong that the knockers' wives and daughters didn't recognize their own menfolk any more. Instead they'd weep and wail over the ugly spriggans—and accuse the knockers of being wicked instead!"

The girl beside Ivy whimpered and hid her face in her hands. Ivy didn't feel like crying, but she did feel a little queasy. She was glad when Mattock raised his voice again: "But the spell would wear off in a few days, isn't that right?"

By then the droll-teller seemed to realize he'd gone too far. He patted the weeping child and said, "Yes, surely it would. No magic lasts forever, after all. But it wasn't long before some of the piskeys decided they'd had enough of that nonsense, and that it was time to make a safe home deep in the rock and earth, where enemies were too cowardly to follow. And that's how the Delve came to be."

He smiled and sat back, as though this was the happy ending. But Ivy wasn't satisfied yet. "What about the other piskeys?" she asked. "The ones who didn't go to the Delve?"

"The spriggans went on attacking them," said the droll-teller, "just as before. But now those other piskeys only won the battle sometimes, and before long they hardly won at all. They were too proud to ask the folk in the Delve for help, you see. So they fought alone, and many died. But whenever our people heard of a piskey village coming to grief, we sent our bravest fighters to rescue the women and children and offer them a place with us. So the Delve grew and the other clans became smaller, until we were the only piskeys left in all Kernow."

On the far side of the circle Mica sat up eagerly, as though he could hardly wait to become a hunter and fight spriggans. Mattock looked solemn and a little troubled. Keeve, on the other hand, appeared to have fallen asleep—but that was no great surprise, since the droll-teller was his grandfather and he must have heard these tales a hundred times.

The droll-teller launched into another tale, but by now Ivy was too tired to enjoy it. She scanned the crowd for her mother, but there was no sign of her. And now her father had gone missing as well, for his chair was empty and his fiddle propped idle against the wall.

"Mica," she whispered to her brother. "I'm going back to the cavern."

"What for? It's not nearly daybreak."

"I want to make sure Cicely's all right." And their mother too, though Ivy didn't say it. Something serious must have happened to keep Marigold away so long.

"Well, you can't go now," said Mica. "You'll have to wait for the rest of us."

Much as it galled Ivy, he was right. The closest entrance to the Earthenbore was down the hillside, too far for a child to go alone. And it was no use asking Mica or Mattock to go with her; they hadn't even got their hunter's knives yet, let alone learned to use them. Sighing, Ivy leaned on a jutting stone and pillowed her head on her elbow. She had slipped into a doze when a cry from the other side of the Engine House startled her awake. Was that her *father* shouting?

Mica was on his feet and running, pushing through the crowd. The music had stopped and all the dancers stood frozen, staring at the doorway. There stood Flint, his hair disheveled and his face a mask of anguish, cradling a bundle of fabric against his chest. He stumbled forward and dropped to his knees.

Ivy scrambled over the green and flung herself down beside him. "Dad, what is it? What's wrong?" Then she saw the cloth that her father was holding. It was, unmistakably, her mother's shawl—but now the pink roses were splotched with ugly gouts of red, and one corner was in tatters.

"Stand back," commanded Betony, and the crowd parted to let the Joan through. She swept Ivy and Mica aside and stooped over her brother. Then she straightened, her expression grim.

"The Lighting is over," she said. "Everyone into the Delve. Now."

At once the piskeys scattered, abandoning half-finished plates and cups of wine, gaming boards, musical instruments, and even shoes and jackets in their haste. Shouts of "Hurry!" and "Go!" rang through the night, as the knockers seized their thunder-axes and the hunters drew their knives. Mica grabbed Ivy's arm, but she struggled against his hold, crying, "Dad!"

"Don't be stupid," snapped Mica, dragging her to the doorway. "The Joan will look after him. Come on!"

Ivy stumbled out onto the hillside, eyes wet and burning. "Mum," she sobbed, but there was no answer—and though it tore at her heart, she knew why.

Her mother had been taken by the spriggans.

1

SIX YEARS LATER

Ivy stood poised on her toes like a dancer, but there was no merriment in her face as she pulled the iron poker from its rack by the hearth and raised it high. A few paces away, a black adder as long as she was tall squirmed across the cavern floor, blood oozing from the gash that should have killed it—but hadn't.

Why hadn't Mica cut the snake's head off before he brought it down from the surface? He'd been hunting for five years now; he should have known better. But he'd been in such a hurry to get to tonight's Lighting, he'd merely tossed his catch through the cavern door and left his sisters to deal with it. And worse, he hadn't even tied the sack tight, so Ivy had to finish off the adder herself.

There was no use shouting for help. Not that her neighbors wouldn't be willing—they'd always been glad to lend a hand, whenever Ivy could swallow her pride enough to ask for it. But by now even the last stragglers had left their caverns and were hurrying for the surface. In fact, if this wretched snake hadn't poked its head out as Ivy was getting dressed, she and Cicely would be running right along with them.

"Oh, Ivy, hurry!" Her little sister crouched at the edge of

her bed-alcove, only her head poking between the curtains. "We're going to be late!"

"Stay where you are, Cicely," warned Ivy, edging closer to the snake. "I'll be done in a minute."

Mind calm and hands steady, that was the way. She mustn't think about what would happen if the snake bit her; she had to strike as quickly as she could. The wedge-shaped head turned toward her, tongue flickering out to taste the air—

And with one savage two-handed blow, Ivy smashed the poker down.

The adder's body whipped into a frenzy, lashing so fast its tail nearly knocked Ivy off her feet. She leaped back, holding the poker ready for another strike. But the convulsions subsided, and Ivy let out her breath. The snake was dead.

"You can come out now," she said to Cicely, dropping the poker with a clang. The floor was a mess and the adder meat would spoil if she left it sitting, but there was no time to fret about that now. "Let me change, and we'll go."

"It's no use," moaned Cicely, knuckling her eyes. "We'll never get through the tunnels in time."

"We're not going through the tunnels," Ivy said, pulling up her breeches. The dress she'd been sewing for months hung by her bed, but she could hardly climb in that. "I know a faster way. Come on."

"Please hurry!" Cicely hovered next to Ivy, her dappled wings fluttering with agitation. "They'll be lighting the wakefire any minute, and Jenny says that's the best part!"

Ivy dug her fingers into the rock, hauling herself up the side of the Great Shaft with stubborn will. She didn't pause to explain that she was climbing as fast as she could; excuses were for the lazy, or so Aunt Betony always said.

Though if it hadn't been for Mica's carelessness, she'd have got Cicely to her first Lighting in plenty of time and found her a good seat into the bargain. But if brooding over what *should* have been made any difference, Ivy would have sprouted wings long ago. She set her jaw and kept climbing.

"It's not fair," wailed Cicely, as sounds of music and laughter drifted down from above. "Ivy, let me go ahead, I don't need light, there's plenty of room—"

"You can't fly the shaft blind," said Ivy firmly. True, compared to the piskeys' own tunnels the Great Shaft was enormous. But there was a cap of concrete and metal over the top, and if Cicely didn't see it coming she'd knock herself senseless. "When you've got your own glow, you can fly where you want. But right now, you stay with me."

Cicely whimpered, but made no further protest. Ivy reached for a grip and pulled herself up again, muscles trembling with the effort. By rights she shouldn't be climbing the Great Shaft at all, and if anyone found out she'd be in serious trouble. But the tunnels would have taken twice as long, even if she and Cicely were running. And it gave Ivy a private thrill to know that she alone, of all the piskeys in the Delve, *could* climb like this.

Her groping fingers brushed wood, slimy and rough with age. She had reached the old ladder. Ivy hooked one arm over the bottom rung and gazed up at the half-rotted wood and rusted metal, chewing her lip in consideration. Once this ladder had carried human miners down the shaft to their day's work. Then the tin mine had closed, and its shafts were caged off to keep careless humans from falling in. Now and then some idle passerby shoved a stick or a stone between the bars and let it drop, but no one had used this ladder in well over a century. If she made herself human size to climb it, would it hold her weight?

She'd soon find out. Ivy took a deep breath, and willed herself to grow.

It would have been easier if she'd practiced first. The shift in size threw her off balance, and she grabbed the next rung just in time. But she had no time to waste on panic. The moment her body stopped tingling she was on the move, scrambling for the top of the shaft. "We're nearly there," she gasped to Cicely. "It's not too—"

"All hail Joan the Wad!" came a muffled shout from above them, and the top of the shaft flared with golden light. Cicely's face crumpled. "We missed it."

Guilt and frustration tumbled like rocks in Ivy's stomach. There'd be another Lighting at midwinter, but what consolation was that to Cicely now? Mica was to blame but he'd never admit it, and Cicely would never dream of reproaching him. Not the older brother who brought her berries and bits of honeycomb, and gave her piskey-back rides around the cavern. In Cicely's eyes, Mica could do no wrong.

"Well," said Ivy, but she couldn't think of anything else to say. She reached for the next rung, and kept climbing.

"People of the Delve, be welcome," Betony declared, with a disapproving glance at Ivy as she and Cicely crept in at the back of the crowd. She took the copper bowl from Nettle's hands and raised it high for everyone around the wakefire to see.

"This is the draught of harmony," she declared. "Let us drink and be one in heart, proud of our heritage and true to our ancient ways, so that enemies can never divide us. A blessing on the Delve, and a curse on faeries and spriggans!"

"A curse on faeries and spriggans!" the others chorused—and Ivy loudest of all. The very mention of those filthy creatures made her burn inside, an ember of bitterness that would never go out. First they had taken her mother from her, and if that weren't bad enough, they had stolen her father as well.

Or they might as well have. After Marigold disappeared Flint had spent days blindly searching the countryside, until the Joan took away his hunting privileges and confined him to the Delve for his own safety. Since then he had done little but work in the diggings, hammering away night and day with his thunder-axe. He seldom spoke, and never laughed; he ate the food Ivy cooked for him without seeming to taste it, and slept poorly if he slept at all. He still came to every Lighting, but only long enough to replenish his glow. And he never played his fiddle any more.

"Curse them," Ivy whispered, but Cicely remained silent, eyes on her lap. Guilt pricked Ivy again, and she gave her sister an apologetic squeeze before reaching for the copper bowl making its way around the circle. The draught inside was clear as spring water, sparkling lights dancing across its surface; Ivy tipped the bowl and drank a mouthful before helping Cicely to do the same.

"Oh, it's *wonderful,*" breathed her little sister, surfacing with flushed cheeks and wide brown eyes. "I had no idea piskey-wine was so nice. Can I—"

"Not until you're older," said Ivy, and handed the bowl on. Cicely's lower lip jutted, but she looked less gloomy as the drink passed from one piskey to another and finally back to Betony, who poured the dregs hissing into the fire.

"And now," the Joan proclaimed, "let us eat!"

Ivy and Cicely jumped up, following the other piskeys toward the long tables. All Ivy's favorite dishes were here tonight—from pasties stuffed with rabbit and chopped roots, to roasted woodlice with wild garlic, right down to the thick slabs of saffron cake waiting at the far end. To drink there was spring water and chilled mint tea, as well as several bottles of the sparkling piskey-wine—though it would be another season before Ivy was old enough to drink more than a small cup, and Cicely was too young to have any more at all. But that scarcely mattered with so many good things to enjoy.

As they ate, Ivy was relieved to see Cicely's mood improving with every bite. Soon she was giggling at the faces Keeve made at her across the table, and Ivy's own spirits began to rise as she realized she hadn't entirely spoiled her sister's first Lighting after all.

But then Mica strolled by, and her smile faded. There he was, relaxed and dressed in his Lighting best—and here Ivy sat with dirty breeches and bare feet. The old aunties gave her pitying looks, and she knew what they must be thinking: *What a shame young Ivy can't take proper care of herself, especially when her brother and sister look so fine. But she's always been sickly, and with no mother...*

"What's the matter?" asked Cicely around a mouthful of saffron cake. "You look like you've eaten gravel."

"Never mind," said Ivy. "It's nothing you need to worry about."

"One-two-three-four!" called the crowder, and the musicians struck up a lively tune that twanged Ivy's muscles and tugged at her bones. As a child, she'd been too shy and short of breath to dance in public. Even when all the other children were skipping about, she'd hung back and pretended she didn't care. But Marigold had seen through her diffidence, and as soon as they got home she'd held Ivy's hands and skipped around the cavern with her until the two of them collapsed in a giggling heap on the floor.

Marigold hadn't worried so much about Ivy's health in those days; she'd told Ivy that her lungs were just a little slower to grow than the rest of her, and they'd soon come right. And she'd promised Ivy that one day she'd be able to dance as well as any piskey in the Delve, if not better.

Well, now Ivy could. But not to this tune. This was a flying dance, where the males tossed the females high in the air and stepped aside as their partners glided down, and Ivy couldn't have taken part even if someone asked her. She walked to Cicely, who was watching the dancers with the same wistful longing, and sat down by her side.

"What is it?" she asked. "Don't you want to dance?"

"I don't have a partner," said Cicely glumly. "And it's already started."

Ivy jumped up and thrust out both her hands. "Then dance with me," she said.

"Me and you? But you're—"

"Stronger than I look," said Ivy, grabbing her little sister under both arms and heaving her into the air. Cicely let out a giggle, her moth-wings fluttering as she drifted back to earth—only to have Ivy whirl her around and toss her up again. Lifting her sister wasn't as easy as she pretended; Cicely was on the sturdy side, and Ivy's muscles already ached from climbing up the shaft. But it was worth the effort to see those brown eyes sparkle, and hear Cicely's squeal of delight.

When the Flying Dance ended another merry reel took its place, and Ivy and Cicely kept dancing. The two of them whirled arm in arm, Cicely tripping over her own feet with laughter, until Ivy was exhausted.

"I'm done," she gasped, waving a hand. "I've got to sit down."

"Me too," said Cicely, collapsing beside her with a happy

sigh. Then she sat up and said, "Is that the moon? I thought it was supposed to be round."

Well, at least she wasn't terrified. Ivy had seen more than a few piskey-girls shriek and hide their faces at their first glimpse of the night sky. "It is, sometimes," said Ivy.

"It's beautiful anyway," Cicely said. She ran a hand over the moss-covered stones. "Everything out here's soft, and smells so good. I wish..."

"What?" asked Ivy, with a distracted glance over her shoulder. The place where her wings ought to be had tingled, as though someone were watching her. But the only thing behind them was the fire, and the benches around it were empty.

"I wish we could do this all the time."

Ivy gave a short laugh. "Do you have any idea how much work goes into a Lighting?"

"I don't mean that." Cicely tugged a loose thread on her skirt. "I mean... being here. Up above. The boys get to when they're old enough, so why can't we?" But before Ivy could answer she made a face and said, "I know. Because of the *spriggans.*"

Gooseflesh rippled over Ivy's skin. Had someone pranked her little sister into thinking spriggans weren't real? "Cicely," she said, fighting for calm, "you know what happened to our mother."

"I know she disappeared," said Cicely. "And all Dad ever found was her shawl. But have you *seen* a spriggan? Has anybody? How do we know they took her, and not... something else?"

"Like what? Giants?" Ivy frowned. "Those are just stories, Cicely."

"No, not that. I mean maybe..." Her eyes slid to the doorway and the darkness beyond. "Maybe she didn't want to be with us any more."

Ivy choked. *"No,"* she said fiercely, when she could speak.

"She would never have left us like that. And spriggans are real, whether anyone's seen one lately or not. Who put these ridiculous ideas in your head?"

"He didn't mean to," said Cicely, shrinking back. "I overheard him and Mattock talking, when they thought I was asleep—"

Fury scorched through Ivy, and she leaped to her feet. "Stay here," she told her sister, and stalked off to look for Mica. Her eyes raked the crowd until she spotted him by the far wall, one arm braced not quite casually against the stone as he tried to coax one of the older girls to dance.

"We need to talk right now," Ivy said as she stepped between Mica and his would-be partner, who gave a nervous titter. "Shall we go somewhere private, or do you want me to shout at you in front of everyone?"

Mica looked startled, but then his expression hardened. He grabbed Ivy's arm and pulled her out into the night.

"Are you mad?" exclaimed Ivy, twisting against his grip. "We're not supposed to leave the Engine House!"

"You're safe enough with me," said Mica. He marched her to the bottom of the slope, then let her go. "All right, we're private. What now?"

"You!" Ivy shoved him as hard as she could, too angry to care that he barely moved. "How dare you tell Cicely that our mother left us on purpose? How could you be so stupid?"

"I didn't tell her that!"

"Maybe not, but you said it where she could hear you. Or are you going to deny that too?"

Mica folded his arms and looked away.

"You disgust me," said Ivy. "You never think about other people at all, do you? You get some slurry-brained idea in your head and you have to blather it to Mattock, no matter who might be listening. And if spilling dross about our mother wasn't bad enough—"

"I wasn't spilling—"

"Now Cicely thinks there's no reason to stay in the Delve, because spriggans don't really exist!"

That struck a vein, if nothing else did. Mica paled, and now he looked worried—even frightened. "All right," he said. "I'll talk to her. First thing tomorrow."

"Good," said Ivy grimly.

"But I'm not going to lie to her."

"Nobody asked you to lie!" Which was a good thing, because most piskeys could only tell a direct untruth if they were joking, and this was no laughing matter. "I'm asking you to stop being so careless, and take some responsibility for a change!"

"Responsibility?" Mica snorted, color flooding back into his face. "That's a fine speech from someone who showed up late, dressed in dirt and patches!"

"I wouldn't have been late if you hadn't chucked a live adder through the door! What was I supposed to do, walk off and leave it there?"

"Adder?" Mica's shock was convincing, as was the look of dawning fury that followed it. But Ivy wasn't about to be distracted. "And I wasn't the only one who ended up late. Cicely missed the start of the wakefire, because of you. So don't—" She broke off, startled, as her brother shoved past her. "Where are you going? Mica!"

But her brother was sprinting up the path, bellowing, "Keeve, you little spriggan! I'll wring your neck!" And before Ivy could call him back, he vanished inside the Engine House.

Ivy stared after him, appalled. He'd left her alone on the darkened hillside, well outside the circle of the Joan's protective spells. How could even Mica be so reckless?

Still, the night seemed peaceful. Surely there was no need to call for help—that would only give her fellow piskeys more excuse to pity her. All she had to do was walk up the slope. It wasn't that far.

Yet she'd only taken a step when her spine prickled with the same feeling she'd had in the Engine House, of being watched by unseen eyes. Her stomach knotted as she remembered how her mother had disappeared, how no one noticed until it was too late...

Ivy blew out an exasperated breath. This was ridiculous. She wasn't weak or helpless; she'd faced down an adder and won. There probably weren't any spriggans lurking, but even if there were a thousand, she wouldn't give them the satisfaction of seeing her panic. She squared her shoulders and started up the path.

"Ivy," said a voice behind her.

She started, then relaxed. So Mica hadn't left her alone after all. There was another piskey out here, probably one of the wood-gatherers or water-carriers for the Lighting, and they could walk back to the Engine House together. She turned, ready to greet him—but the words died on her lips.

It was too big for a piskey and too small to be human, a spidery figure wrapped in dark clothing. It wore a hood, no doubt ashamed of its hideous features, but no shadow could hide the sickly pallor of its skin, or the hunger in those glittering eyes.

Spriggan.

2

If Ivy had wings, she might have been tempted to risk everything on a dash for the Engine House. But though she was quick on her feet, she wasn't sure she could outrun a spriggan. Especially since he'd crept up behind her so stealthily that she'd never heard him coming—if he could do that, there was no knowing what else he could do.

Ivy took a step backward, feeling the dirt crumble beneath her bare feet. She was acutely aware of the hairs standing up on the nape of her neck, the *boom-boom-boom* of her heartbeat, the stench of her own cold sweat. "How—" Her voice wavered. "How do you know my name?"

The spriggan moved closer, teeth gleaming in the shadow beneath his hood. "That's good," he said. "I didn't even have to warn you not to scream. I think we're going to get along very well."

The amusement in his tone made Ivy feel sick. She could smell him now, a sharp dry scent like fir needles, and all her instincts screamed at her to turn invisible. But what good would that do? He'd still be able to hear her, and probably smell her as well. She retreated another step, groping with her toes for a loose stone, or a clump of soil. Anything that might hurt him, distract him, buy her a few precious seconds to escape—

"Ivy!" came a shout from up the slope, and the spriggan hissed a curse and darted away. Sagging with relief, Ivy turned to find Mattock sprinting down to her, hair gleaming copper in the light of their shared glow.

"Are you all right?" he exclaimed. "When Mica came back without you, I knew something was wrong. But I didn't expect to find you all the way down here!" He seized her by the shoulders and gave her a shake. "What were you thinking?"

She'd nearly been caught by a spriggan, and he was giving *her* a lecture? Indignant, Ivy smacked him. Then she jabbed a finger in the direction the spriggan had gone.

But the slope was empty, the heather and bracken undisturbed. The only sign of life was a tiny bird, fluttering off into the night.

"I know what I saw," Ivy insisted as she and Mattock headed back to the Engine House. "It was a spriggan, I'm sure of it."

"Well," said Mattock, rubbing his ear where she'd clipped him, "if you're that convinced, I suppose you'd better tell the Joan. But I wouldn't mention it to anyone else."

"But if there's one spriggan out there, there could be more," she said. "We have to warn the others—"

"They're safe enough right now," said Mattock. "I'll stand guard if it makes you feel better, but no spriggan's going to take on two hundred piskeys at once." He quickened his stride as they reached the doorway, where Mica was leaning with a sour expression on his face. "Did you find Keeve?"

"No," said Mica. "But when I do, I'm going to give him the

thrashing of his life." His gaze shifted to Ivy. "What are *you* doing here?"

"You left her down in the valley," said Mattock before Ivy could answer. "You're lucky I was the one who found her, or you'd be explaining yourself to the Joan."

"*Left* her?" Mica said. "She's got legs, hasn't she? If she didn't have enough wits to follow me, it's not my fault." He gave Ivy a contemptuous glance and stalked inside.

"I hate him," said Ivy flatly.

Mattock put a hand on her shoulder. "He's half-drunk, and angry at Keeve for pranking him. In a few hours he'll think better of it."

"And I'll still hate him then." She shook him off. "I'm going to find Cicely."

She found her little sister sitting with the other children by the droll-teller, listening raptly as he spun a tale about a tribe of piskeys who could magically leap from one place to another at will. Ivy had heard such stories and dismissed them as wishful thinking, like the legends that claimed her piskey ancestors had power to heal every kind of sickness, or that they could change their bodies into any shape they pleased. Surely, if her people had been able to do such wonderful things in the past, they'd still be doing them now.

But the spriggan had appeared out of nowhere, and Ivy had to wonder if there might be some truth to the legends after all. Maybe piskeys couldn't transport themselves from place to place with a thought, but what if spriggans could? It would explain how Ivy's mother had vanished so quickly, and why they'd never found any trace of her but her shawl...

Shuddering at how close she'd come to sharing that fate, Ivy sat down next to Cicely. She couldn't tell her sister what had happened: Cicely was in no danger at the moment, and it would be cruel to steal away her joy in her first Lighting. But if Mica couldn't convince her to take the threat of spriggans seriously, then Ivy would have no choice but to tell her. A few nightmares were a small price to pay for Cicely's safety.

She glanced across the Engine House to where the Joan sat with her consort Gossan—the Jack O'Lantern by title, though he wasn't the sort to stand on ceremony. By rights Ivy ought to tell him her story, for he was the leader of the hunters, and it was his duty to help defend the Delve. But right now he was engrossed in a conversation with Keeve's father Hew, and it would be hard to talk to him or Betony without drawing attention.

Maybe Mattock was right. Maybe Ivy should hold her peace until tomorrow, when she could talk to the Joan in private. After all, the spriggan had vanished, so what were the chances of anyone finding him now?

"Now then," said the droll-teller, clapping his bony hands on his knees. "What would you like to hear about next?"

"Giants!" piped up one eager boy, and "Dwarves!" shouted another. Ivy, who was interested in neither, was about to get up when Cicely called out, "Faeries!"

"Ah, I can't refuse a pretty lass," the droll-teller said. "Faeries it is." Some of the boys groaned, and he gave a chuckle. "No worry, lads, there's something for you in this tale as well. Let me tell you of the last great battle between the Small People and the Fair Folk, many years ago..."

He went on to tell how the old piskey clans of Cornwall—or Kernow, in the old speech—had banded together to defend their territory against an invading army of faeries. The fight had been long and bitter, with terrible magic wielded on both sides, but in the end the piskeys had won and the faeries had retreated to their own lands.

"And after that day," he finished, "they never dared march upon our borders again. Once or twice a troop of them came sneaking across the Tamar, claiming some patch of woodland as their *wyld* and pretending they'd always lived there. But they soon gave it up once a few of our boys paid them a visit, and now there's scarcely a faery to be found from Launceston to Land's End."

Probably for the best, Ivy thought. Faeries might not be as vicious as spriggans, but they were too cunning and ruthless to be trusted. Still, she couldn't blame Cicely for being curious about them, because they were said to be eternally young and beautiful, with wings clear as crystal, and when she was little Ivy had often longed to see a faery herself.

"Where's Mica?" asked Cicely, as the droll-teller strolled off for a drink. "He said he'd play jump-stones with me—oh, there he is." She started to get up, but Ivy caught her arm.

"He's in a foul mood right now," she said. "I'd leave him alone, if I were you. Why don't we play a game instead?"

As usual, the Lighting ended with the first rosy glimmer of dawn. The wakefire was quickly doused, and the tables and benches whisked back into storage. The Joan pronounced her blessing on the company, and with that all the revelers—yawning musicians and sore-footed dancers, pranksters and victims, knockers and hunters, aunties and maidens—headed back into the Delve for some well-earned sleep.

"I'm telling you, it was a spriggan," Ivy said, as Mica laid the slumbering Cicely in her alcove. "If Matt hadn't shown up when he did..."

"And I'm telling you it was Keeve, hiding in the gorse-bushes with a tablecloth over his head," said Mica. He sat down on the edge of his bed and started pulling off his boots. "He did the same thing last year, remember? Jumped up behind the droll-teller and made everyone scream." He flopped onto the mattress. "I should have throttled him then."

"It wasn't Keeve," said Ivy. Keeve's eyes were bright with boyish mischief, nothing like the slate-gray stare that had so chilled her. "And I know what a tablecloth looks like. Why can't you believe—"

But Mica's eyes had closed, and a snore was bubbling up between his lips. He wasn't pretending, either. Her brother could drop off in an instant, and Ivy, who often struggled to sleep, found it one of the most infuriating things about him.

Meanwhile, the adder's body still lay in the middle of the cavern, its blood clotted on the granite. And though Ivy understood now that Mica wasn't to blame, she resented him for not even offering to clean up the mess.

Flint wouldn't help either, even if Ivy had dared to ask him. He'd left the Lighting early and his thunder-axe was gone from its place by the door, which meant he'd already slept as long as he cared to before heading off to the diggings again.

Wearily Ivy crouched, pulled the sack over the snake's mangled head and started shoving the rest of it back in. She'd stick it in the cold-hole for now, and give it to Keeve later—along with a piece of her mind. Maybe then he'd think better of switching sacks on his fellow hunters, especially without making sure the snake was properly dead first.

When Ivy woke hours later, the cavern was quiet, the only light her own skin-glow reflecting off its copper-tiled walls. It had taken her father years to refine all that metal and hammer it into shape, but he'd worked every spare moment until it was done. He'd also polished the floor to bring out every fleck and ripple in the granite, and as if that weren't enough, he'd begun inlaying the stone with silver around the edges.

He'd only half finished the work when Marigold disappeared. A few chiseled swirls continued where the silver left off, but they'd never been filled, and in the end Ivy had dragged an old trunk over those forlorn two paces of stone so she wouldn't have to look at them.

She padded to the water-channel and splashed her face, then opened the wardrobe she shared with Cicely and took out a sleeveless blouse and skirt. Close to the surface the Delve could be cool, but not here, and where Ivy was going it would be warmer still. Once dressed, she studied herself critically in the mirror. Should she leave her shoulder-length curls down, as she usually did? Or would she look older and more serious with her hair up?

"You look nice," said Cicely sleepily from her alcove. "Where are you going?"

Ivy put the mirror aside. "To talk to the Joan."

"What about?"

She didn't like to frighten Cicely, but she couldn't lie to her, either. "I saw a spriggan last night, outside the Engine House," she said in an offhand tone, hoping Cicely would assume she'd only glimpsed it from a distance. "It ran away before I could show anyone, and Mica thinks it was only Keeve playing a prank. But I thought the Joan and Jack should know."

"Oh," Cicely said in a small voice, and Ivy could tell she was troubled. Well, maybe that was for the best—it would make easier for Mica to talk to her when the time came. Ivy slid on a pair of copper arm-rings, then stooped to kiss her sister's forehead.

"I'll be back soon," she said. "Wish me luck."

"You'll need that and a hammer to get Aunt Betony to listen," said Mica from his alcove. He swept back the curtain and clambered out of bed, scratching his bare chest. "What's for dinner?"

"There's plenty of adder in the cold-hole," said Ivy sweetly, and walked out.

As Ivy headed down the steps to the lower tunnels, she was struck by how quiet the Delve was. Usually at this time of day there'd be children chasing each other through the corridors, matrons carrying baskets of laundry up from the wash-cistern, knockers returning from the diggings with their thunder-axes over their shoulders. But most of the piskeys were still sleeping off last night's revels, and Ivy walked the passages alone.

Soon another set of stairs took her down to Silverlode Passage, where threads of precious metal still glittered against the stone. It was one of the main thoroughfares of the Delve, a direct route to the cavern where the piskeys held their market. Yet even this passage was empty, which made Ivy feel lonely and strangely liberated at once. She appreciated the close-knit community of the Delve, where everyone looked out not only for their own interests but also for everyone else's. But there were times when her fellow piskeys' company became stifling, and it was a relief to be alone for a while.

The Joan's stateroom stood at the far end of the Silverlode, its entrance marked by lit torches on either side—a sign that Betony was awake and ready to hear petitions. But the door was closed, and Ivy had to knock three times before anyone answered.

"All right, all right," said Nettle's gravelly tones from within, "I'm a-coming." The door opened with a creak, and her thin, wizened face appeared. "Right then, what's your business?"

"I need to talk to the Joan. I think..." No, she didn't just think. She'd looked into those cold eyes, and she *knew*. Ivy drew herself taller. "I saw a spriggan last night."

Nettle seemed taken aback, but then her expression softened. She leaned closer and murmured, "Ah, Ivy-lass, your mother was a good woman, and what happened to her was a shame. But you can't go about saying—"

"Let her in, Nettle." Betony's voice carried across the cavern. "I'll deal with this."

Nettle shut her mouth so hard her teeth clicked, and opened the door. Ivy walked into a broad, fire-lit chamber, its daunting size made cozy by copper panels, a knotted rug, and draperies in rich, earthy hues. The far end of the room was dominated by a desk of carved granite, and Ivy's aunt sat behind it.

"You believe you saw a spriggan," said the Joan. "Where?"

Looking at Betony always made Ivy feel small. Her strong bones and striking features, the smooth waves of hair falling about her shoulders, made Ivy keenly aware of her own unruly curls and slight, unpiskeylike figure. Not to mention her aunt's creamy, bronze-dappled wings, so much like Cicely's that Ivy couldn't help being reminded of what her own wings could have—*should* have—been.

"In the valley below the Engine House," she said, subdued.

"And what were you doing there?"

This was the awkward part. Exasperating though Mica could be, he was still Ivy's brother, and she didn't want to make trouble for him. But she wasn't about to take the blame for his carelessness, either. "Mica and I needed to talk in private. He said I'd be safe with him."

"So he was with you when you saw the spriggan?"

Ivy winced. "No."

"I see," said the Joan. "Go on."

"He didn't mean to leave me," Ivy said. "He thought I was behind him when he ran up the hill. But the spriggan arrived before I could catch up."

"Arrived how? From which direction?"

Her pointed questions were making Ivy feel defensive. "I don't know. He turned up all of a sudden. It was like he was just... there."

"And he didn't touch you, or bespell you, or hurt you in any way?"

"No," Ivy said, "but I'm sure he would have if Mattock hadn't come looking for me."

"So Mattock saw the spriggan?"

"It ran off before he arrived. I tried to point it out to him, but—" She spread her hands, feeling more foolish than ever. "It was already gone."

The Joan leaned back, fingers tapping the edge of the table. "And when you told Mattock and your brother about this spriggan, what did they say?"

"They said it was Keeve playing a prank. Only I know it wasn't, because—"

She was about to say *he talked to me*, but Betony cut her off. "Clearly you feel that wasn't so. But for a spriggan to appear the instant you were alone, frighten you without doing any harm, and vanish before anyone else could see him... It does seem unlikely, don't you think?"

"But I felt him watching me, when I was sitting by the wakefire," Ivy said in desperation. "He could have singled me out then, and waited until I was alone to—"

"How could he know you would go outside the Engine House, much less that your brother would leave you alone? And when he had a chance to seize you, why didn't he take it?" She paused, then went on more gently, "No one could blame you for hating spriggans, or wanting your mother avenged. But you were not yourself last night, and the mind can play tricks sometimes."

So because she'd showed up late to the Lighting with old clothes and dirt on her face, the Joan thought she was losing her wits? Ivy gripped her arm-rings, calling on their cold strength. "I didn't imagine it! Why doesn't anyone believe me?"

But her aunt only looked at her, a faint pity in her gaze. And all at once Ivy remembered what Cicely had asked last night: *Have you ever seen a spriggan? Has anybody?*

She drew a sharp breath. "You don't believe in spriggans." And neither did Mica or Mattock, judging by their reactions. How could she have been so naïve?

"You mistake me, Ivy. I would never deny that spriggans are real."

"Really?" Ivy was angry enough for sarcasm, though she knew she might regret it. "When was the last time anyone saw one?"

"Must be thirty years ago now," came the rasping answer, and Ivy started; she'd forgotten Nettle was there. "A thin, miserable thing it was, all by its lonesome. But it fought like a demon 'til young Hew smashed its head in, or so he and the other lads said."

Could it be true? She'd spent her whole life terrified of spriggans, and all the while they'd been practically extinct? "Then why are we still hiding underground?" Ivy demanded. "If I only imagined what I saw last night, and my mother wasn't taken by the spriggans—"

"There are more enemies in the world than spriggans," said Betony, with a hard look at Nettle. "And good reason for our women and children to stay underground, even now. As for your mother... I would let that be, Ivy, if I were you."

"You think she left us," Ivy said, struggling to breathe. "You think my mother went away on *purpose.*"

"I don't know what became of Marigold that night," the

Joan replied, unruffled. "She may indeed have been caught by spriggans for all I know." She rose and walked around the table. "But you will not bring her back by making yourself miserable—as I have told your father many times." She put her fingers under Ivy's chin and tipped her face up. "You have been working too hard. It would do you good to get some rest. Let Mica and Cicely look after you for a change."

I'm not sick, Ivy wanted to protest, but she'd heard the warning in her aunt's tone: the discussion was over. And Nettle was holding the door open in case she hadn't taken the hint. Ivy bowed her head. "Yes, my Joan."

It wasn't self-doubt that made Ivy change course halfway through her walk home. It was sheer stubbornness, and as she turned west into Tinners' Row where Keeve and his family lived, Ivy clenched her fist in determination. She'd get to the bottom of this, never mind what Betony said. She'd *prove* she hadn't been pranked, or imagined something that wasn't there.

"Keeve!" she shouted at his door, her knock ringing loud as a thunder-axe in the narrow tunnel. "Wake up! We need to talk!"

"He's not here," came a muffled reply.

Ivy was surprised. Last night Keeve had danced harder and drunk more piskey-wine than anyone else she knew; it seemed impossible he'd recover so quickly. "Where is he, then?"

The door creaked open and Keeve's mother Teasel looked out, her face pinched with anxiety. "He didn't come back last night. Hew's gone looking for him."

That was odd. Keeve had reason to fear Mica's wrath after his prank with the adder, but he liked a good sleep as much as anyone. "I'm sorry to trouble you, then," Ivy said. "But when Keeve gets back, would you let me know? I've got something of his I need to return, and—"

Teasel didn't wait for her to finish. She gave a tight-lipped nod and shut the door.

"He's still not back," said Mica, several hours later. "And Teasel didn't want the adder."

It was night again, and Ivy was brushing out Cicely's hair before they went to bed. Not that any of them would sleep well, knowing Keeve was missing.

"So Hew couldn't find him?" Ivy asked as she gave Cicely's hair a final stroke and started to braid it again. "Is Gossan going to send a search party?"

"Two of them," Mica said, heaving the adder back into the cold-hole. "Gem and Feldspar are leading the first, and Matt and I'll be on the second. But I doubt it'll be worth the trouble. He's probably just gone off to town for a pint."

"You mean with the humans?" Cicely twisted around so eagerly that Ivy lost hold of her braid. "You really think so?"

Mica shrugged. "It wouldn't be the first time." But Ivy could see the crease between his brows, and knew that he was more worried than he let on. Keeve might be reckless, but he'd never stayed away from the Delve this long before.

"They've checked the milking barn, I suppose?" Ivy asked. The piskeys kept no cattle, but one of the nearby human farmers did, and Keeve was an expert at coaxing them to give up a few extra pints for the piskeys. "The cows are bound to miss him, if nobody else does."

She spoke lightly for Cicely's sake, but her little sister wasn't fooled. "Do you think the spriggan took him?" she asked in a small voice.

Mica's eyes flicked to Ivy's, then away. "What would a spriggan want with Keeve? He wasn't carrying any treasure, and he's too tough to be good eating. Off to bed with you, skillywidden." He tweaked Cicely's nose and went out.

That was all the reassurance Cicely needed, and she went to sleep without protest. Even Ivy managed to coax herself to rest, telling herself Keeve would surely be back by morning.

But the search parties returned empty-handed, and by the time another day had passed even Mica stopped acting casual. The atmosphere in the Delve grew tense and the piskeys spoke in whispers, as though at a funeral. Gifts began to pile up in front of Hew and Teasel's cavern.

And before long, Ivy's story about the spriggan wasn't a joke any more. Mattock came to the door and apologized, his square face sober beneath his mop of rusty hair. Betony called Ivy back to the Joan's chambers and questioned her again, this time without condescension. Cicely woke sobbing that a spriggan had come to get her, and when she found Mica pulling on his boots for the evening hunt, she clung to him and begged him not to go.

"Don't be such a pebble-head," he said gruffly, prying her off. "I'll be safe enough with Mattock, and we can always jump down a hole at the first sign of trouble. Or run like rabbits, if it comes to that."

It was the right thing to say to Cicely, who managed a watery smile. But Ivy wasn't so reassured. Mica might be lazy and prone to boasting, but he was no coward; what he could do if a spriggan came after him and what he actually *would* do were different matters. "Be careful," she said, as Mica headed for the door.

Two days ago her brother would have rolled his eyes and

told her not to be such an old auntie. Now he gave a sober nod, and left without another word.

"Ivy! Wake up!"

It surely couldn't be morning. Ivy raised her head blearily from the pillow to find Mica stooping over her. "Ugh," she said, "you stink. What have you been doing?"

"Guess," said Mica, baring his teeth in a grin.

Ivy sat up, suddenly awake. "You found him?" Alive, it would seem, or Mica wouldn't look so pleased with himself. "Is he all right?"

Mica gave her an odd look. "After Matt and I beat him senseless, I should say not. Why, did you want to question him? I'd leave that to the Joan if I were you."

"Beat him—?" For a moment Ivy was too shocked to believe it. Then her sleep-addled brain caught up with her, and she understood. "You don't mean Keeve."

Mica gave a snort. "I wish," he said. "No, we didn't find him. We caught the spriggan."

3

"Won't speak a word, I'm told. Just sits there with his ugly mouth shut, and stares at nothing." Keeve's mother tugged a fresh coil of roving onto her shoulder, her drop spindle whirling as she spun the soft wool into yarn. Only someone who knew her well would have noticed the tremor in her hands.

"Maybe he doesn't know how," piped up one of the younger girls from her seat on the rug. Teasel's cavern was as well furnished as any in the Delve, but not even she had enough chairs for twenty. "Has anyone ever heard a spriggan talk?"

I have, thought Ivy. But the memory of that soft, insinuating voice made her feel slimy all over, and it wasn't as though he'd said anything useful. Teasel needed answers, not mockery.

"Tch! You'd get more sense out of an animal," said another woman. "It's useless if you ask me—meaning no offense to you, Teasel," she added as Keeve's mother bristled. "Of course we all want to see your lad safe home again. Only that I can't see how that nasty creature down below is going to help us find him."

"Well," said Teasel, pinching the yarn tight between finger and thumb, "if that creature won't give me back my son, then at least we can make him pay for it. That's what I say, and

Hew's of the same mind. My man killed a spriggan all by himself once, you know. Smashed its head in with his thunder-axe, and kicked its carcass into the sea."

The other women sat up, eager for details, but Cicely edged closer to Ivy. "I don't like when people talk about killing," she whispered.

"It's a spriggan," Ivy replied, not looking up from the wool she was carding. "And if he won't tell what he did with Keeve, then he deserves it."

Yet later that evening, after she'd tucked Cicely into bed, Ivy found herself wondering *why* the spriggan hadn't talked. Perhaps he was afraid of being executed, but he must know that was going to happen anyway...

Make him pay for it, murmured Teasel in her memory, and then with grim relish, *My man killed a spriggan all by himself once.*

But that had been thirty years ago, according to Nettle. If the spriggan had managed to hide from the hunters of the Delve for so long, how had her brother and Mattock caught him so easily? Especially if he'd killed Keeve and eaten him right down to the bones, as everyone feared. Surely after committing such a horrible murder, the spriggan would put as much distance between himself and the Delve as he could?

"How am I supposed to know what goes on in a spriggan's head?" asked Mica irritably, when Ivy questioned him. By that time Cicely was asleep, so they could talk freely. "Ask the Joan, if she can get him talking before he starves." He poured himself a tankard of small beer and sat down at the table. "Anyway, why do you care? I thought you'd be happy to see him caught. Revenge for our mother, and all that."

"All that?" Ivy repeated in disbelief. "You caught a spriggan with your own hands! How can you talk as though—" She dropped onto the bench across from Mica. "You can't still think our mother left on purpose."

"Why not?" he snapped, then flinched as Cicely mumbled and turned over. "All I'm saying," he went on more quietly, "is that nobody knows what happened to her. And I don't see how you can keep on about spriggans, when you of all people should know—" He pushed back from the table, his lip curling. "Oh, what's the point? You never listen to me anyway."

"I'm listening now," said Ivy, with an effort at patience. Maybe Mica had forgotten the tenderness in Marigold's face as she kissed her children goodnight, or her radiant smile as she danced to the music of Flint's fiddle. Maybe he thought he knew some reason their mother would have wanted to leave. "What is it I'm supposed to know?"

"About the fight, of course."

"What fight?"

"Between Dad and Mum, the night before she disappeared." He glanced at the archway to their parents' bedchamber—the only separate room in the cavern. "They were in there with the door closed, so there's no telling how it started. But once they got going you could hear nearly every word. Don't you remember?"

It seemed impossible. Flint had always doted on Marigold, and neither of them were the quarrelling sort. Ivy was tempted to suggest it had been a nightmare, but the look on Mica's face forestalled her. She shook her head. "You'll have to remind me. What were they fighting about?"

"She said she was leaving, and she wanted to take you and Cicely." His voice wavered on the last phrase, and he made a face at his tankard. "Dad was furious. He said he couldn't stop her throwing her life away, but she wasn't taking his daughters anywhere. Then she started to cry and I couldn't make out what she was saying anymore, and he didn't say anything at all. And when she came out of the chamber she was still crying, but quietly, like she didn't want us to know. So I pretended I was asleep."

Ivy's stomach felt heavy, as though she had swallowed a stone. "I don't remember any of that."

"Well, you should. Because you sat up and asked her what was the matter. And then she climbed into your alcove and shut the curtains, and the two of you were whispering in there for ages." He ran a finger around the rim of his cup. "So you knew she was going away, like I did. You just couldn't bear to face it, so you..." He shrugged. "I don't know, blocked it out somehow. Told yourself it was the spriggans who took her instead."

"I didn't *tell myself* anything!" Ivy knotted her fists, so furious she felt sick. "What makes you think your memory's any better than mine? Maybe it was you who couldn't bear to think our mother was taken by the spriggans, so you invented this story and talked yourself into believing it! You think she bled all over her shawl on purpose, then hung it on a gorse bush for Dad to find? So she could do what? Go dancing with the faeries?"

Mica hunched his shoulders. "I don't know why she wanted to leave," he said. "And I don't know what happened to her either. Maybe the spriggans did get her in the end. But I'm not going to waste my life brooding over someone who—"

"Don't you dare," warned Ivy. "If you want to tell yourself that Mum was selfish and uncaring and that we're well rid of her, then I can't stop you. But I remember what she was like, and I will never believe that. *Never.*"

"It doesn't matter," Mica muttered into his beer. "Either way she's gone, and she isn't coming back. Believe whatever makes you happy."

All at once Ivy thought she understood. "Is that why you never said anything to me about it?" she said more softly. "Because you thought I was happier not knowing?"

"No," said Mica. "I never said anything because I knew

you'd be like this." He drained his tankard, shoved it toward her, and marched off to bed.

Ivy sat unmoving, staring into the foamy dregs. She felt a little dizzy, as though she'd cut herself by accident and was just starting to feel it. Could she really have forgotten something so enormous, so shattering? Even if she had, shouldn't she be able to remember it now?

Yet when she forced her mind back to that night six years ago, she found only a blank fuzzy space. Could she really have been so weak, so desperate, as to erase her own memories? She'd never heard of such a thing, but maybe...

No. She wasn't going to blame herself, or her mother, until she knew Mica's story was true. Which meant she'd have to wait until her father came home, and ask him.

Or better yet, she could go find Flint herself, and settle the question at once. After all, what was the worst he could do? Even a blow or a curse would be better than the silence she lived with every day.

Ivy pushed back from the table. "I'm going for a walk," she said. "Don't wait up."

By this time of the evening most piskeys were in bed, and the others were on their way. But Flint had given up regular hours a long time ago, so he could be anywhere.

Most likely he was working in the deepest part of the mine, but by now he'd tunneled so far that Ivy had no idea where to find him—a problem that became clear the instant she climbed down the ladder to the diggings. If any other knockers were working, she could have asked them to point her in the right direction. But without being familiar with the labyrinth of rough tunnels the piskey miners used, she could wander half the night before she heard the telltale crack and rumble of her father's thunder-axe.

She shouted his name, but there was no answer. If her father had been less capable, Ivy might have worried about him. But Flint was a true knocker, able to sense every strength and weakness of the surrounding granite, and he never caused a rock-fall unless he meant to. He was safe enough, and he'd come home when he was ready. But who knew how long that would be?

Frustrated, Ivy climbed up the ladder and shut the trapdoor behind her. What to do now? It was no use going home to bed in this state: she'd be tossing and turning all night.

At last she decided to take a walk around the Delve. Perhaps she'd bump into her father, or at least hear him working, along the way. And even if she didn't, at least the exercise would tire her out enough to nap a bit before he came in.

Ivy made two long winding circuits of the tunnels, climbing every ramp and staircase she could find. But by the time she'd finished, she felt no sleepier than before.

There was only one place she hadn't been yet. Ivy walked to the end of the tunnel and braced her hands on the iron railing, gazing up the Great Shaft to the faint glimmer of moonlight above. Should she climb to the top? The effort would certainly be tiring, but–

"Bind up my wounds," rasped a voice.

Ivy jumped, clapping both hands over her mouth. "Who's there?" she tried to ask, but her lips could barely form the words.

The voice hadn't come from behind her. It was floating up from the depths of the shaft, from the old human diggings where no piskey had reason to be.

"Soft! I did but dream. O coward conscience, how dost thou afflict me!"

Nobody in the Delve talked like that. Not even the oldest piskeys used such formal language, and the droll-teller himself had never spoken with such tortured passion. Ivy gripped the railing and leaned over it, dreading what she might see. She'd never believed in ghosts, but...

"The lights burn blue. It is now dead midnight. Cold fearful drops stand on my trembling flesh..." Then the speaker faltered and began to moan, "Light! *Light!"* with growing desperation, like a sick child begging for water. It was the most pitiful thing Ivy had ever heard.

Could it be a human, who'd wandered into one of the old adits and got lost in the depths of the mine? Ivy would have been glad to think so, for it would be easy to play will-'o-the-wisp and lead him back to the surface. But in her heart she knew better. The words might be strange and garbled, but the voice was all too familiar.

It was the spriggan.

She'd never suspected that his cell was so close to the Great Shaft. All she'd heard was that he was being held somewhere deep in the mine, and only the Joan and Jack were allowed to see him.

But she'd also been told he wasn't talking, and he was definitely talking now.

"What do I fear? Myself? There's none else by: Richard loves Richard; that is, I am I..."

He'd calmed down enough to stop wailing for light and start muttering to himself again. Was Richard his name? It sounded oddly human. Ivy hadn't thought of spriggans as having names before; to her they were all just spriggans, as snakes were snakes.

But if he had a name, he had a personality. If he could talk about feeling pain and guilt and fear, he might be willing to talk about other things as well. Like what he'd done with Keeve...

Or what had happened to Ivy's mother.

Did Ivy dare? Could she climb down into the depths of the shaft, find the cell where the spriggan was kept prisoner, and knock on the door? If she offered him a taste of the light he craved, would he tell her what she needed so badly to know?

Mind, if anyone found out she had gone near the spriggan, Ivy would be in big trouble. But he could hardly hurt her while locked up in a cell. And if she didn't take the chance now, she might spend the rest of her life wondering what would have happened if she had.

"I am I," the spriggan repeated, then muttered, "Whatever that means." And with that he began to laugh—but it dissolved into coughing, and ended in a gasp like a sob.

Ivy inhaled, summoning strength and courage. Then she swung her leg over the railing and lowered herself into the darkness.

She had never climbed this part of the Great Shaft before, much less backward. Every new foothold had to be carefully tested, lest it crumble away and send her plummeting into the fathomless sump below. After several minutes of spidering her way down the rock, Ivy's curls stuck to her forehead with sweat. Yet she thought of her mother, and kept on.

She swung her left leg sideways, toes groping for another ledge. But her foot dangled into empty air, and no matter how far she stretched she could find no place to put it. Had she reached the tunnel to the dungeon already? Digging her fingers into the rock, Ivy eased herself downward, then arched her back, swung her hips, and let go.

The tunnel was deeper than she'd expected, and for a heart-stopping instant she feared she'd made her last mistake. But then her bare feet smacked stone, and she landed with barely a stumble. Relieved, Ivy straightened up—

And found herself face to face with the spriggan.

At first she was too stunned to say anything. Not only because she'd never guessed his cell would open straight onto the shaft, but because he was so different from the monster she'd imagined. Pale as a dead thing, yes, and thin—he could never have passed for a piskey. Nor was he pleasant to look at, with one eye swollen half-shut and a split lip twisting his mouth into a sneer. But apart from that there was nothing gruesome about him, and he was *young.* Older than Ivy to be sure, more a man than a boy. But he couldn't be more than a couple years older than Mica.

Yet he was a spriggan, and that made him dangerous. Even crouched against the wall with one arm cradled to his chest, he had a menacing air about him, a tension that might explode at any moment into violence. Ivy dimmed her glow and backed toward the shaft, though she knew it was too late: he'd heard her land, seen her skin shining in the darkness, and now...

"Is there a murderer here?" he whispered, pushing himself to his feet. He lurched forward—but then came a rattling noise, and he jerked to a halt.

So that was why the Joan hadn't feared him escaping, even with an open shaft mere paces away. While the spriggan was unconscious, Mica and Mattock had clapped an iron manacle around his ankle and chained him to the floor. He couldn't go more than two strides in any direction, so Ivy was well out of reach—and if she remembered the legends, the iron would keep him from using magic, too. Only those with knocker blood could endure the touch of cold iron.

"You tell me," she said, feeling bolder. She could see him clearly with her night vision, but to him she'd be nothing more than a ghostly shape and a tantalizing hint of light. "Are you a murderer?"

The spriggan let out his breath. His head drooped, and he muttered, *"No. Yes. I am: Then fly..."*

If only she could. "I'm not here to play riddle-games," snapped Ivy. Had he lost his wits? "Did you kill Keeve?"

The spriggan watched her sidelong out of one gray eye. *"I*

am a villain," he said at last, then added quickly as Ivy tensed: *"Yet I lie. I am not."*

"Stop talking nonsense and tell me the truth, then!"

The spriggan leaned against the wall, his distorted mouth closing tight. He did not reply.

Had she been too harsh with him? Would he refuse to speak any more? Ivy took a step forward—though not too close, since she had no desire to feel those thin fingers around her neck. "You want light, don't you?"

His breath caught, just the briefest hitch, but it was as good as an answer. "I'll give it to you," Ivy said, "if you answer some questions."

She waited, but the spriggan didn't respond. Did he not believe her? Or was he too slurry-brained to understand?

Ivy increased her glow a little, hoping to tempt him. "See?" she said. "I'll give you more, if you'll tell me what you did with Keeve. And even more if you tell what happened to my mother. She was beautiful, with light brown hair, and her wings..."

What had Marigold's wings been like? For some reason she couldn't remember. Ivy cleared her throat and went on. "Anyway, she disappeared six years ago. Did you spriggans take her? Is she still alive?"

The prisoner raised his fever-bright eyes to hers, lips parting as though to speak. But then his chin dropped and he looked away.

Ivy threw up her hands. "This is useless." The stench in the cell made her queasy, and she was tired of looking at those hollow cheeks and sunken eyes. The spriggan was delirious or mad or both, and she wished that she had never come. "I give up. Stay here and rot." Defiantly flaring brighter so he'd know what he was missing, she turned to walk away.

"Ivy."

Startled, she looked back to find the spriggan stretching out his one good hand. "Don't go," he said, and now his voice sounded ordinary, the formal cadence lost. "I didn't know... I couldn't be sure it was you, until now."

Was he trying to make her pity him? If so, it wasn't going to work. And she wouldn't ask how he knew her name, either—he'd probably just overheard it at the Lighting. Ivy tapped her foot. "Well?"

"I didn't kill Keeve." He rubbed his temple, as though concentrating were an effort. "I don't know where he is."

"But you were there the night he disappeared," Ivy said. "Who else could have taken him?"

"I have no idea. But it wasn't me."

"Why didn't you say that to the Joan, then?" Ivy asked. "Did you think she wouldn't believe you?"

"I had to give her a reason to keep me alive," he said. "Until I could talk to you."

"Me?" Ivy was startled. "Why?"

The spriggan straightened, brushing sweat-damp hair from his brow. "Because," he said, "your mother sent me to find you. She's alive, and safe. And if you let me go... I'll take you to her."

4

Ivy stood still, wide green eyes fixed on the spriggan. For a moment there was no sound except the slow drip of water down the Great Shaft and the creature's labored breathing. Then she said in a strangled voice, "You're lying." She didn't know if spriggans could lie, but what other explanation could there be?

"I'm not."

"Yes, you are." She spoke quickly, almost gabbling with panic. She had to stop this before it got out of hand—before she was tempted to believe him. "You heard me say I was looking for my mother, and now you're using that to try and trick me."

"Her name is Marigold."

His quiet certainty shook her, but Ivy wasn't about to give in. There were any number of ways he could have learned her mother's name—including under torture. "Why would she send *you*? If my mother was alive, if she wanted to see me so badly, she'd come herself."

"I didn't ask about her motives. Marigold asked me to give you a message, and I agreed because I owed her a debt. If you want explanations, you'll have to ask when you see her." His look turned sly. "Unless you don't *want* to see her."

Ivy barely resisted the urge to hit him. "Of course I do," she snapped. "Or would, if I believed a single word you've said. Where did you see my mother, then? In the bottom of your stew-pot?"

"Actually, it was in Truro." He paused, then added with a hint of condescension, "That's a human city and not a recipe, in case you were wondering. I don't eat piskeys, even irritating ones."

"That's ridiculous," Ivy said, folding her arms so he wouldn't see her hands shake. "My mother would never live in a human place when she could be here with us. And even if she couldn't come back to the Delve for some reason, she'd never make a bargain with a—a filthy, lying *spriggan.*"

The prisoner pinched the bridge of his nose, as though she had given him a headache. Then he said with infinite weariness, "I don't even know what a spriggan is."

Ivy's legs wobbled. "What? But then... what are you?"

"A faery. What else?"

What indeed. Between the dirt and blood that smeared his body, his torn clothes and unkempt hair, she would never have taken him for one of the so-called Fair Folk. Yet now that he mentioned it...

"Oh," she said faintly.

"Marigold warned me to be careful about showing myself. She said your people had been underground for a long time, and that they didn't take kindly to strangers. But even so—" He touched his injured arm and grimaced. "I wasn't expecting quite this level of hostility."

He sounded reasonable now, and sane. But Ivy wasn't ready to let her guard down yet. "Is your arm broken?" she asked.

"Out of joint." He moved his hand, revealing an ugly swelling around the elbow. "Your brother seemed to think he could make me talk by trying to rip my arm off, but I can't say it inspired me to much more than yelling."

Ivy almost asked how he'd known Mica was her brother, but then she remembered: he'd seen the two of them arguing outside the Engine House. "So why didn't you tell him about my mother?"

"Because I was too busy yelling, perhaps?" His words were mild, but tinged with sarcasm. "Not to mention fighting for my life."

Ivy couldn't help feeling a twinge of sympathy. Faeries might be as deceitful as the legends said, but the stranger was clearly in pain. Maybe that was why he'd been raving earlier.

"Mica doesn't always think before he acts," she said, resisting a traitorous impulse to add, *I'm sorry.*

"I got that impression," said the faery dryly. "I don't suppose you have some kind of magical healing potion that would put my arm right?"

"Not really," said Ivy. Yarrow's herbs might ease the pain and bring down the swelling, but they wouldn't solve the underlying problem. "And even if I did, don't you think the Joan would notice that someone had healed you?"

"I doubt it, unless she can see through rock." He jerked his head at the windowless slab of granite behind him. "She hasn't bothered to see me once since I woke up here. And it seems she's not planning to give me food or water either, unless I start talking."

Ivy was silent, troubled by the revelation. Did Betony really mean to starve the spriggan—or faery—until he confessed to killing Keeve? But what if he hadn't?

"I don't know what you've heard about faeries," said the prisoner, "but if there's one thing my people honor, it's a bargain. Help me, and I'll do you a favor in return."

"Like you did for my mother?" Ivy asked, moving a little closer. After all, he could hardly overpower her with only one working hand. "What exactly did she make you promise, anyway?"

"To tell you that she's alive, and wants to see you," he said. "And if you're willing, to bring you back to Truro with me."

Ivy had no idea how far away Truro was. But she'd never heard Mica or any of the other hunters mention it, so it must be out of their usual range—a few hours' journey on foot, or more. How could she travel so far from the Delve without anyone knowing that she was gone?

And yet, if her mother was truly alive... how could she *not* go?

She was still struggling to decide when she noticed the stranger extending his injured arm toward her, wincing all the while. "What are you doing?" she asked.

"I told you. Help me, and I'll help you." He hesitated, then added with obvious reluctance, "Please."

Ivy sighed. "What do you want me to do?"

"Take my hand, and slide your other hand under my elbow."

Suppressing her distaste, Ivy took his limp, white fingers in her own. She half expected to find his skin cold and slimy, as a spriggan's ought to be—but his hand was warm, even feverish, in her grip. Gingerly she slipped her other hand beneath his swollen joint, feeling the dislocation. "What now?"

"Hold my elbow steady," said the prisoner between his teeth, "and pull my wrist toward you. Not too fast, but—*aaaaah!*" There was a sickening pop beneath Ivy's palm and he staggered, gasping. But when he lifted his head the relief on his face was close to ecstasy.

"You have my *profound* gratitude," he breathed, flexing his arm. "So do we have a bargain?"

Ivy sat down heavily on a jutting rock, her thoughts and feelings in a tangle. Had she really just helped one of her people's oldest enemies? What would happen to her, if anyone found out? When she'd left the cavern looking for answers about her mother, she'd never imagined it would turn out like this. "I don't know," she said. "I don't know what to do."

"Yes, you do." He dragged his chain across the floor and crouched beside her. "It's simple. You get me out of here, and I take you to Marigold."

He made it sound so easy. "But how would we get there? And when would we leave?"

"As soon as you like, or near enough. As for how..." He tapped a fingernail against his teeth. "It would be easiest to leap there by magic, but you've never been to Truro before, so that won't work. And you haven't got wings, so..." He shrugged. "I'll have to carry you."

"*Carry* me?" asked Ivy, in baffled outrage. "I can walk perfectly well, in case you hadn't noticed!"

"Of course. But you can't fly, which is more to the point."

"And you expect me to believe that you can?" Faery or not, he was a male, and had no more wings than she did. Was the stranger mad after all, or did he think she was stupid? Disgusted, Ivy pushed herself to her feet. "I've had enough. I'm going to bed."

"Wait." His voice sharpened. "You can't leave me here."

"I don't see why not," Ivy said. "You've had your fun, and got your arm fixed into the bargain. What else do you need me for? Wait a few days, and you should be thin enough to slip out of that manacle and *fly* out of here." She made a cynical flapping motion and turned away.

"You really don't know what I'm talking about." He sounded incredulous. "I knew piskeys were different, but I had no idea... Ivy, listen to me!"

Annoyed as she was, his desperation stopped her short. She stood with her back to him, waiting.

"Of course I don't have wings," he said. "Not in this form. But I can change shape—all male faeries can. If I turn myself into a bird, and you make yourself small, I can fly you to Truro and back again before anyone knows you're gone."

"That's ridic—" Ivy started, but the word dissolved on her

tongue. The little bird she'd seen two nights ago, right after the spriggan disappeared—could that have been him?

She wanted to believe. Not only that magic could turn a wingless faery into a bird, but that everything else he'd told her was true as well. That Marigold was alive and longing for Ivy, and that one short flight would bring them together again.

And that was why she couldn't listen to him any longer. Because if she did, she might end up making the worst mistake of her life.

"I have to go," she blurted, and fled.

"I shall despair. There is no creature loves me; and if I die, no soul shall pity me..."

Ivy buried her head in the pillow, the stranger's last words still echoing in her mind. She'd had to listen to him all the way up the Great Shaft last night, gabbling about villainy and murder and vengeance, and guilt had pricked her as she realized he was tumbling back into madness. Even without the agony of a dislocated arm, being locked up in absolute blackness with iron around his ankle must be torture, and if that weren't cruel enough, he was dying of hunger and thirst as well.

Ivy kicked back the covers and pulled open the curtain of her alcove, grimacing at the dirty smears her fingers left behind. She'd been so tired when she got home, she'd climbed into bed without washing or changing her clothes. Had Mica and Cicely noticed? What would she say if they asked where she had been?

Ivy hopped down onto the rug and glanced about. All the beds in the cavern were empty, and the door to their father's bedchamber stood open; bowls and spoons littered the table, and Cicely had forgotten to put the cream back in the cold-hole. It was mid-morning, and they'd all left hours ago. What must they have thought when they woke and found Ivy still asleep?

She heated water and scrubbed herself clean, then tidied up the dining table and the bed Mica had left unmade. It irked her that he never cleaned up after himself, but if she didn't do it Cicely would, so there was no point leaving it. Next she'd sweep the floor, make some bread, and finish curing the skin from Keeve's adder, and after that...

Ivy collapsed into a chair, fingers worrying at her black curls. It was no use trying to distract herself, or pretend that her conversation with the spriggan hadn't happened. What if Marigold really had sent him? Could Ivy afford to miss her only chance to find her mother, just because she was afraid of being taken in?

Yet she had to be careful before she agreed to anything. Faeries might consider a bargain sacred, but the old stories said they had a knack for finding loopholes in nearly any promise. The last thing Ivy wanted was to risk her life for this stranger, only to end up betrayed.

"You're up," said Cicely, peering in through the outer door. "I thought you were ill. I was going to ask Yarrow to come and look at you."

Ivy forced a smile. "I'm not sick. I just got to bed late last night." She rose and dusted her hands. "Why don't we make some bread?"

"Did you talk to him?" asked Mica at supper, taking the last roll from the basket.

Ivy choked. "What—who?"

"Dad. It was him you were looking for, wasn't it?" He gave her a pointed look. "To ask him about... you know."

She hid her face behind her drinking cup. Why was Mica always oblivious to her feelings except when she *didn't* want him to notice? "Oh. No, I didn't. I couldn't find him in the diggings, so I went for a walk instead."

"What are you talking about?" asked Cicely. Mica didn't answer, and the silence thickened until Ivy said, "Just something that Mica remembered and I didn't. I thought he was mistaken, so I was going to ask Dad. But then I realized maybe he was right after all."

"Took you long enough," muttered Mica, but she could tell he was both surprised and pleased. It must have been frustrating for him these past few years, hearing Ivy claim their mother had been taken by the spriggans when he was certain that deep down she knew better. Not that it excused his rudeness—he still deserved a good smack about the head for that, and Ivy wished she were tall enough to give it to him. But it explained a lot about the way he'd been behaving.

"It's about Mum, isn't it?" Cicely turned accusing eyes on Ivy. "You always get that look on your face when you're thinking about her. What did he say?"

"Leave it," Mica cut in. "Ivy's tired of talking about it and so am I." He stabbed another slice of rabbit off the platter and began cutting it up. "Matt and I are going to Redruth tomorrow. Is there anything you want?"

Ivy poked at her meal, torn between gratitude and guilt. Every now and then, along with the small animals they hunted, the fish they caught and the wild greens, mushrooms and berries they foraged, the hunters of the Delve took human shape and journeyed to the nearby towns for more exotic fare: glittering white sugar and flour ground fine as dust, currants and saffron and citrus peel, slabs of chocolate or sweet marzipan. It was nice when Mica remembered to ask Ivy what she needed, but if he knew where she'd been last night, he wouldn't be offering to do her any favors.

"I'm running out of cinnamon," she said at last. "And I wouldn't mind a couple of oranges." Cicely loved oranges, so perhaps that would be enough to keep her from brooding over Mica's reprimand—though judging by the mulish look on her face it was already too late.

"I told Yarrow I'd help her grind herbs tonight," Cicely said, pushing her plate away. "I should go."

Ivy waited until her sister left the cavern, then turned to Mica. "Have you heard anything about the spriggan? Has he talked yet?"

Mica shook his head in disgust. "I told Gossan they should hang him up by his ankles over a smelting-pot and see what he has to say then, but he said *we piskeys ought to be better than that,* whatever that's supposed to mean. They're going to leave him another day or two before they question him again."

"And if he still won't talk?"

He shrugged. "Gossan said they'd mine that vein when they got to it." Though the contempt in his tone said how little he approved of the Jack's forbearance. "But whether he tells what he did with Keeve or not, there's no way that spriggan's going to see daylight again. If the Joan doesn't make sure of that..." He clenched the hilt of his hunting knife. "Then I will."

It was raining as Ivy descended the Great Shaft that night, fat drops falling between the bars and running down the rock walls in rivulets. But this time she'd brought a rope, tying one end by the foot of the iron railing and the other around her waist, so if she slipped she wouldn't fall into the stagnant waters below.

She'd expected to hear the spriggan muttering to himself, as he had before. But the shaft remained silent, and as she lowered herself into his cell the only sounds were the rasp of hemp on stone and the slap of her own bare feet. "It's me," she whispered, brightening her glow so he could see her. "Are you awake?"

The prisoner sat against the wall, hands dangling between his knees. He looked like a corpse at first, eyes glazed and features slack. But as Ivy approached he stirred, and gave a feeble smile. *"But soft!"* he murmured. *"What light through yonder window breaks?"*

"What are you talking about?" asked Ivy, sharp with the effort to hide her relief. "There aren't any windows here."

"It's a quote from Shakespeare," he replied. He must have seen Ivy's blank expression, because he went on patiently, "He was a human playwright who died four centuries ago. You understand plays? Stories made up of speeches, and acted out for an audience?"

"You mean a droll-show," said Ivy. "Like at midwinter, when the children dress up and pretend to be warriors, or... monsters." She had almost said *spriggans.*

The prisoner's nostrils flared. "I suppose. In a crude fashion."

Time to change the subject, before he made her feel any more ignorant. "I've been thinking about what you said to me. And... I'm ready to bargain."

At once his expression changed. "Go on."

"I'll get that iron off your ankle, so you can take me to see my mother. But I won't ride on your back."

She spoke firmly, determined not to betray any hint of weakness. After all, even if he could turn into a bird, there was no guarantee that he wouldn't fly away without her. Or worse, take Ivy somewhere she didn't want to go.

"Ivy," said the stranger in exasperation, "you can't expect us to *walk* there. Even at human size—"

"No." Her heart was fluttering, but she kept her voice calm. "Teach me to change shape, like you do. I won't go anywhere with you until I can fly."

He stared at her. "You? But you're a piskey. A *female* piskey, at that. You think I can teach you to become a bird?"

"Why not? You learned."

"Piskey magic and faery magic aren't the same," he said with forced patience. "There are things my people can do that yours can't. And even among faeries, changing shape isn't something females do."

"How do you know? Just because you've never seen one do it? I wouldn't bother turning into a bird either, if I had wings of my own. But I don't, so I have to try." She folded her arms. "And if you want to get out of here, you're going to have to try too."

He made a faint, disbelieving sound. "You drive a hard bargain, lady."

"Harder where there's none," she said tartly.

The prisoner sighed. "Even if you're right, it won't be easy. Before you can take the shape of a bird or animal, you have to understand it. You need to be completely familiar with how it looks and moves, and know its habits as well as you know your own." He spread his lean hands, inviting her to look around. "Do you see any birds here?"

Ivy bit her lip. She'd thought all he'd have to do was explain the process to her, and she'd be able to try right away. But if she had to actually *look* at a bird in order to become one...

"You'll have to go up to the surface," the stranger went on, "in the middle of the day, and spend a few hours bird-watching before you find the one that feels right to you, the one you *need* to become. And that's just the first step." He shifted his weight, wincing as the iron band tugged his ankle. "Are you ready to do that?"

Was she ready to go above in broad daylight, under the merciless eye of a sun she'd never seen before? To defy all the rules and traditions she'd been raised with, risk the Joan's wrath, and make herself a hypocrite for telling Cicely it was too dangerous to go above? What if Keeve's murderer was still out there, waiting for another careless piskey to cross his path?

Any one of those thoughts was terrifying, let alone all of them. And yet to trust herself to a strange faery, to climb on his back and let him carry her wherever he pleased, was even more unthinkable. Either way she'd be taking an enormous risk. But better to choose her own path than to have someone else choose for her.

And besides, if she *could* do this, she wouldn't just have a chance to find her mother, she'd have wings as well.

"Yes," said Ivy, lifting her chin. "Whatever it takes, I'm ready."

5

The good thing about sneaking out through the Earthenbore was that it gave Ivy plenty of places to hide. Smaller tunnels branched off in every direction, so she could easily duck into a side corridor if she heard someone coming.

The problem was, Ivy couldn't be sure she wouldn't get caught anyway. Turning invisible would keep her from being seen, but it couldn't mask her scent, or stop other piskeys from bumping into her. And since she couldn't see unless she glowed at least a little, it would be useless unless she planned to grope her way through the tunnels with no light at all.

But it was early afternoon, the time when the older knockers taught the younger men to refine and work metal, and piskey-wives did their washing and sewing while their daughters looked after the Delve's small menagerie of livestock, and all the children were at lessons. As long as Ivy didn't stay outside too long, there was no reason anyone should notice her missing.

She followed the passage to its final branch, as far from the Delve as she could travel underground, and began climbing toward the surface. Soon the scent of sunbaked earth wafted toward her, and the blackness in the tunnel grayed with light. Ivy crept forward until the ceiling became so low she had to stoop, then crawl. At last the tunnel ended in a lattice of green foliage, with a sliver of sky above it so blue it hurt to look at. She squinted and shaded her eyes.

Ivy's heart began to hammer. To leave the earth's cool embrace and step out into that blazing emptiness, alone and weaponless, was something no piskey she knew had ever done. Even Mica had been guided by two seasoned hunters on his first daylight journey, and he'd come back with a headache so fierce he'd spent the rest of the day in bed.

But if Ivy didn't do this, she'd never learn to fly.

Ducking low to avoid the prickly overhang, Ivy crawled out of the tunnel. Not until she emerged from the underbrush and felt the sun's heat on her black curls did she sit up, and crack her eyelids open.

She'd only seen this landscape before at night, when its colors were soft and soothing. Now it shone with a hectic brightness that made her dizzy. How could she spot a bird, let alone get close enough to study it? Her eyes burned and watered until she could hardly see. If an enemy crept up on her, she'd never know until it was too late.

Yet she wouldn't give up yet. Learning to climb hadn't been easy either, and she'd had to start small, scaling the walls of an abandoned stope. Even after months of practice, her first climb up the Great Shaft had been terrifying. But Ivy would never forget the thrill when she pulled herself up onto the concrete lip at the top, and felt the rain falling on her upturned face. Fresh air had never tasted so sweet.

She was stronger than anyone knew. She could do this. Ivy straightened up, shielded her eyes, and began picking her way down the hillside.

Hours later Ivy sat cross-legged in the shade of a holly bush, searching the sky. Her head throbbed, and sweat trickled down her spine. But her eyes had got used to the sunlight, so she no longer feared that anyone would sneak up on her unnoticed. And she'd already spotted several kinds of birds.

Some had been solitary, winging past with smooth, unhurried strokes; others flew in clusters, dipping and soaring in patterns intricate as any six-hand reel. She'd seen birds big as Mica and small as Flint's fiddle, birds with pointy beaks and stubby ones, birds pale as the spriggan's hair and dark as her own. But though she'd listened intently to their chirps and cries, none had stirred any answering call in her heart.

Maybe she was just too distracted. A few minutes ago a horse and rider had come trotting out of the nearby wood—tiny with distance, but still the sight sent a stab of envy through Ivy's heart. Though she'd only seen them in pictures, the love of horses was in her piskey blood, and she longed to ride one.

But a horse couldn't take her to Truro and back before anyone knew she was missing—not like her own wings could. Ivy had to concentrate on finding the right bird, so she could learn how to take its shape. Even if the spriggan turned out to be lying about her mother, at least that way she'd get *something* out of meeting him.

Time passed, and more birds flew overhead. But none felt right to Ivy. She told herself to stop dithering and choose the next bird that came along, but when she saw it—a ragged black creature with a scrap of carrion in its beak—her soul rebelled. No matter how eager she was to see her mother, she couldn't shape a bird like that.

The shadows were growing longer, the sun slipping toward

the horizon. If Ivy didn't get home soon, Cicely would come looking for her. Reluctantly she got to her feet, and started back toward the Delve.

A dark shape flashed by, and instinctively she whirled toward it. A little bird with wings like a bent bow, body tapering smoothly to a two-pronged fork of a tail. It swooped over the valley, moving so fast that Ivy's eyes barely had time to focus before it was out of sight.

Swee-ree, swee-ree, swee-ree, came its song in the distance, a piercing call that plucked at Ivy's heart. "Wait!" she cried. "Come back!"

And to her delight, the bird did. Skimming the treetops, it darted toward her and circled her head, bright eyes watching her all the while. She'd heard piskeys had a special rapport with animals, but she'd thought that was something only hunters did. She'd never guessed she could do it, too.

"What are you?" Ivy asked, soft with wonder. The bird didn't answer, but it dipped lower, as though making her a bow. And then another fork-tailed bird came flashing over the hillside, and the two of them chased each other in dizzying spirals across the sky.

It was like magic, and music, and dancing, all at once. And as Ivy's heart soared with them she knew, as surely as she knew her own name, that this was the bird she was meant to be.

"Are you sure?" asked the strange faery, tearing a piece off the loaf Ivy had brought him. "Small, forked tail, dark all over? And it stayed aloft the whole time, without coming to land?"

Ivy nodded. She'd lingered so long studying the little birds, she'd nearly bumped into Mica and Mattock coming back from their trip to Redruth. A quick invisibility spell had protected her, but she shuddered to think how close she'd come to being caught.

Still, it had been worth it. "So what kind of bird is it?" she asked. "Do you know?"

"It's a swift. They're not resident birds. They winter in Africa, and stay here only for the summer. You're *certain* that's the one you want?"

"Why do you keep asking that?" asked Ivy. "I thought you'd be pleased. If I fly, so do you, remember?"

"Believe me," said the prisoner, "I couldn't forget that if I tried." He chewed another bite before going on, "It's just unusual. I've never met anyone who shaped a swift before. So are you ready for the next step?"

"Of course."

"Good. What do swifts eat?"

She was taken aback. "I'm... not sure. Insects?"

"Well, you'd better find out, because you're going to be eating it yourself." His gaze held hers, relentless. "How does a swift drink? Where does it sleep? How long can it fly, how high, how far? What predators does it fear, and how does it escape them? How does it behave around other swifts?"

"Why does it matter?" asked Ivy. "All I want to do is fly."

"Because," he said, "swifts are communal birds. If you don't behave like a proper swift the other swifts will sense it, and instead of welcoming you, they'll attack. Predators will notice, and see you as easy prey. You could be driven miles off course, or killed before you ever see your mother. Do you want to take that chance?"

Ivy blew out a frustrated breath. "But I don't know *how* to find out all those things," she said. "I can't spend days chasing swifts around the countryside—"

"Then find out as much as you can. But you can't turn

yourself into a swift until you know more than you do right now."

It wasn't what she'd wanted to hear. But he had no reason to lie, not with his own freedom at stake. So she nodded, and held out her hand for the water bottle.

"You're not going already?"

"Why not? What else is there to talk about?"

His mouth flattened. He tossed her the bottle and turned away.

"Richard," Ivy began, then faltered as he shot her an incredulous look. "Isn't that your name?"

Abruptly the prisoner began to laugh, a dry and horrible sound like bones clattering down a mineshaft. *"I am justly served with mine own treachery,"* he gasped.

Ivy started to back away, but he held up a hand. "No, don't run. I'm not angry. *Richard..."* He rolled the two syllables around in his mouth. "Why not? It's as good a name as any."

But not the one he was used to, obviously. "So what do other faeries call you?"

"It doesn't matter. Richard will do." He stretched his arms above his head and yawned. "Now if you'll excuse me, I'm going to sleep."

Ivy's gaze traveled across the cell, taking in the rough-hewn floor without even a heap of straw to soften it, the chain that restricted him to two steps in any direction, the iron that clamped his ankle. Not to mention the acrid stench from the corner—if it was unpleasant now, it would soon be unbearable.

Yet she didn't dare do more to help him, not yet. Bringing him food and water was risky enough.

"Good night, Richard," Ivy said quietly, and left.

"You're awfully brown," said Cicely in a tone that was half puzzlement, half admiration. "Have you been rubbing something on your skin?"

Ivy looked up from the water-channel, washcloth in hand. "I... no, I haven't," she said, flustered. She'd returned from her second trip to the surface in plenty of time, brushed off her clothes and combed her windblown curls. But she hadn't noticed what the sunlight had done to her complexion. "Why would I?"

Cicely blushed. "I thought you might be trying to make yourself pretty. Not that you aren't—I mean, I know you don't usually fuss about that sort of thing, but you've been away from the cavern a lot these last few days and Jenny said—I mean, I was wondering—"

"Jenny said what, exactly?" Ivy dropped the cloth and put her hands on her hips. "And when did the two of you start talking behind my back?"

"It wasn't like that!" said Cicely, indignant. "I was feeding the chickens when Jenny came to get some eggs, and she asked me where you were and I said you were at home, and she said you weren't because she'd knocked and got no answer, and then she said she hadn't seen Mattock either and maybe..."

So Jenny thought she and Mattock were sweethearts, sneaking off together. Well, Ivy couldn't blame her, even though the idea was laughable—not only because Matt was Mica's best friend and Mica would probably thump him for even considering it, but what piskey-boy would want a mate with no wings?

"I'm not prettying myself up for Matt, if that's what you're asking," Ivy said. "I've just been... working on something."

Cicely's face lit with excitement. "Is it a surprise? Will I get to see it?"

For one wild moment Ivy was tempted to tell her the truth. Keeping secrets was a lonely business, and Marigold was Cicely's mother too. But then she'd have to explain about her nighttime visits to Richard, and that was too much dangerous knowledge for an eleven-year-old to carry.

Better to leave it until she'd learned to fly, and found Marigold. There would be plenty of time to share the good news then.

"Soon," she said, smiling at her sister. "Wait and see."

"I'm ready," Ivy told Richard as she dropped to the floor of his cell. "And I've brought supper."

Richard's lips moved, but only a croak came out. He had to take a long drink from the water bottle before he could speak. "Lovely," he rasped, wiping his mouth. "I see you've been enjoying plenty of sunshine on my behalf."

Ivy took a loaf from her pack and set it down beside him, along with a hunk of cheese she'd saved from her own meal. "Ask me what I know about swifts," she said. "Anything you like."

"I'll take your word for it," said Richard. "Why don't you ask me something you *don't* know?"

That was easier than Ivy had expected. In truth she knew the answers to fewer than half the questions he'd asked her, but she couldn't think how to learn more on short notice. "Do they ever land?" she asked. She'd watched a swift skimming over a river to scoop up water with its beak, and seen another snatch insects from the air in mid-flight. But though there were plenty of low trees and shrubs nearby, they hadn't stopped to perch on any of them.

"Only to nest," he said. "They eat, drink, mate and even sleep in flight. Have you seen their legs?"

"They're short."

"Yes. Far too short to land easily, even in a tree. They only perch on vertical surfaces, like rock faces and old walls. And they build their nests under the eaves of houses—the higher, the better." He popped the cheese into his mouth and said around it, "Anything else?"

"I'm not sure about predators," Ivy admitted. "I saw a few birds that looked dangerous, but they didn't seem fast enough."

"Most aren't. But watch out for the hobby—it's a small falcon that can dive very quickly. That's about the only thing that can catch a swift."

Ivy waited, but he only bit off another chunk of bread and kept eating. "So," she said, "what now?"

Richard swallowed with an effort. "Picture," he said, "a swift in your mind. Every detail, from beak to tail-feathers. Don't let any other thoughts come in."

The moment he said that, it was impossible *not* to be distracted. All Ivy could think about was Cicely's expression as she said, *You're awfully brown...*

"You've lost it already, haven't you?"

"Don't talk to me," she said irritably.

"You're going to have to do this with every kind of noise and distraction around. You might as well start learning now."

Ivy scowled, trying to marshal her scattered thoughts. Meanwhile Richard, blast him, started *whistling*—no, not so much whistling as trilling, a persistent chirrup-noise she'd never heard before. What bird sang like that?

And now the swift-image was gone again. She screwed her

eyes shut for another attempt. Mentally she traced and retraced every line of the swift's small body, down to the tiny patch of white feathers beneath its chin—until Richard exclaimed and Ivy opened her eyes to find a perfect illusion of a swift flashing around the cavern.

She threw up her hands, and the glamour vanished. "That's not what I meant to do!"

"No," said Richard, "but it's not a bad start." He ran a finger thoughtfully over his split lip. "Maybe if you create the illusion first, and focus on that..."

"And then what?"

"Then will yourself into its form."

That didn't sound so hard. Ivy brushed a curl back from her forehead, conjured the swift-image again, and silently commanded her body to take its shape. Harder and harder she concentrated, until her skin began to tingle. It was working! She could feel her muscles shifting, her bones beginning to shrink...

But when she opened her eyes, she was still in piskey-form. She'd made herself as small as a swift, but she hadn't taken its shape. "Ugh!" said Ivy, changing back to her usual size. "Why isn't it working?"

"I was afraid of this," said Richard. "Without being able to show you how I take bird shape, it's impossible to teach you how to do it. Did your mother ever have to explain to you the steps that go into creating a glamour? Of course not. You watched her a few times, and you *knew.*"

It was true. Magic was a matter of instinct rather than learning, for piskeys and all magical folk. But Ivy could see where this was leading, and she didn't like it. "So you're saying that unless I take the iron off your ankle and let you go, I'll never be able to fly."

Richard opened his mouth, made a face and closed it again. Finally he said, "There are a couple of things you can try first.

You might find it easier to change shape outside, where there are no walls or ceilings to hold you back. If that doesn't work, try it by moonlight."

"Moonlight? What difference would that make?"

"It'll make your magic stronger. A full moon on a clear night would be best, but any moonlight's better than none."

Ivy glanced back at the darkened shaft. She was too tired to climb to the top right now, after so many long nights and daytime trips to the surface. And Mica had come back later than usual that evening, so she didn't have much time to spare.

"All right," she said. "I'll try tomorrow."

"Then I wish you good luck," said Richard. "But if you could speed up your experiments a little, I'd appreciate it. One meal a day isn't much to go on, and I'm not sure how much longer your Joan plans to keep me alive."

He spoke casually, but the wildness in his eyes reminded Ivy of when she'd first seen him, clutching his injured arm and babbling Shakespeare. Battered, starving, and desperate for light, he might not keep his sanity much longer. Then what would Ivy do?

"I can't promise anything," she said as she reached for her rope. "But I'll do what I can."

When Ivy returned the only sound in the cavern was Mica's rattling snore, and for once she was glad of it. Keeping her glow dim, she tiptoed to her bed-alcove and climbed in. If she could stop fretting about swifts and Richard and her mother for a few minutes, maybe she'd be able to—

"Ivy?"

It was only a sleepy mumble, but Ivy's heart dropped into

her stomach. It took her several seconds to collect her wits and whisper, "It's all right, Cicely. I'm here."

She waited, but there was no answer, and finally Ivy relaxed. Most likely Cicely was just talking in her sleep, and wouldn't remember it in the morning.

"Sleep well, little sister," she murmured, as she lay down and closed her eyes.

Tired though she was, Ivy woke early enough to rouse Mica for the morning hunt, though he looked even more sour than usual about it.

"You were out late last night," she said, as she packed up a cold pasty and a bottle of small beer for Flint's lunch. His thunder-axe was still propped outside the bedroom door, so maybe she'd be able to get some breakfast into him before he vanished again. "What happened?"

Mica poured himself a mug of hot chicory and gulped half of it, making a face as he set it down. "I brought coffee back from Redruth," he said. "Why are you still making this muck?"

"If you don't like it, make coffee yourself," said Ivy. "Why are you changing the subject?"

Mica shot her a baleful glare. Then, with a glance at Cicely's curtained alcove, he leaned close and muttered, "Gem and Feldspar spotted someone—or some*thing*—sneaking about the Engine House last night."

Ivy's lips formed a silent *oh.*

"But it disappeared before they could get a proper look. So Gossan sent a few of us out to see if we could track it, but..." He shrugged, and took another swig of chicory. "No luck. Whatever it was came and went like the wind."

"You think it's another spriggan?" asked Ivy. She'd been so caught up watching the swifts, she'd forgotten that Keeve's murderer could still be out there.

"Maybe." Mica dropped the empty mug onto the table and picked up his hunter's knife. "But we're not supposed to talk about it, so keep that to yourself."

"Ready, Mica?" The voice came so quietly through the crack in the door that only piskey ears could have heard it. It always amazed Ivy that a boy as big as Mattock should be so soft-spoken.

"I'm coming." Mica swung his pack over his shoulder, gave Ivy a last warning glance and disappeared.

Ivy stooped over the hearth and stirred the porridge, her brows creasing in a frown. Who was the shadowy figure that Gem and Feldspar had seen creeping about the hillside? Could Richard have had a companion, who was now looking for him? It seemed unlikely that two strangers would turn up around the same time, if they weren't connected...

"Is there any porridge left?" asked Cicely, climbing out of her alcove. But her gaze was downcast, and she spoke without her usual spirit. Had she overheard Mica? Or merely sensed Ivy's troubled mood?

"Yes, of course," Ivy said, doing her best to sound cheerful. "With berries and cream too, if you like."

The two of them were sitting down to eat when Flint emerged from his bedchamber, dressed in the same dusty clothes he'd worn the day before. Once he had been handsome, and so like Betony that the two of them might have been twins. But now his features sagged as though his skin were too big for him, and his eyes were dull as pebbles.

"Come and have porridge, Dad," Ivy said, offering him her bowl. But he shook his head, and reached for his thunder-axe.

Ivy wanted to grab her father and shake him, but she knew it would do no good. She heard him coughing in the night sometimes, but he never took any of Yarrow's medicines to make it better. His hands shook whenever he gripped anything lighter than a shovel, and his teeth were yellow with neglect—yet he didn't seem to care about those things, either. So why should he bother eating breakfast?

"Take this, then," Ivy said, pushing the packed lunch against his chest. He curled his arm around it, swung the magical pick-axe onto his shoulder and walked out without another glance.

Oh, Mother, Ivy thought, leaning wearily on the table. *Even if you stopped loving him, surely you didn't want him to end up like this?*

Going up to the surface today, with half the Delve's hunters on alert, would be the biggest risk Ivy had taken yet. But she couldn't let that stop her. Because if Marigold was alive, she needed to know how much her family missed her, and how desperately they needed her to come back.

Ivy waited until Cicely went off for her lessons, then crept out of the Delve with all her usual caution. All seemed well at first, though as she turned into the Earthenbore she had an uneasy feeling that she was being watched. But no one stepped out to challenge her, so after a brief hesitation she kept on.

Once outside she found a good spot on the hillside from which to launch herself, and went through the steps Richard had taught her. *Picture the swift. Focus on the swift. Become the swift.* Yet despite several minutes of jaw-clenching effort, it was no use. No matter how hard Ivy concentrated or how much magic she put into her efforts, she was still the same wingless piskey-girl as always.

Ivy sat down and hugged her knees, doubt snaking into her mind. When she'd seen her first swift and felt that powerful connection, she'd felt certain she was meant to fly. But what if Richard's first instinct had been right, and she *couldn't* change shape? What if her piskey blood, or some quirk of her female nature, made it impossible?

Well, she'd find out tonight, one way or the other. Maybe moonlight would do for her what will alone could not. But after so many failures, it was hard to believe that such a small thing would make any difference.

She was back in the cavern, making a fish pie for supper, when Cicely came in. "Did you have a good lesson?" she asked, but Cicely didn't reply. She kicked off her shoes and climbed into her bed-alcove, pulling the curtain shut.

That wasn't like her at all. Ivy wiped her hands on her apron and followed. "What's the matter?" She opened the curtain and found her little sister lying on her side, her eyes squeezed shut. Her cheeks were flushed, her forehead warm to the touch.

No wonder she'd been so quiet earlier. "Does your stomach hurt?" Ivy asked. "Or your chest? Shall I get Yarrow to make a potion?"

"No," mumbled Cicely. "I just want to rest. Please go away."

Ivy stepped back and let the curtain drop. Perhaps her sister had become overheated running around with the other children, and would be better in an hour or so.

"I'll get you some water," she said. "Drink as much as you can. If you're not well by suppertime, I'll call for Yarrow."

To Ivy's relief, Cicely got up and joined her for supper. She wasn't her usual talkative self, but she ate a generous helping of fish pie, and helped Ivy wash up afterward. She spent the rest of the evening working on the socks she'd been knitting for Mica, then climbed into bed without complaint.

By the time Mica returned, Ivy had snuffed out the day-lamps and was pretending to be asleep. She waited until his breathing deepened into the usual full-throated rumble, then dropped lightly to the rug and tiptoed out.

All seemed quiet as she made her way through the tunnels, but halfway up the Hunter's Stair she froze, her skin prickling. Had she heard a footstep? She turned, ready to confront her pursuer and brazen it out. But she saw nothing behind her, not even the tiniest glimmer of light.

Ivy climbed faster, silently rebuking herself for letting her nerves get the better of her. Yes, it would be disastrous if someone caught her sneaking out of the Delve. But she'd already taken that risk three times by daylight, so there was no reason to turn coward now.

When she emerged onto the hillside, she had to look both ways before she spotted the moon. Only half-full, and dimmed by streaks of cloud, but it would have to do. Now, where to begin? She couldn't return to the spot she'd tried earlier, with its too-gentle slope that reeked of fear and failure. If this were her last chance to change shape, she had to be bolder. Ivy set off at an angle across the hill, crunching through the heather and bracken.

Soon she reached a spot where the rocks broke through the soil, and the ground dropped steeply away. It would have been a long jump to the bottom even for a human, and at piskey size it was high enough to make her nervous. But it was the perfect place to launch from, if she became a swift.

Ivy tilted her head back, closing her eyes as the moonlight tingled on her skin. Summoning the familiar bird-image in her mind, she spread her arms wide, stepped forward...

And a scream rang out behind her.

Ivy whirled—and her foot slipped. Arms flailing, legs twisted together, she let out a cry of her own as she toppled over the edge. But the shout became a shriek, keening high in her ears, and her skin changed to feathers as she fell. She skimmed a hand's span over the rocks and zoomed upward, into the open sky.

She was flying! Joy filled Ivy, from her crown to her forked tail-feathers. Though she'd never flown before, she felt no fear; her new body was the perfect shape to bend the air currents to her bidding, and she could change speed or direction with a flick of a feather. How could she ever have thought wind had no substance? The updraft beneath her wings felt solid as the earth itself.

Ivy soared higher, the landscape beneath her dropping away. Her swift's eyes were sharper than her piskey ones had ever been, and she could pick out every feature of the countryside below—hills and valleys, houses and barns, and here and there the silhouettes of old whim-engine and pumping-engine houses, remnants of the hundreds of tin mines that now lay abandoned and overgrown. Lights dotted the horizon like bits of shattered crystal—not merely the small clusters of human dwellings she'd grown used to, but whole towns and cities glittering in the dark. And in the distance lay more houses, more towns, open land both wild and tame... and beyond, the gray rolling waves of the ocean.

Excitement surged in Ivy. She could fly anywhere she wanted, now. In fact, if she'd known where Truro was, she could have flown to her mother this very minute.

Then she remembered the cry that had startled her, and the warmth in her chest turned chill. It might have been an animal or a passing bird, but what if it wasn't? Ivy doubled back toward the familiar hillside, searching for signs of life. But all that greeted her were the dull hues of wild greens and shrubberies, earth and clay and stone. And though she listened closely with her bird-keen ears, the only sound was the wind whispering through the bracken.

It was a relief to think she'd imagined it. She'd barely stretched her wings yet, and there was still a glorious infinity of open sky to explore. But the night wouldn't last forever, and now that Richard had proved himself, it was time Ivy set him free. Maybe, if she moved quickly, there'd still be time for him to take her to her mother.

Ivy hurried down the tunnel to her home cavern, giddy with the thrill of flight. Before heading underground she'd transformed into a swift and back again several times, until she could leap aloft easily as blinking and land with barely a stumble. Changing shape felt so natural now, she felt sure she wouldn't need moonlight to do it again.

I can fly! Ivy's heart sang. She wanted to burst into the cavern and shout her triumph, wake up Mica and Cicely so they could see the miracle. But she had to free Richard first. Dimming her glow, she eased the door open and tiptoed in.

Flint's thunder-axe was propped against the wall, with his well-worn boots beside it. Ivy glanced at the bed-alcoves, making sure all the curtains were drawn. Then with painstaking care she lifted the magical pickaxe and carried it out the door.

Lowering herself down the Great Shaft was a nerve-wracking business. Every time the pick's weight shifted Ivy caught her breath, fearing the precious tool would slip free of her makeshift harness and fall into the flooded depths below. But at last she made it to Richard's cell.

"I did it," she panted, as she loosened the ropes around her chest and lifted the thunder-axe. "Now let's get that iron off your ankle."

Richard looked blank, and Ivy wondered if he'd understood. "I said," she began more loudly, but he cut her off.

"I heard you," he replied. "I'm just a bit unused to *pleasant* surprises, that's all. Are you really planning to strike off my manacle with that thing? From the way you're staggering about, it seems more likely you're going to smash my foot to bits."

"I'll try not to," said Ivy tartly. She crouched beside him, examining the iron band. "How did they put this on?"

"I don't know. I was unconscious—" But then Ivy slipped her fingers between the manacle and his skin, and his words ended in a gasp.

"Did I hurt you?" Ivy snatched her hand back. "I didn't mean to."

"Not that." Richard sounded shaken. "It's—you. You touched iron on *purpose.*"

Of course. She'd forgotten what a shock that would be to him. "My people have been working with rock and metal for centuries," Ivy said, feeling her way around the band. "If we lost our magic every time we touched iron, how would we get anything done?" She frowned. "I can't find a hinge or a keyhole anywhere. They must have spelled it onto your ankle."

He stared at her. "You mean piskeys can use magic on iron, too?"

"Some of us can. Unfortunately for you, I'm not one of them. That's why I borrowed this." She nodded at the thunder-axe. "But we'll need to put some padding around your ankle first."

Richard pulled off what was left of his shirt and handed it to her. His skin was sickly-pale beneath the bruises, his ribs clearly visible. "Try not to swoon," he said dryly.

"I've never swooned in my life," said Ivy. She tore the shirt into strips, and pushed as much of the fabric as she could beneath the manacle. "Ready?"

Richard looked apprehensive, but he nodded.

"Just one question," Ivy said as she hefted the pickaxe. "And tell the truth. When you came here looking for me, on Lighting night—did you bring someone with you? Did you tell anyone where you'd gone?"

She searched his face for a hint of guilt. But he only looked puzzled. "Your Joan asked me the same thing this morning," he said. "But no, I came alone. And the only one who knew I was coming here was Marigold."

If he was a liar, he was a very good one. "All right," said Ivy, and swung the thunder-axe down.

The blade struck with a ringing *clank* and a spark of brilliant blue light. Richard made a strangled noise, and she knew the blow had hurt him—but when Ivy's dazzled vision cleared, the band was still unbroken. Maybe if she pushed a bit of magic into it first? With scarcely a pause, Ivy raised the thunder-axe and brought it down again.

This time the spark was so bright, Ivy nearly dropped the pick. The iron manacle cracked apart, and fell clattering to the stone.

"Finally," Richard breathed. He sat back and rubbed his ankle, which was cruelly blistered where the iron had touched it. She waited for him to do some magic—heal himself perhaps, or spell himself clean, or mend his tattered clothes. But he didn't move.

"Well?" she asked. "Aren't you going to fly?"

Richard raised his eyebrows. "After wearing iron for a week? It'll be hours—maybe days—before I can do magic again. I'm not flying anywhere tonight."

Ivy recoiled as though he'd slapped her. "You can't be serious. You promised—"

"I said I'd take you to your mother. I never said I could

do it right away." But there was no triumph in his tone, only resignation. "I can't even get out of this cell, unless you lead me out yourself."

Ivy's hands tightened on the thunder-axe. She'd been prepared for everything from passionate gratitude to cold-blooded betrayal, but she'd never anticipated this. "I can't do that. If we're caught..."

"Then go, and leave me here." He spoke wearily, as though he'd expected nothing better. "Maybe I can find somewhere to hide before your Joan comes to execute me tomorrow."

Alarm stabbed into Ivy. "She told you that?"

"Oh yes. Quite matter-of-factly. I'm to be hanged in the Market Cavern, with someone called Hew knotting the rope, and my body left in the Engine House as a warning to my accomplice. Whoever that is."

Ivy wished she could believe he was lying, but his story was far too likely. Keeve's family were still crying out for vengeance, and if Richard's body was left to deter whatever creature had been skulking about the Engine House, it would satisfy the hunters as well.

"But you never know," Richard went on. "Maybe in a few hours I'll be strong enough to fly out of here—though that's going to be tricky with no light." His mouth twisted ruefully. "Pity I never learned bat-shape."

He was right, Ivy thought in dismay. If she'd been worried about Cicely flying up the Great Shaft without any light, how could she expect Richard to do better? The only way to get him safely to the surface was to guide him there herself.

Yet to free a prisoner that the Joan had condemned, and lead him through tunnels that no one but piskeys were allowed to see—it was unthinkable. If Ivy were caught, not only would she bring disgrace on her entire family, she'd probably be executed as well.

I can't do this, her mind cried out, *there has to be another way.* But it was too late for that. First she'd fixed Richard's arm, then she'd fed and watered him, and now she'd freed him. And she'd sworn to help him get out of the Delve.

Ivy drew a deep breath, mustering strength. Then she hefted Flint's thunder-axe and said, "All right. Follow me."

7

If carrying the thunder-axe down the shaft had been hard, getting it back up was even more of a challenge. Growing a little made the pick lighter for her to carry, but it also made Ivy heavier and put more strain on the rope. She'd only climbed a short way before she had to shrink to her customary size, and by the time she reached the iron railing she was exhausted.

"I'm up," she panted to Richard, making her glow as bright as she dared so that he'd have enough light for his own climb. "Tie the rope around your waist, and I'll—"

But Richard was already pulling himself up toward her, bare feet braced against the rock. His strength surprised Ivy—if he could manage such a climb even in his weakened state, how strong had he been before? But when he reached the railing he stopped, leaning back on the rope.

"That's iron," he said flatly. "I can't touch it."

"You have to," she whispered, but he shook his head.

"Touching iron's like an electric shock to a faery—it doesn't just take away our magic, it *hurts*. It can even knock us unconscious. If I grab it, I may not be able to hang on." He shifted his footing and stretched his hand up toward her. "I'll have to jump, and let you pull me over."

This was ridiculous, thought Ivy. They'd never get out of

the Delve at this rate. Still, there seemed no other solution, so she leaned over the railing and gripped his hand in hers.

"One," mouthed Richard, crouching against the rock. "Two. *Three–*"

He sprang upward, while Ivy braced her feet and hauled with all her might. The iron groaned as Richard's weight landed on it, then blazed white as it touched bare skin. He gasped and convulsed–but in the same moment Ivy dragged him over, and the two of them landed in a heap.

"Ow," Richard moaned, pressing one hand to his stomach. Dizzy with relief, Ivy sat up and crawled over to the railing to untie her rope. She coiled it up, slung it across her body and picked up the thunder-axe.

"Come on," she said. "We've got a long way to go."

"This is incredible," murmured Richard. "Is that *silver?"*

She'd told him to stay close and put his hand on her shoulder, so she could keep her glow dim. Not only because she feared some late-wandering piskey might spot them, but because no outsider should ever see the treasures of the Delve. Unfortunately, the faery's night-vision was better than she'd thought.

"Stop it," she hissed, quickening her pace. "Keep your eyes down."

He obeyed, or at least kept silent, until they turned the corner. But then he made a disbelieving noise, and Ivy knew he'd just seen the thousands of tiny gemstones set into the tunnel walls. Only total darkness could have hidden them, and she didn't dare extinguish her light or they'd never get anywhere. But hearing Richard's slow, wondering exhale made Ivy feel more like a traitor than ever.

She hugged her father's thunder-axe, arm muscles burning with the strain of carrying the heavy pick so long. She didn't dare try shifting it to a more comfortable position—if she dropped it, the crash would be loud enough to wake the whole Delve. Richard might be willing to take it, but she hated to look weak, and she didn't trust him enough to hand him something he could use as a weapon.

They'd only gone a few more steps when a stone spiked into her heel, throwing her off-balance. Ivy staggered, bumping into the tunnel wall. The thunder-axe's head tipped away from her, and she felt the haft twisting from her grip—

Richard leaped forward, his hands locking over hers and catching the pickaxe a hand's-breadth from the floor. For a few uneven heartbeats the two of them stared into each other's eyes, breathing hard. Then Ivy gave a shaky nod and hefted the pick again.

By the time they reached her home cavern, Ivy's nerves were jangling. Little shivers ran over her skin as she crept inside, and she felt horribly sure that at any moment Mica or Cicely would fling open their curtains and confront her. When her brother mumbled as she was lowering the thunder-axe to the floor, she had to clamp her teeth shut on a scream. But then the familiar snores returned, and she managed to quell her panic and carry on.

"Done it," she whispered to Richard as she slipped out, easing the door shut behind her. Then she grabbed his arm and hurried up the tunnel. She couldn't bear to keep skulking about; it was too unnerving. Better to make a bold rush for the surface while they could.

They'd passed the Narrows and were starting up the Hunter's Stair when Richard seized her wrist. Annoyed, Ivy was about to demand he let go when she heard the voices.

There was no time to discuss it. Backing hastily down the steps, Ivy pulled Richard into the first hiding place she could find—a shallow curve of the tunnel, barely wide enough for the two of them. Flattening him against the wall with one outstretched arm, she pressed beside him, extinguished her glow, and fervently willed them both invisible.

"...doesn't mean he won't come back," said Feldspar's voice from above. "Next time he'll bring friends, and we'll have a battle on our hands."

"You think so?" That was Gem, boots clomping as he headed down the steps. "I can't see it. We've always kept our heads down when their kind were about, and we haven't lost a hunter in years. Excepting young Keeve, of course. But he always was a wild one, and I wouldn't be surprised—" He stopped. "What?"

"Hush a minute." Feldspar sounded tense. "Did you hear that?"

Ivy's heart was pounding so hard, she felt sure it would smash right out of her chest. She closed her eyes, willing the invisibility glamour to hold. The hunters were close by, their combined glows banishing every shadow, and if she let the illusion waver even for an instant...

"What's to hear?" asked Gem with a snort. "You think a spriggan could follow us right into the Delve? If he's that crafty and we're that blind, we may as well hand over our treasure now."

Richard's chest rose sharply beneath Ivy's arm, and she could practically hear his thought: *Treasure?*

Her lips flattened. If he turned out to be a spriggan after all, she'd never forgive herself.

Above them, Feldspar chuckled. "All right, I'll quit trying to prank you. But I'm not joking about there being more of those creatures. Two sightings in a week—that can't be an accident. And who's to say that killing one won't just make the rest of them angry?"

"Ah, you're a twitch-nosed rabbit. We're safe enough in the Delve, so let 'em come, I say..."

Lost in friendly argument, the two hunters continued down the tunnel into the Narrows, passing so close to Ivy that she could feel their glows warming her skin. But they never looked around, and soon even the sound of their footsteps faded.

Ivy relaxed, but her mind was racing. So Gem and Feldspar had been out all night, looking for spriggans. How close had she come to meeting them earlier? Had they heard the scream that startled her into flight?

Richard gave a little cough, and she realized she was still pressing him against the wall. Embarrassed, Ivy let go.

"We'd better hurry," she whispered as she stepped out into the corridor, rekindling her light. "It's safe now, but there isn't much time."

By the time they reached the surface the moon had vanished, and a light rain was falling. Ivy rubbed her bare arms, but Richard flung his wide as though to embrace the sky.

"Finally," he crowed. "I thought I'd never breathe fresh air again."

This was the moment Ivy had dreaded. He was stronger and faster than she was; if he chose to betray her, she'd have no way to stop him.

"You taught me to fly," she said. "Now I've set you free, as we agreed. But there's one more thing. Swear to me that you'll tell no one what you saw in the Delve tonight. *No one.*"

"A good mouth-filling oath?" Richard turned, his smile

fading to seriousness as his pewter-gray gaze met hers. "I swear it," he said. "By my blood and by my name. My *true* name."

Maybe she could depend on him after all. "But you still have to take me to my mother," she said. "I'll come and find you when I get the chance, but—"

"You're not coming now?"

"I can't." It hurt to admit it, but she had to face the truth. "If I don't get home soon, my family will wake up and find me missing. And when they realize you're gone as well..."

"They'll think we've eloped?" said Richard with a quirk of the eyebrows, but when Ivy glared at him he relented. "My apologies. They'll think I've taken you hostage, of course."

Ivy nodded. "That's why I have to go. But..." She drew herself up. "I risked my life for you tonight, and I hope you won't make me regret it. Promise that when I call for you, tomorrow night or the next, you'll be here."

A muscle jumped in Richard's cheek. He wrapped his arms around himself, as though he'd just remembered he was shirtless. "Tomorrow *or* the next, you say. And if you can't come by then?"

"You'll be free to go." She couldn't expect him to wait forever, after all. "But if you leave a note telling me where my mother is, I'll be able to look for her on my own. So you'll have kept your word to both of us."

Richard gave her a narrow look. "Not to the letter, which is how we faeries make our bargains. But perhaps Marigold will see it differently. As you wish." Without another word, he walked off down the hillside.

"That's gratitude," called Ivy after him, but the faery didn't look back. Telling herself it was foolish to feel hurt—what could she expect from someone who wasn't even a piskey?—Ivy swept the bracken aside and vanished into the Delve.

Ivy dreamed that she was flying, and at first she was sorry to wake—until she remembered she *could* fly, and broke into an involuntary smile. But her bones ached, and her eyelids felt so heavy. Surely it wasn't morning yet?

But there was no doubting her piskey sense of time; it was as unfailing as her sense of direction. She had to get up and wake the others, or they'd suspect something was wrong with her. Repressing a sigh, Ivy struggled out of bed and lit the day-lamps. She prodded Mica with the broom handle until he swore and slapped it away, then crossed to Cicely's alcove, opened the curtains...

And found her sister's bed empty.

"Cicely?" Ivy turned, searching the cavern. She passed a hand over the pillow, then the bedclothes, but felt no trace of warmth. "Mica, did you hear Cicely get up a while ago?"

Mica poked his head out between the curtains, his black hair tousled with sleep. "What? No."

A fearful suspicion stirred in Ivy. She went to the door and opened it, looking both ways. "Cicely! Are you there?"

"Don't be ridiculous," said Mica, muffled by the shirt he was pulling over his head. "Where would she go at this hour?"

He had a point, but Ivy wasn't about to acknowledge it. She grabbed her wrap off its hook. "I'm going to look for her," she said, and dashed out.

An hour later she had visited all of Cicely's favorite places, knocked several sleepy families awake, and walked a circuit of the neighboring tunnels, calling all the while. Jenny joined her, as did Mica and Mattock, and between them they searched the Delve from Market Cavern to Earthenbore.

But there was no sign of Ivy's little sister anywhere. Cicely, like Keeve, had vanished.

8

Ivy sat shivering by the hearth in the Joan's stateroom, one of Cicely's hair ribbons crumpled in her hand. She barely noticed Betony pacing the rug as she questioned Mica about when he'd last seen Cicely, or Gossan's frown as he listened, or Flint standing in the doorway with a face as stony as his name. All Ivy knew was that her little sister was gone, and it was her fault.

After the first shock of Cicely's disappearance, it hadn't taken Ivy long to realize what had happened. The uneasy feeling she'd had yesterday, both times she went to the surface... she ought to have trusted her instincts. Because Cicely had been following her all along.

Perhaps it was Ivy's sun-browned skin that had roused Cicely's suspicions, or hearing her slip back into the cavern in the middle of the night. Perhaps she'd simply been eager to find out what "surprise" Ivy was preparing. But for whatever reason, Cicely had turned herself invisible and tiptoed behind her, only to discover that her older sister had been sneaking out of the Delve alone.

Cicely probably hadn't gone outside the first time—the afternoon light would have blinded her. Instead she'd retreated to her bed, to brood over what she'd seen. But when she heard

Ivy getting up in the night, it was the perfect chance to follow her a second time, and discover what she was up to.

It sickened Ivy to think she'd led her little sister into danger. But worse was knowing that the wailing cry that had startled her on the hillside must have been Cicely's. If she'd flown to investigate straight away, she might have been in time to save her. But Ivy had been caught up in the joy of her new swift-form, and by the time she turned back her sister was already gone.

"WHAT?" exploded Mica, and Ivy nearly dropped Cicely's ribbon in the fire. "That's impossible! I chained that spriggan up myself. There's no way he could have escaped!"

"And yet he did," said Betony crisply. "Perhaps the iron was not as pure as you thought, or perhaps he found some way to weaken it. But the prisoner has gone, and taken Cicely with him."

No, thought Ivy in dismay. *He couldn't have, he was with me.* But how could she say that?

"I'll kill him," Mica's voice was savage, his big hands clenched so tight they shook. "I'll track him all the way across Kernow if I have to, but I swear I won't rest until I break his skinny neck."

"There's a search party heading to the surface," said Gossan, "and our most seasoned hunters and trackers are among them. They will do everything in their power to find Cicely."

"No doubt," Mica said flatly, "but they can only go so far before they have to come back again. That's not good enough." He dropped to one knee. "Jack O'Lantern, Joan the Wad," he said formally to Gossan and Betony in turn, "I ask your permission to hunt the spriggan, for as long as it takes to find him and get my sister back."

"Alone?" asked Betony. "Leaving Ivy with no one to provide for her?"

She didn't even glance at Flint; they all knew that Ivy's father was unfit to look after anyone, even himself. He was safe enough working in the mine, but send him to the surface and he might well drown in a bog, or walk off a cliff into the sea.

"Mattock would take care of Ivy, if I asked him," said Mica quickly. "Or Jenny's clan could take her in until I get back."

And there it was again. Just because Ivy was wingless, because she was small and skinny and sometimes struggled to breathe, they talked about her as though she were an invalid. Never mind that she'd been managing a household for six years and doing the bulk of the chores as well. That didn't count, apparently.

Betony and Gossan shared a look. Then the Joan said, "Cicely must be found, yes, and her kidnapper punished. But this is not a task that any piskey should undertake alone."

"Then I'll put together my own search party," pleaded Mica. "I'll take Mattock with me, and Gem and Feldspar too if you want. But you have to let me go!"

"*Have* to?" Betony said coldly. "The Jack and I will do what is best for the Delve, Mica. Not only for you, but for *all* our people." She walked behind her desk and sat down, wings folded primly behind her. "I will consider your request, and inform you when we reach a decision."

Mica's expression turned mutinous. He sprang to his feet and stalked out.

"That one will make trouble," warned Nettle, as she poured the tea and handed a cup to Gossan. "He's moody, like his mother. And if he's not kept busy..."

"He will be," said the Joan, and now she sounded weary. Then she turned to Ivy and said, "Did you bring something of Cicely's with you? Give it here."

Silently Ivy got up and handed her the hair ribbon. Betony smoothed it out against her palm, then laid her other hand over it and closed her eyes. She must be casting a spell to try and find Cicely, Ivy thought, and held her breath. Of course the Joan would have tried the same spell when Keeve went missing, but perhaps this time...

"Nothing," said Betony. "I fear she is already beyond the range of my spells." She laid the ribbon down. "Tell me, Ivy. You said you and Mica had warned Cicely against going to the surface. Do you have any idea what drew her there, and made her disobey?"

"I–" Ivy's throat was so tight she could hardly speak. "I don't–"

"My love." Gossan leaned close to his wife's ear. "She has already lost her mother, and now her sister as well. Give her time to grieve."

Gratitude rushed into Ivy, followed by a hot wave of shame. She didn't deserve the Jack's compassion after the things she'd done. But if she confessed, they'd lock *her* up in the dungeon. And then she'd never get the chance to search for Cicely as only a swift could do.

"Very well," said Betony, waving a hand at Ivy. "You may go."

As Ivy walked to the door, Nettle followed her. "I know how it feels, to lose a sister," she said in a cracked whisper. "It's a hard, hard thing. I'll never see my poor Gillyflower again, but I hope you find your Cicely." She gave a last, sad smile, and closed the door.

Ivy was left alone with Flint, who stood like a statue with his thunder-axe over his shoulder. "She's gone, Dad," Ivy said, clutching at his free hand. "Cicely's gone. What should we do?"

She searched his face, but Flint didn't even blink. He pulled out of her grip, hefted his pickaxe, and walked away.

"What is wrong with you?" Ivy's voice rose high, breaking on the final word. "Don't you care about Cicely, or anything? Is this all you can do–bury yourself in the ground and hammer away until you drop dead, and we're left with no parents at all?"

Flint's head drooped a little, but he didn't answer. He kept walking past the stairs and the entrance to the Market Cavern, heading for the trap door that led to the diggings.

Ivy stared after him until he was nothing but a watery blur in the distance. Then she wiped her eyes angrily on the back of her hand, and ran to catch up with Mica.

"I can't believe Aunt Betony just dismissed me like that." Mica paced around their cavern, kicking at the rug. "Cicely's my sister; I should be the one to look for her. And I was the one who caught the spriggan in the first place. But from the way *she* was acting, you'd think it was my fault he'd escaped!"

Ivy sank into a chair, arms wrapped around her chest to hold the hurt inside. "I know," she said unevenly. "It's not fair."

"I can't understand how he got out," muttered Mica. "The iron was good—I made sure of it. He couldn't have got past that slab door, and he couldn't climb the shaft without a rope..."

Apprehension stirred in Ivy. If she let him go on, it wouldn't be long before he figured out someone had helped Richard escape. "What are you going to do?" she asked, to change the subject. "If Betony won't let you go..."

"She will. She's *got* to." Mica dropped onto the sofa, fists clenched on his knees. "I know the surface as well as any hunter in the Delve. I'm not afraid of spriggans. And I won't give up until I find Cicely, however long it takes. Who else can say that?"

I can, Ivy thought, but she didn't dare speak it aloud. Not until she knew she could trust him. "But if Betony doesn't listen, what will you do?"

His face creased with anguish. "What do you want me to

say? That I'd disobey the Joan and Jack, break every rule in the Delve if I had to, to find Cicely? You know I would. You would, too."

Ivy's eyes prickled, and she looked down at her lap. So Mica did understand. If she could only explain that she'd felt the same way about finding their mother...

"So if someone told you Cicely was alive, and they knew where she was," she said, "you'd do whatever it took to get to her? Even if—if everyone else said it was too dangerous, and you shouldn't go?"

"Of course." His voice sharpened. "I'm not a coward. What are you getting at?"

She must be careful now, very careful. If Mica guessed that Ivy had anything to do with Richard's escape, he'd turn against her in a heartbeat. "I've heard stories," she said. "About our ancestors, and other magical folk. How some of them could change into the shapes of animals, or—"

His face twisted with revulsion. "You want me to turn myself into an *animal?"*

Ivy hadn't even considered that possibility; she'd only meant to prepare him for the shock of seeing her change into swift-form. But perhaps it was a good thing he'd misunderstood. "Is that wrong?"

"Of course it is!" He flung himself to his feet and began to pace again. "If you'd ever *seen* a wild animal, let alone hunted one—"

"I don't understand."

Mica made an exasperated noise and raked his fingers through his hair. "Look, it's common sense. Piskeys have a special relationship with animals—you know that much?"

Ivy nodded.

"Well, when we become hunters, we swear to help any sick or injured creatures we find, and never kill them for sport. But they're still animals, and we have to eat. If we started turning ourselves into them, how could we hunt them? That's why it's forbidden."

"Who says?" asked Ivy. "I've never heard such a thing. And animals eat each other all the time. Maybe you wouldn't want to kill the exact kind of animal you become, but—"

Mica cut her off. "It's not just bad, it's against our nature. Piskeys are solid like the earth, not changeable like air or water. That's how we've survived."

That sounded like something Aunt Betony would say, though it made no sense to Ivy. If shape-changing was impossible for piskeys, why bother forbidding them to do it? "But the droll-teller said our ancestors used to change shape sometimes," she protested. "And some faeries still—"

"Faeries!" Her brother's mouth worked as though he were about to spit. "We don't go near their kind. Why should I want to do anything they do?"

"Because," said Ivy, controlling her impatience with an effort, "if you could turn into a bird and fly over the countryside instead of having to search it all on foot, you might have a better chance of finding Cicely."

Mica gave a harsh laugh. "A bird! Do you have any idea—" Then he stopped and repeated softly, "A *bird,*" as though it were a revelation.

Had he finally understood? It was on the tip of Ivy's tongue to tell him he was wrong about piskeys not being able to change, and prove it by transforming into a swift before his eyes. Maybe then he'd see how foolish it was to cling to some old hunters' superstition, and let her help him find Cicely.

"So that's how he did it," Mica went on, gazing past Ivy as though entranced. "I wouldn't have thought he could, but maybe..."

"Mica?" asked Ivy, wary now. "What are you talking about?"

His eyes focused on hers, alight with fervor. "I know how

the spriggan escaped," he said. "And I know how to catch him, too."

"What? How?"

"Never mind that. This is hunter business. I'm going to talk to Gossan." He started toward the door, then paused and turned back. "But if I were you, I'd forget all that dross about shape-changing. If the Joan knew you'd even suggested it..." He gave her a bleak smile. "Trust me. You don't want to know what she'd do."

Ivy slumped in her chair, more disheartened than ever. For one brief shining moment she'd dared to believe that she might not be alone, that she and Mica could put aside their differences and work together. And that if she explained it carefully, he might even understand why she'd gone outside the Delve and learned to change shape—because she'd truly believed it was the only way to find their mother.

But she'd been wrong, more wrong than she'd ever imagined. Because shape-changing wasn't merely unusual, it was forbidden. If Mica saw Ivy turn into a swift, he wouldn't just be surprised, he'd be horrified.

And now she'd put Richard in danger, too. She'd never meant Mica to guess that the so-called spriggan could become a bird, much less use that knowledge to trap him. Now he had a plan—one that might even work—and she had no idea what it was, or how to stop it. All she could do was warn Richard, and urge him to be on his guard.

But how could she meet him without giving herself away? The whole Delve was buzzing with the news of Cicely's disappearance, and there'd be searchers going in and out of the Earthenbore all day—not to mention all the neighbors coming by to offer Ivy their sympathies. Getting away would be impossible until tonight at the earliest, and it would be tricky even then.

A knock at the door startled Ivy from reverie. She got up and opened it, to find Mattock with a basket of flat cakes in one hand and a bottle of cream in the other. "My mum sent these for you," he said.

"Did she make the hevva cakes or did you?" asked Ivy, and he blushed. A few years ago Mica had caught Mattock helping his mother make saffron buns and had never let him forget it. "It's kind of you," she added, managing a smile. "We'll have them for tea, if Mica gets back in time."

"He's not here?" asked Mattock. "I'd have thought... well, with everything going on, I expected you'd be together."

"Mica doesn't like brooding over bad things," said Ivy. "He'd rather be doing something about them. Right now, he thinks he's figured out a way to catch the spriggan and get Cicely back before—"

Her throat closed up, and she couldn't finish. She took the gifts from Mattock's hands and turned away before her face betrayed her as well.

He followed her to the kitchen, his big frame looming over her as she set the bottle and basket down. She could feel his warmth against her back as he said quietly, "Ivy, it's no shame to cry."

"I'm not crying." She ground the words between her teeth. "Cicely's alive, and I'm going to find her. There's nothing to cry about."

"*You're* going to find her? How?"

Ivy wanted to beat her head against the counter and curse her own stupidity, but she forced a laugh. "I mean we are. All of us. Together."

And now she was babbling. Why wouldn't Mattock leave her

alone? Surely he could tell she didn't want anyone's company, didn't want to eat his stupid cakes or drink the cream that only Cicely really liked, didn't want anything except to find her sister, only no one would let her try—

Then Mattock put his hands on her shoulders, and Ivy's resistance crumbled. She turned and buried her face against his chest. "I can't believe she's gone," she whispered. "I should have known, Matt. I should have seen it coming."

He didn't say anything, only held her tight. It felt amazingly good to lean against him, feeling his strength like armor all around her—the last person she remembered holding her like this was Flint, and that had been years ago.

But she couldn't cling to Mattock forever, and surely he wouldn't want her to. Ivy straightened up, brushing at her cheeks. "I appreciate you coming by," she said with all the dignity she could muster. "Please tell your mum I'm grateful."

Mattock nodded and backed out of the cavern, closing the door with such exaggerated care that Ivy had to smile. Simple, honest Mattock. Sometimes she wished he were her brother instead of Mica, but that wouldn't be fair to him.

And it wouldn't be fair to drag him into her scheme for finding Cicely, either. She could only hope he wouldn't guess, after her foolish slip of the tongue, that she planned to do anything at all.

It was a grim and mostly silent meal that Ivy and Mica ate that night. Without Cicely's bright chatter the atmosphere in the cavern was oppressive, and even phrases like "pass the butter" fell with the weight of an anvil. Ivy soon found herself wishing that Flint would come and join them, just so she'd have someone else *not* to talk to.

But she hadn't seen her father since the morning, and when she'd met Hew coming up grimy-faced and coughing from the diggings, he'd told Ivy that Flint meant to stay later than usual to make up for the time he'd missed. As though losing Cicely had been merely an interruption to his work. As though it mattered whether he dug any more tin or copper out of that tunnel, or dug any more tunnels at all.

"He's a knocker, lass," Hew had reminded her gently. "He's only doing what he's made for. And maybe it's the best thing for him. Same as your brother, with the hunting. It's how we menfolk grieve."

What about me? Ivy wanted to shout at him. *I can't sense ore or shape metal. I'm not allowed to hunt. All I want to do is help look for my sister, but that's forbidden. How am I supposed to grieve?*

But there was no answer to that, at least not that Hew could give her. So she'd nodded politely, and then she'd gone back to the cavern and made a whole week's worth of meat pasties to keep in the cold-hole, since that at least was something she could do.

"What did Gossan say about your plan?" she asked Mica, when he'd finished his last bite and she could endure the silence no longer. "Did the Joan agree to let you look for Cicely?"

"They said I could go out tonight," replied Mica, wiping his mouth, "If Matt and Gem go with me. Only we have to stick together and be home by dawn, so what's the use?" He threw the napkin down. "We might as well not bother."

"But you will," said Ivy. She knew Mica too well to believe otherwise, no matter how much he complained. "When do you leave?"

"In a couple of hours." He walked toward his alcove. "But

Matt said he'd come by and wake me, so you needn't worry about it. I'm going to sleep."

Mechanically Ivy put what was left of the food away, then climbed into bed. She was drifting in and out of consciousness, too miserable to sleep but too tired to stay awake, when the door creaked and she heard Mattock tiptoe in. Mica groaned, there was a rustle, and a few minutes later the two of them went out.

Now was her chance. Ivy waited a few minutes to be sure Mica and Mattock were well on their way. Then hurriedly she dressed and slipped out into the passage, heading for the Great Shaft.

The sky above the Delve was clear, the moon a neat half-circle among the stars. To the west, a trio of dim lights bobbed along the ground—Mica, Mattock and Gem. Confident that they'd never recognize her in swift-form, Ivy glided through the ruins of the Engine House, then swooped toward the nearby wood.

It wasn't a large wood: only a scattering of trees and undergrowth, with a well-worn footpath through the middle. Ivy flew from one end to the other looking for signs of life, and landed in piskey-shape on the far side. "Richard?" she asked, quietly at first and then louder. But though she listened and called again, there was no reply.

"Richard!" She was shouting now, not caring if anyone heard. Surely Mica and the others wouldn't recognize her voice at this distance. "Where are you?"

Still no one answered, and Ivy's impatience grew. She couldn't hang about all night—she had to find Cicely. But she'd wanted to warn Richard about Mica's plan. Why didn't he answer?

Maybe he was too far away. Ivy walked to the center of the wood, cupped her hands around her mouth, and yelled "Richard!" one more time. Then she sat down on a fallen branch and waited.

Minutes passed, each more slowly than the last. Something rustled in the leaves above her, and Ivy glanced up in hope—but no, it was only a squirrel. A little while later a bird began to sing, but it was a liquid, melancholy tune, nothing like the trilling noises Richard had made in the dungeon.

Ivy rubbed her palms on her thighs, fidgeting with anxiety. What if Richard had broken his promise? What if he'd seen the search for Cicely, and decided it was too dangerous to stay?

"Richard!" she called hoarsely. "You'd better come! I'm not going to wait forever!"

But still there was nothing. Not a word, not a sign.

The faery was gone.

Ivy took a deep breath and let it go. Then she leaped to her feet, snatched up a stick and hurled it into the underbrush. "Curse you!" she stormed. "You liar, you oath-breaker, you—you demon blackguard wretch of a *spriggan!*"

There was a long silence while the wind murmured in the treetops. Then a light, ironic voice said, "I see my reputation is at stake."

Ivy spun around. There on the path, as though he had been there all along, stood Richard. But not Richard as she had last seen him, covered in filth and dressed in rags. His hair hung straight and clean almost to his shoulders, and his jacket and slim trousers looked new. If not for the purple shadow around one eye and the scab on his upper lip, she would scarcely have recognized him.

But before she could speak he vanished. A tiny bird with a

blue-black head, shadowy wings and white underbelly flicked past, landed on her other side, and changed into Richard again.

"I was a few hundred feet up when I heard you calling," he said. "And I needed to be sure you'd come alone."

Blood rushed into Ivy's face. She'd been so busy worrying if she could trust him, it had never occurred to her that he might have similar doubts. "You thought I'd betray you?"

"Not willingly, no. But if your Joan found out that you'd helped me, she might not have given you a choice."

He had a point. Ivy's fury subsided, and she gave a reluctant nod.

"Ready to go?" Richard asked. "It's a little late, but we should be able to get to Truro in time."

"I can't." Ivy passed a weary hand over her curls. "My little sister's gone missing."

He frowned. "You mean she just disappeared? Like that other one—Keeve?"

Ivy hoped not, since she suspected Keeve was dead. But she couldn't deny the similarity. "Yes. Do you have any idea where she might have gone?"

Richard looked sober. "None at all."

No easy answers, then. She'd hoped she wouldn't have to do this, but she could see no other way. "Then I'll have to say goodbye," Ivy told him. "I can't go to my mother until I find Cicely. Besides, my brother's guessed you can take bird-shape, and he thinks he's got a way to catch you. It's not safe for you to stay here."

"What do you want me to do, then? Go back to your mother and tell her you aren't coming?"

How could one little word be so hard to say? "Yes. But," she added quickly, "don't leave it at that. Tell her everything that's happened—especially about Cicely." If Marigold knew her youngest daughter was missing, maybe she'd come and help with the search. "And tell her that if she has any more messages, she'll have to deliver them herself. You've done enough."

The faery's brows lifted, and he gave her an appraising look. Then he bowed without a trace of irony, and vanished. He didn't even turn into a bird; he was simply *not there.* Ivy stared at the place where he'd been until her eyes began to burn. Then she shook herself into swift-form and flew away.

Ivy hunted for Cicely all night, gliding low over the rocky ground. She glimpsed a badger digging in the underbrush, and fox cubs tussling at play; she passed fields where rabbits browsed in the grass, and watched an owl wing silently by. The twin lamps of a human car swept the roadway, turned into the drive of a little farmstead and winked out, while in the distance hundreds of twinkling lights marked the edge of some great city. Yet she found no sign that Cicely had passed that way.

She turned west and flew along the Cornish coast, skimming past sweeping curves of sand and coves where foam-capped breakers smashed against the rocks. The sea-cliffs were riddled with holes, many of them adits from abandoned mine workings that might even connect to the Delve. But still she found no trace of her sister.

Absorbed in her search, Ivy scarcely noticed the thread of gold creeping along the horizon. Not until the sky lightened from black to deep blue and the air began to fill with squawking gulls did Ivy realize it was dawn—and that she should have been home long ago. Cursing herself for being so careless, she wheeled and flashed toward the Delve. Mica would be returning any minute, and if she didn't make it back to the cavern before he did, there'd be trouble.

Then she caught sight of her brother at the top of a ridge, with Mattock and Gem by his side. From the way he was waving his arms he must be furious about something, but that was of no matter. All Ivy cared about was getting down the Great Shaft.

Only she couldn't, because birds zoomed at her from every direction, warbling and squawking in a cacophony of avian speech. A pair of swifts darted around her, black eyes staring cold and bright into hers—and then the whole flock dived beneath her, a whirlwind of beaks and feathers, heading for the hillside where Mica and his companions stood.

Bewildered, Ivy hung back as the mixed multitude of birds spiraled around the hunters, still uttering their wordless cries. Had Mica sent them to look for the spriggan? Were they reporting to him somehow? She was still puzzling over it when Mica waved his hand and the flock scattered, flapping off as quickly as they had come.

Except for the swifts. They hovered before him, uttering staccato shrieks, while Mica stood still as though listening. Then he made a sharp gesture, and the swifts shot off like twin arrows—straight at Ivy.

For an instant her mind went blank. Then she remembered what Richard had told her: *Swifts are communal birds. If you don't behave like a proper swift the other ones will sense it, and instead of welcoming you, they'll attack...*

Panic erupted in Ivy's breast. She whirled and fled, wings drumming frantically as she shot toward the Engine House and the capped shaft beside it. But the other swifts were more experienced fliers, and they quickly cut her off. Forced into retreat, Ivy swerved toward the wood, with the other swifts in close pursuit.

"Stop!" she screamed, but it came out as a shriek—and then the swifts were on her, all stabbing beaks and beating wings. Buffeted by their rage, Ivy struggled vainly to fend them off. But escape was impossible, and hopelessness filled her as she realized they were herding her toward Mica and the other piskeys.

Tsier-sier, sang another bird as it passed above, mocking her with its freedom. Ivy cried out as a swift's beak jabbed into her breast, piercing feathers and skin. She had to get away, or they would tear her to pieces. She folded her wings and dropped earthward—then snapped them wide and shot up the slope in a last, desperate run for the Engine House.

Mica shouted, and the whizzing sound of his sling rippled the air. Ivy sensed the stone hurtling toward her and rolled—a second too late. Heat scored her back, and the muscles of her shoulder separated in a blaze of dazzling pain. The ground spiraled up to meet her, and she knew it would only be seconds before she hit—

A freak wind blasted the hillside, thrashing the gorse bushes and rippling the heather in its wake. Flapping helplessly, Ivy felt herself tossed upward on the breeze. She was still trying to fly, despite the blinding pain, when a figure loomed before her and ruthless hands snatched her from the air.

Ivy gave a final shriek of agony and terror. Then she willed herself into piskey-form, and let the darkness take her away.

She had thought fainting would be like sleep, a quiet place where she knew nothing and no one could touch her. But though darkness hazed her vision and she had a fuzzy sense of being disconnected from her body, she could hear a voice, sounding faint and far away.

"—don't know where you fell yet, but they'll be here any—"

A moment of merciful oblivion, then it returned, louder and closer.

"–hide you somewhere. But if they find us–"

The words rose and fell in gasps, as though the speaker were running. Strangely, Ivy felt as though she were rising and falling, too. But she had no idea where she was or who had caught her. A dull pain radiated through her shoulder and out from her chest, but she couldn't tell what any of it meant.

"–stop it. Do you hear me? You have to–"

The words faded again, and the next time she became aware, the up-and-down sensation had stopped. An earthy smell rose around her, damp seeping through her clothes. She was lying down and someone was covering her up, but why were the blankets so wet and heavy?

Then the darkness shattered, and pain smashed into her like rocks falling. Ivy tried to scream, but a hand clamped over her mouth, muffling the cry. "Stop glowing!" her rescuer snapped. *"Now!"*

Ivy was too dazed to protest. She willed herself not to glow, and tried to breathe through the pain instead. Soon all was black except for a few glints of gray light above her, and she found herself half-buried in dirt, her head resting on something warm that smelled like fir needles...

Richard.

"...can't have got far," said a soft voice from above, and Ivy felt sure she must be dreaming, because it sounded like Mattock. "But how could he disappear like that?"

"Quiet," came the reply, lower and harsher. "Keep looking. He could be anywhere."

Mica. Ivy caught her breath, but agony stabbed her chest and she let out a feeble moan. The foliage above rustled, and Richard covered her mouth again, all his muscles tensed.

Don't move, his body told her. *Don't make a sound.*

Ivy dug her fingers into Richard's arm and bit her lip to

keep from screaming. How long had she lain in this dank hole? It felt like forever, and the fiery knots of pain in her chest and shoulder blotted out all other sensations. She would have surrendered to Mica and Mattock gladly, if only it would make the hurting stop.

"...Ivy, it's all right. They've gone."

She should have been relieved, but now it hardly seemed to matter. Was it getting brighter? It could be the sun's rays angling into the hole, but daylight had never seemed so inviting. It bathed her wounds, taking away the pain and lifting her tenderly as her own mother's arms.

"Ivy?"

The light was all around her now. A blissful peace enfolded her, and she could feel the world slipping away...

"Oh no, you don't." Richard's voice was harsh. "Stay with me. Ivy!"

She sighed, melting against him. Then a hand smacked her injured shoulder, and Ivy's eyes flew open. The golden light vanished, and cold fire seared through her body. She would have screamed, but the pain was so intense it took her breath away.

"Live!" Richard shouted, as a second wave of power shocked through her. Ivy convulsed, bolted upright—and slapped him across the face.

For a moment Richard froze, eyes wide and neck twisted with the force of her blow. Then he collapsed against the wall of the muddy hollow and broke into rasping laughter. Only then did it dawn on Ivy that the pain in her shoulder had faded, and her chest no longer stabbed with every breath. She felt weak and a little dizzy, but...

"I'm alive," she whispered.

Her skin was glowing again, and now she could see everything: the burrow lined with soil and dead leaves, the mushrooms crowded into one corner, the roots that kept the ceiling from falling in. Some abandoned fox's den or badger scrape in the depths of the wood, so shallow that Richard had been forced to shrink himself and Ivy to fit.

And yet he'd done it. She'd told him to go, but he'd stayed, and when he saw her in trouble, he'd been ready. He'd flown to meet her, cast a spell to throw off her pursuers, and transformed into faery shape to catch her as she fell. Now he'd brought her back from the very gates of death, and what had she given him? A smack hard enough to rattle his teeth.

Richard was still laughing. There was more than a hint of hysteria about it, and Ivy wondered if she might need to slap him again. "What's so funny?"

He let out a last snort, wiped his eyes with one filthy hand and sat up. "It's just... there's a delicious irony to you hitting me, that's all. *The law hath not been dead, though it hath slept.*"

Which meant nothing to Ivy, but she didn't really care. "You saved my life," she said, as her hand crept to her shoulder. It felt stiff and tender, but the bones and muscles were whole and even the skin was unbroken. "I don't know how to..." No, she wasn't about to *thank* him, that would put her eternally in his debt. But she owed him a great deal, and it would take her a long time to repay it. "I don't know what to say."

"Then don't say anything," said Richard. "You saved my life too, when you freed me from that dungeon. Now we're even."

His gaze held hers until Ivy began to feel self-conscious. She brushed the soil from her legs and edged away. "Well," she said, "we're certainly evenly dirty."

Richard climbed to his feet, one hand braced against the ceiling. "We need to get away from here," he said. "I don't think your brother saw you change out of swift-form. But soon he'll realize you're missing, and I don't want to be around when that happens. Especially not now that I've seen what he can do."

The fevered energy that had filled Ivy since her healing

drained away, leaving her shaken. "Mica," she whispered. "I knew he had a plan to catch you, but I never guessed..." She looked up at him miserably. "Richard, I can't go home."

"Why not?"

"It's too late, and Mica knows too much. Even if he hasn't guessed yet that I was the swift he shot, it won't take him long to figure it out. I'll be punished for going above—locked up, or put on watch at the very least—and then I'll never get the chance to—"

She broke off, pushing her fingertips against her eyes. The thought of how badly she'd miscalculated, what a disaster she'd made for herself and all the people she loved, shook her to the core. "I can't go back until I find Cicely. Maybe not even then."

Richard was quiet, his face unreadable. At last he said, "It's your choice. But if I were you, I'd talk to Marigold first. You'll have a better chance with her help than you would on your own."

Ivy longed to agree, but she felt selfish for even considering it. She wanted to see Marigold so badly, to know the comfort that only a mother could give. But surely she didn't deserve that after the way she'd failed Cicely? Especially now that she'd abandoned Mica and her father as well?

And yet punishing herself wouldn't help Cicely either. "I suppose you're right. But..." She flexed her shoulder, wincing at the pull in her muscles. "I'm not up to flying yet. I'm not even sure I could hold on, if I rode on your back." Especially since his bird-form was so tiny, she couldn't believe he'd made the offer in the first place.

"Well, we can't go any farther by magic. I could leap a short way with you because you'd been in the wood already, but after that it was back to running." Richard tapped his fingers on a root, frowning in thought. "What if we make ourselves human size, and you turn us both invisible? If we've got to walk, we'll cover more ground that way."

Ivy still felt wobbly from her near-death experience, and the thought of casting spells made her head ache. But what choice did she have?

"All right," she said, trying to sound confident. "Let's go."

On the far side of the wood the ground dropped away, sloping down into a little valley where a stream gurgled among the rocks. Richard set the pace, and Ivy did her best to keep up. But though nervous energy sustained her for a while, it wasn't long before her strength began to falter. She'd been up all night, eaten nothing for hours, and her shoulder was starting to throb again—first in occasional spasms, then with a steady pulse that made her queasy.

"So," said Richard as the path turned away from the riverbank and began to rise, "now that I've convinced you I'm not one, what *is* a spriggan? Some kind of hideous monster, obviously, and I'm trying not to take that as an insult. But how are they different from other magical folk?"

"I don't know that much about them," Ivy said, struggling to put one foot in front of the other. Her chest was hurting as well now, and she found it hard to breathe. "Only that they're thin and pale and ugly, and bring bad luck and bad weather. They love only two things—food and treasure. And they steal piskey-women, because they haven't any women of their own."

"And they only live in Cornwall? Nowhere else?"

"I'm not sure," she panted, wiping sweat from her brow. "Why?"

"Because I've been to quite a few places in my time," Richard replied. "I've traveled across England and Wales, and even spent a few months in Scotland. This isn't the first time

I've been to Cornwall, either. But I've never seen one of these so-called spriggans—*look out!"*

Head down, eyes half-shut, Ivy didn't even see the loose rock until she tripped over it. She tumbled forward, too startled to cry out—but when Richard caught her arm, Ivy let out a swift's shriek of agony. Hastily the faery switched his grip and helped her to safer ground.

"This shouldn't be happening," he said, as Ivy sank down on an outcropping. He crouched in front of her, seizing her chin and lifting her head up. "How long have you been in pain?"

She averted her eyes. "A while. I thought I was just tired."

"I put a lot of power into that healing." His fingers traced the purpling bruise on her bare shoulder, and Ivy flinched. "Why is it coming undone?"

"I don't know." She tried to get up, but her knees buckled. "But I can't walk any farther. Just... go. Leave me here."

"I don't think so," said Richard. He slid one arm beneath Ivy's legs, lifted her from the ground and set off, carrying her as though she weighed nothing.

Ivy wanted to tell him to stop, so she could make herself small and save him the effort. But her head was pounding with the strain of keeping them both invisible, and the pain in her arm was getting worse with every step he took. All she could do was hide her face against Richard's neck and try not to be sick...

Then she lost consciousness, and dropped into a bottomless shaft of oblivion.

Ivy woke in a world of dusty golden light. Above her stretched a ceiling braced by dark, square-cut beams, and she lay against a wall of stone and mortar.

She was in a human building of some sort—a barn, perhaps. But if so, how had Richard brought her here? She'd always heard that faeries couldn't enter human dwellings without permission.

There was an itch behind her shoulders, where her wings ought to be. Ivy squirmed and stretched with one arm and then the other, trying to get at it. Then she realized she'd twisted her injured shoulder to its limits, and hadn't felt any pain at all. Wondering, she touched the place on her chest where the swift's beak had pierced her. There was no tenderness there, either.

So Richard had healed her again, and this time he'd succeeded. But it must have used up all his strength, because now he lay sprawled on the straw beside her, so deep in slumber that he didn't even twitch when Ivy spoke his name.

Well, let him sleep; he'd earned it. Ivy rose, brushing dust from her breeches. The building was old but in good repair, a low rectangle with a corridor down one side and the other half divided into pens by half-doors and wooden walls. A pungent, earthly smell mingled with the scent of dried grass. Ivy stepped through the doorway, avoiding a heap of muck in the middle of the corridor, and went to investigate.

She expected to find pigs or goats in the neighboring pens, or even a cow. But when she reached the last box a shaggy brown head rose to greet her, ears pricked and nose quivering. Ivy held out her human-sized hand, delighted when the horse lipped her palm. "Hello, you beauty," she whispered to it, rubbing the smooth arch of its neck. "What are you doing in here?"

The horse gave a whinny and stamped one foot—but gingerly. And when Ivy leaned over she saw the problem at once: its left foreleg was injured, and it couldn't gallop until it was better. "Oh, what a shame," Ivy said, unlatching the door and slipping inside. Rubbing soothing circles over the horse's chest, she crouched to examine the bandaged limb.

Even through the wrappings it felt swollen and hot to touch, and the horse shied away from her fingers. "It's all right," Ivy murmured. She blew gently into the horse's nostrils, soothing it, and smiled when it tucked its head against her chest. "I can't heal you, but when Richard wakes up, maybe—"

A creak echoed through the barn, and Ivy froze. The outer door swung wide and another horse pranced in, an elegant dapple-gray with a haughty air that reminded her of Betony. And beside it walked a human girl perhaps two years younger than Ivy, with a braid of dark hair swinging down her back.

Ivy turned invisible, but not quickly enough. The girl's head turned, her pert features creasing in a frown. "Hello? Is someone there?"

The brown horse chose that moment to sidle over and squeeze Ivy against the wall. A gasp escaped her and she shoved at its curving ribs, but it refused to budge. She flattened herself against the wood and tried to slide sideways, but something sharp stung her leg and she let out an involuntary yelp.

"Right, whoever you are," said the girl sternly. "Come out." With a slap she sent the gray mare trotting into the neighboring stall, then strode toward them. "Budge over, Dodger." She shoved the brown horse and it danced sideways, leaving Ivy backed against the wall with blood trailing down her calf.

"What are you doing here?" the girl demanded—but as soon as their eyes met, her expression changed. "You're a faery! No, wait." She cocked her riding helmet to one side, looking puzzled and awed at once. "What *are* you?"

Gooseflesh prickled over Ivy. How could a human see through her invisibility spell? She was desperately wondering what to say when a laconic voice spoke up:

"She's a Cornish piskey. And she's with me."

The girl spun around, and Ivy took advantage of the distraction to turn piskey-size and dart out into the corridor, taking refuge behind a nearby bucket. Once more, Richard had put himself between her and danger. But how were they going to get out of this?

"Faery man?" breathed the girl, unlatching her helmet and pulling it off. "Is it really you?"

Without hesitation Richard stepped out to meet her. His clothes were still rumpled and muddy and there were bits of straw in his hair, but his eyes were wickedly bright.

"Hello, Molly Menadue," he said. "It's good to see you again."

10

The situation had changed so unexpectedly, Ivy felt as though she were having some strange dream. The human girl had recognized Richard, even knew that he was a faery, and he didn't appear to mind at all. He'd even greeted her by name, as though she were an old friend. How could that be?

"I thought I'd never see you again!" The girl flung her arms around Richard and hugged him. Then she pushed him away and scolded, "You just disappeared! Without even a note!"

"Something came up and I had to go," he said, but his eyes had darkened, and Ivy could tell it wasn't a pleasant memory. "There was no time to explain."

"You don't know what it was like, coming here and finding you gone." Molly sniffed. "It was *horrible.*" She scrubbed her eyes, then went on more briskly, "But enough of that. You're here now. What brought you back? And what are you doing with... did you say a *piskey?*"

"Her name is Ivy, and we're travelling together," said Richard. "We got into a bit of trouble and needed somewhere to hide. This was the safest place I could think of."

"Safe from what?"

Richard hesitated, and for a moment Ivy thought he was going to tell Molly their whole story. But all he said was,

"That's faery business—or rather, piskey business. But you needn't worry, you're in no danger."

Molly put her fists on her hips. "I don't care about that," she said. "I'm just dying to hear what you've been up to. It's been *ages.*"

"It has," Richard agreed solemnly. "How old are you now? Eighteen? Twenty-two?"

Molly broke into a reluctant smile. "Fourteen, silly. It hasn't been *that* long."

Ivy couldn't restrain her curiosity any longer. She stepped out of hiding and grew to human size. "How do you know Richard?" she asked the girl.

"Richard?" Molly frowned at the faery, who gave a tiny nod. "Oh. Well... he's my faery godfather."

Richard spluttered, and Ivy was torn between disbelief and a mad desire to laugh. She was still wrestling with the impulse when Molly grinned at her, and then it was hopeless: she had to smile back.

"I was out riding Dodger last spring," Molly went on, gesturing to the brown horse, "and I saw a... a bird, fall out of the sky. So I went to see if it was hurt, and when I got there, I found him—Richard, I mean—lying in the grass."

She hadn't been about to say *bird*, Ivy could tell. She'd started to say something else, but changed her mind. Why?

"He tried to act human," Molly went on, "but I knew right away he was a faery, and I got so excited. I'd seen a couple of faeries before, but they always ignored me, and my mum got really angry at me for talking to strangers. But he didn't seem to mind talking, even though it was mostly nonsense, and he looked so thin and tired I felt sorry for him. So I brought him home."

"*Home* in this case being the barn," said Richard. "Since we both agreed her mother wouldn't think much of the arrangement. And then she wrapped me up in blankets and fed me until I could hardly move, which probably saved my life."

Molly blushed, but she looked pleased. Ivy turned to Richard. "Why were you so weak? What happened?"

"That's another story," said Richard shortly. "Let Molly tell hers."

"He wouldn't tell me either," Molly confided. "I think he likes being mysterious. Anyway, he stayed for a few days and we got to be friends, and I told him my mum wants me to be a teacher like her, but what I really want is to be an actress. And he turned out to know loads about theater, and I did a speech for him and he told me I was really good, and two weeks later I tried out for our school play and got the lead. So that's why I call him my faery godfather."

"Did you!" said Richard, with a warmth in his tone Ivy had never heard before. "Well done, Molly. What did your parents say?"

"I emailed the video to my dad, and he said I was brilliant. But Mum said I shouldn't let it go to my head."

Richard's lip curled. "Your mother suffers from a grievous lack of imagination. Never mind her, Molly. There'll be more starring roles in your future."

Molly beamed at him. "I've got to head in for supper," she said, jerking a thumb at the open door. "But I'll come back later and bring you something to eat." She looked from Richard to Ivy. "You're not going to run away again, are you? You'll stay the night at least?"

"We can't stay long," said Richard, with unusual gentleness. "But yes. For now, we'll stay."

The sun was slipping past the horizon, its last rays slanting across the field. In the neighboring stalls the horses stamped and snorted, while Ivy and Richard lay on a makeshift bed of old blankets, waiting for Molly to return.

Richard's eyes were half-closed, with blue shadows beneath them, and the bones of his face stood out sharply in the fading light. He'd carried Ivy over miles of countryside to this barn, then poured the last of his strength into healing her a second time—if she hadn't owed him before, she surely did now. But Richard hadn't mentioned that, and Ivy had a feeling that he'd rather she didn't either.

"How far from the Delve are we?" she asked. "Are we safe here?"

"Not far by human standards, but far enough that your people aren't likely to find us," said Richard. "And besides, there's some charm about this place that makes it hard for magical folk to see—I'd never have found it myself, if Molly hadn't shown me. Some protective spell set up by her grandmother, perhaps."

"You mean," said Ivy, propping herself on one elbow, "you think her grandmother was a faery?"

"Or some other relative, I suppose," Richard replied, gazing thoughtfully into the rafters. "It's hard to say. But there's magic in Molly's blood somewhere, if she's been seeing faeries all her life. On her father's side, probably—it doesn't seem likely to be her mother's."

"Where is her father, then?" asked Ivy. "Doesn't he live here?"

"Sometimes," Richard said. "But his work takes him away

for weeks at a time, so Molly doesn't see much of him. I've never seen him at all." He sat up, ran his hands down his dark jacket and trousers, and the mud that had crusted them vanished. "I think I could heal that leg of yours now."

"I'd rather you healed Dodger's," said Ivy, getting up. She showed Richard the horse's bandaged leg, but the faery shook his head.

"I don't have your people's gift with animals," said Richard. "And my sorry experience with this one is that he'd as soon bite me as look at me. He can heal on his own, as far as I'm concerned."

Ivy wanted to protest, but she owed Richard too much to demand anything. She was about to close the door when a thought occurred to her. "I cut my leg on something in here," she said. "Maybe that's what happened to Dodger, too."

She slipped into the box, pushing away the horse's inquiring muzzle, and crouched to examine the dividing wall. At first she saw nothing, but when she allowed her skin to glow a little brighter she caught the glint of dull metal protruding from the wood. She closed her fingers around it and felt a faint tingle.

"An iron nail," said Richard. "Probably worked its way out over the years and no one noticed it. Tell Molly, when she comes back."

"Tell me what?" asked Molly from the doorway, and Ivy pointed. The human girl gasped. "Is that how Dodger cut himself? We thought he did it outside, but we could never find where. *Thank* you!"

Ivy went rigid with shock, but by the time she recovered, Molly had found a hammer and tugged the nail out. "You hurt yourself on it too, didn't you?" she said to Ivy as she held it up—a crude-looking thing, rusty with age. "That's why I could see you."

"I... hadn't thought of that," said Ivy. She'd been immune to iron when she lived in the Delve, but perhaps Richard's healing spells had changed her more than she'd realized. Could he have made her part faery by accident? Ivy wasn't sure she liked that idea at all.

Molly tossed the nail into the waste bin and plopped down on an overturned bucket, crossing her ankles. "My mum's in her study working on some project or other. We should be all right for a while." She pulled out a cloth bag and began rummaging inside. "I found a packet of fairings—"

"Fairings?" asked Richard.

"Ginger biscuits," said Ivy, helping herself to one.

"And sausages—sorry they're cold. Oh, and pears." Molly made a face. "It's not much of a meal, is it?"

"Don't apologize," said Ivy. "It's kind of you to bring us anything at all."

Molly looked at her curiously. "You're nothing like I expected. I thought piskeys were little brown men, full of wrinkles and mischief."

"That's just legend." Richard cut in before Ivy could speak. "Piskey women don't get out much, but they do exist. And magical folk don't have wrinkles. Unless you know what to look for, you couldn't tell the difference between a piskey of twenty or two hundred."

"Two hundred!" exclaimed Ivy. "That's ridiculous. The oldest piskey I know is Nettle, and she can't be more than a hundred and ten. And she does have wrinkles; all the old aunties and uncles do."

Richard looked surprised. "My mistake, then," he said. "Perhaps faeries and piskeys are more different than I'd thought."

"Tell me more about piskeys," said Molly, turning eagerly to Ivy. "I want to know everything about them."

Ivy hesitated. She hadn't meant to give away any secrets, and she had a feeling she'd already said more than she should. Not that she was worried about Richard; by now she felt almost sure she could trust him. But although she liked Molly, she didn't know the human girl well enough to speak freely.

"Well," she said, trying to think of an answer that was honest but harmless, "piskeys do enjoy a good prank, or at least the younger ones do. It's a sort of game with our people, to play tricks on each other without being tricked ourselves. And if we can all laugh about it together, that's the best of all."

Yet even as she spoke, Ivy had to admit there wasn't nearly as much laughter in the Delve as there had been when she was a child. The older folk had a weary air about them, and some of the oldest—especially the older knockers—looked positively grim. Was it Betony's strict rule that had sobered them? Or was it something more?

"Go on," said Molly. "Where do you live? Richard told me once about some faeries who live in a hollow oak tree. Is it something like that?"

"No," said Ivy. "But it's a safe place. A good place. And it's... beautiful." Homesickness welled up in her, and she couldn't speak any more. She had spent nearly two days away from the Delve now. Would she ever see her home and people again?

"I'm taking Ivy to visit a relative of hers," said Richard, filling in the silence. "Someone she hasn't seen in a long time. Once that's done, I'll be on my way."

"Where?" asked Molly.

Richard shrugged. "I'm not sure yet," he said. "I like to keep my options open." But a shadow crossed his face as he spoke, and it dawned on Ivy that he might not be a wanderer by choice—that he might not have anywhere to go.

"I didn't mean *you*," said Molly reproachfully. "I know not to meddle in your business by now. I meant Ivy. Where are you taking her?"

"Truro," said Richard. "There's a dance and theater school in the city where her relative's been staying."

Ivy straightened up sharply, the blood draining from her

face. That was where her mother had been all these years? Surely he must be pranking her. She opened her mouth, but Molly spoke first:

"Dance and *theater?* Really? Can I come?" She must have caught Richard's dubious look, for she went on quickly, "Mum lets me go to Truro on the bus sometimes, as long as I take my mobile and promise to call her when I'm coming home. And she likes it better when I'm out of the house anyway. She won't say no if I tell her I'm going with friends. *Please."*

Richard glanced at Ivy, but she was too choked with anger to reply. So her mother had abandoned her family to go dancing after all—not with the faeries, but with the humans. No wonder Richard had kept this from her.

But why was he telling her now? Did he think it was safe because Ivy had already committed herself, because she needed Marigold's help too badly to walk away? He was right about that, but she hated the thought that he'd manipulated her—and that she'd been fool enough to let him.

"You never told me what she was doing," she accused, when she could speak. "Did she ask you not to? Or was it your idea to keep me in the dark?"

Richard's jaw tightened, and she could see she'd offended him. He turned to Molly and said, "I know we're in your debt, but I don't think it's a good idea. As you can see, Ivy's a little sensitive at the moment."

"Oh, and now it's *my* fault?" exclaimed Ivy. How dare he make her seem ungrateful for Molly's kindness? "I apologize," she said hastily to Molly, who had turned pale and then very red. "If there's anything else we can do to repay you, I'd be glad to know of it."

"Don't bother," Molly said, her eyes on Richard. "I won't interfere in your faery—or piskey—business. But if you had any idea what mum's been like..." A spasm of anger distorted her face. "Never mind. I suppose that's all just *human business* to you." She leaped up from the bucket and ran out.

"Wait," Ivy called, but Molly had already slammed the door.

"Don't worry," said Richard. "She'll be all right by tomorrow. And so will you, once you've had a proper night's sleep."

Ivy bristled. "What's that supposed to mean?"

"I told you your mother was at a dance school," he said. "If I thought that was some dark secret, I wouldn't have said it. I've never lied to you yet, Ivy. Not that I expect you to be impressed by that, but you should be, because I'm one of the few faeries who can." He pushed himself upright and went to the window. "Marigold will explain herself to you tomorrow. Tonight, you need to rest."

"I'm not tired." Ivy spoke crisply, to deny the embarrassment crawling inside. Perhaps she had leaped to the wrong conclusion, but she hated being caught off guard. "Why can't we go to Truro now?"

"Because you're not ready to fly again, even if you think you are." His hands tightened on the windowsill. "Do you have any idea how damaged your body must have been, to need two complete healings in a day?"

The reminder of how much she owed him shamed her. But she couldn't let that hold her back. The sooner she found her mother, the sooner they could find Cicely. "Then we'll fly slowly. But I'm not staying here."

He gave an exasperated growl and spun to face her. "Why are you so stubborn? What are you trying to prove?"

"Cicely needs me!" she shouted at him. "She's out there somewhere, and she's scared and she's hurting, and nobody's going to find her if I—"

Richard cut her off with a gesture—literally, because though Ivy's mouth kept moving no sound came out. "Quiet," he said. "Or Molly's mother will hear us." He held her gaze until she gave a sullen nod, then motioned again to remove the spell and went on. "I know you want to find your sister. But you're not going to help her by killing yourself."

So not only did he see Ivy as weak, he thought her too stupid even to know how weak she was. No wonder he'd taken such pains to protect her. "I'm not a fool," she retorted, barely controlling her fury. "I know what I'm capable of."

"If that were true," Richard said, "we wouldn't be here right now. It took a lot of power to heal you, and I'm not going to let all that effort go to waste. Stop behaving like a petulant child, and lie down."

Ivy's fists clenched. "And if I don't?"

"Then I'll knock you out myself."

He would, too. She could see it in his face. "Fine," Ivy said bitterly. "I'll do as you say. For now."

"Good," said Richard, and walked away.

"Where are you going?"

"Out," he replied shortly. "Don't wait up for me." He took one more step, and changed to a little black-and-white bird. It flitted around Ivy, paused on the windowsill to fix her with one coldly glittering eye, then flew off into the darkening night.

With her thoughts still raging at Richard, her clothing stiff with mud and nothing but a layer of horsey-smelling blankets beneath her, Ivy didn't expect to sleep well. But once she'd made herself piskey size and dragged a piece of sacking over herself for protection, she dropped into a deep slumber at once.

Still, it seemed only moments before the door of the barn creaked, and Ivy's eyes opened to the first pale light of morning. The horses stamped and shook themselves, and Ivy got up quickly, thinking it must be Molly coming in. But then among the earthy smells of grass and manure she caught a thread of an unfamiliar scent. Surely Molly wouldn't smell like that, all drenched in musk and strange spices? Ivy crept to the corner of the box stall and peered into the corridor, staying small so she wouldn't be noticed.

A woman stood in the corridor, fitting a bridle over the gray mare's head. She wore trousers and a fitted jacket, and her auburn hair curved smoothly against the nape of her neck. Her skin was pale as cream, far lighter than Molly's. Still, she had the same upturned nose and determined chin, and there could be no doubt she was the human girl's mother.

The mare snorted and shied as her mistress led her out into the corridor, but the woman kept a firm hand on the bridle until the horse settled. She heaved a saddle onto the mare's back and cinched the strap tight, then led her into the yard. Keeping to the shadows, Ivy crept to the door and watched as Molly's mother swung into the saddle and cantered off.

To ride like that must be glorious, thought Ivy with a tinge of envy. She retreated to her stall and sat down, pulling the blankets around her. There was no sign of Richard yet, but surely he'd come back soon, and they'd fly to Truro together.

"Hello?" came Molly's voice from the far end of the barn, and Ivy jumped to her feet. The sun had fully risen, slipping its golden fingers between the shutters, and the place was growing stuffy with its warmth.

"I'm here," Ivy said, mouth watering at the rich, buttery scent wafting off the sack in Molly's hand. Even after finishing off last night's provisions, she was starving.

Molly handed her the paper bag, then glanced about with a frown. "Where's—er, Richard?"

"I don't know," Ivy said, pulling out a pastry and biting into it. It tasted as good as it smelled. "I saw your mother a little while ago."

Molly's face turned hard, a strangely old look on her still-young face. "Oh," she said, and picked up Dodger's currying combs.

Ivy ate two pastries and a hunk of cheese before forcing herself to stop—Richard would probably be hungry too, when he returned. It seemed odd that he wasn't back yet, but after their quarrel she could hardly blame him for wanting to go elsewhere. She still resented his high-handedness, but she hadn't exactly been reasonable either, and she hoped he'd return soon so they could both apologize and move on.

"The food's very good," she said to Molly. "I appreciate it."

Molly paused in her currying, and her set expression relaxed. "You're welcome," she said, and went back to brushing the horse again. There was a long silence, until she spoke without looking up:

"My mum didn't used to ride much, but lately she's been taking Duchess out every day. I asked her once if I could ride with her, but she said no, she needed time to be alone." Her voice turned acid, and her hand clenched in Dodger's mane. "Like she doesn't get plenty of that already. Sometimes I wonder why she even bothered to have me."

Ivy was silent.

"Sorry." Molly rubbed her face against her forearm. "You don't want to hear all that human stuff. It just... gets hard sometimes, not having anyone to talk to. I mean, I have friends at school, but..."

Ivy felt a pang of sympathy. She knew too well what it was like to wonder if her parents cared. And though she had friends in the Delve, the things she'd been through in the past week were more than she could expect any of them, even Jenny or Mattock, to understand. "You don't need to apologize," she said. "I'm glad to listen."

Molly gave her a watery smile. Ivy smiled back, feeling happier already. It was good to know that she'd brought the human girl some comfort, however small.

Yet she couldn't stay here much longer, even for Molly's sake. "I'm going to find Richard," Ivy said. "I'll be back." Then she changed to swift-form and flashed out the door.

The yard dropped away beneath her, the stone barn and Molly's house receding to tiny squares as she soared higher. She flew over drystone hedges and scrubby clumps of woodland, bare ridges and grassy valleys, slate-roofed human dwellings and dark ribbons of paved road. Other birds flitted across her path, some much larger than she was and others smaller, but nowhere did she see a bird with Richard's markings. Where had he gone?

Ivy wheeled and began to circle, sharp eyes scanning the air. Perhaps she'd just missed him, or perhaps he'd flown back to the barn already. Surely there was no reason to fear...

But she did. Because deep inside Ivy, an instinct as sure as her sense of direction told her that Richard should have returned hours ago. And if she didn't find him soon, she wouldn't find him at all.

11

Ivy paced the barn floor, her thoughts a whirl of confusion, impatience, and worry. What could have happened to Richard? Had he been captured? Hurt? Perhaps even killed?

"I don't think he's the sort to take risks unless he has to," said Molly, when Ivy voiced her fears. "If you'd heard the way he talked the first time I met him... he doesn't fancy himself a hero." She stroked Dodger's nose as the horse lipped the last fragments of apple from her palm. "I think he might just have decided it was time to go."

But he promised my mother, Ivy protested silently. *He said he'd bring me to her.*

Yet hadn't Richard done more than anyone had a right to expect of him already? He'd risked his life and nearly lost it, delivering Marigold's message. He'd taught her wingless daughter to fly. And if that weren't enough, he'd saved Ivy's life twice over.

No wonder he'd been so frustrated by Ivy's stubbornness and ingratitude. No wonder he'd flown off to cool his temper—and if he'd decided it wasn't worth coming back, who could blame him?

"You're probably right," she replied, though there was a knot in her chest that wouldn't go away. Maybe Richard considered himself well rid of her, but she wished she'd had a chance to say goodbye.

"Anyway," said Molly, wiping her hands and tossing the rag aside, "my mum's gone shopping and she won't be back for a while. Why don't you come inside and wash up, and I'll make you some tea?"

Ivy ran a hand through her filthy hair. She longed to accept Molly's invitation, but did she dare? If the girl's mother came back early and found an oddly dressed stranger in her house, there was no telling what might happen.

Yet she could hardly go to Truro covered in dirt and dried blood. And if Richard didn't show up in the next hour or two, going on without him was exactly what she'd have to do.

"Yes, please," Ivy said. "I'd like that."

Such a strange place to live, thought Ivy as she followed Molly into the house. The caverns of the Delve had rounded ceilings and gently bowed-out walls, but everything here was straight lines and sharp angles, like the inside of a box. Instead of displaying the beauty of the surrounding stones, the humans had covered them with plaster and paint. And there were windows everywhere, which made Ivy feel like the whole world was staring at her.

"Here you go," said Molly, leading her to a white-tiled room. "Leave your clothes outside the door, and I'll wash them for you."

"Wait," said Ivy. "Where do I wash?" She could see no water-channel where she could splash her face and hands, or a pool she could pump full and step into. There was a bit of standing water in one basin, but she couldn't imagine trying to get clean with it.

Molly broke into a grin. "You really don't know, do you?" she said, and Ivy would have blushed, except that the younger girl looked so delighted by her ignorance. "Well, if you want a proper soak you can use the tub, right here. First you put in the plug, and then you turn the taps like this. And you can use this towel to dry off after." She started the water running, poured in some liquid that made it froth and bubble, then waved cheerfully to Ivy and shut the door.

There was one alarming moment when Ivy couldn't make the water stop, but she figured it out in time. Soon she was blessedly clean, and shaking out her damp curls as she dressed in the clothes Molly had left for her. First came a blouse with short sleeves and a softly gathered neckline, then a pair of dark blue breeches that came halfway to her knee—both of them too wide for Ivy's slight frame, but once she'd tucked in the shirt and tightened the belt they fit well enough. She hung up the towel, drained the bath, and went out.

She found Molly in the kitchen, pouring tea into two flower-painted cups. The human girl had laid out a plate of split buns spread with butter, strawberry preserves and clotted cream, and when Ivy came in she pulled out a chair for her. "I could cut up some cheese, if you like," she said. "Or make watercress sandwiches."

"This is lovely," said Ivy. She helped herself to one of the splits—they were as good as anything Mattock could make—and was chewing happily when Molly spoke.

"How are you going to find your relative, if Richard doesn't come back? Have you been to Truro before?"

The bun caught in Ivy's throat, and she took a hasty sip of tea to wash it down. "No, but I'm sure I'll find her somehow." Though since she had no idea where the dance school was, it might take a while.

"I see," said Molly. "And when are you leaving?"

Ivy's hands tightened around her teacup. There was a hollow feeling inside her, and she realized that she'd given up hoping Richard would return. "As soon as I'm finished here."

"And this relative of yours..." began Molly, then gave an apologetic smile. "Sorry, I'm asking too many questions, aren't I?"

Guilt stirred in Ivy. This girl had been so kind to her, and asked for so little. Was it fair to leave her in the dark?

"It's my mother," she said. "She disappeared six years ago, and I never knew what happened to her. Until Richard told me she was alive, and wanted to see me."

"And she's been in Truro all this time?" Molly frowned. "That's a bit odd, isn't it? Why didn't she come and find you herself?"

That part of the story had never made sense to Ivy, either. "I'm sure there's a reason, but I won't know until I talk to her. The problem is..."

She was about to tell Molly about Cicely, but a crackling noise from outside interrupted her. "That's my mum's car!" Molly exclaimed, snatching away Ivy's teacup. "Quick–hide in my bedroom. Third door on the right."

Ivy didn't have time to argue. She ran down the corridor to Molly's room, darted inside and pushed the door shut behind her. Heart pounding, she pressed her ear to the wood.

"Mum!" exclaimed Molly brightly from the kitchen. "I made lunch. Would you like some?"

"It looks more like tea to me," the woman replied, disapproval in her tone. "What a mess you've made! Go and get the other bags from the car, please."

"Right," Molly said, and the front door banged as she ran out. Ivy kept listening, afraid to move. What if Molly's mother guessed that her daughter wasn't alone? What if she came looking for Ivy? But no steps sounded in the corridor, and at last Ivy relaxed. She slid her hands from the door, turned—and her mouth fell open.

Molly's bedroom was full of faeries.

Printed on the bedclothes and curtains, dangling from the ceiling, framed in wood or casually stuck to the wall, pictures of the Fair Folk were everywhere. Faery dolls of all sizes formed a teetering pile in the corner, and the shelf by the window was cluttered with little statues of them, from a glass-winged faery in pewter to a pottery piskey with a look as impish as Keeve's.

That was her answer—the window! If Ivy opened it, she could take swift-form and fly out. Ducking the shelf, Ivy took hold of the right-hand pane and tugged. The glass creaked, but it didn't budge.

"What's that?" came a sharp voice from the kitchen, and Ivy's mouth went dry. She looked about for a hiding place, but she could already hear the woman's footsteps, and there was no time. She backed into the corner and turned herself invisible as the door opened, and Molly's mother strode in.

She had changed out of her riding clothes into a floral dress that emphasized her willowy shape, and her hair fell in a smooth bell to her shoulders. She was pretty in a fine-boned way—though Betony would have said she looked unhealthy—but the hard, suspicious look on her face made Ivy shiver. Her gaze swept the room, searching.

"Mum?" asked Molly from behind her. "What's wrong?"

She sounded perfectly innocent, as though she had no idea. No wonder Richard had encouraged her to become an actress.

"Never mind," said the woman, her gaze flickering past Ivy. "It must have been the wind." She kicked a prop into place to hold the door open, and walked away.

Molly waited a few seconds before stepping into the room. "Ivy?" she mouthed.

"I'm here," Ivy whispered back. "Open the window for me, please?"

The girl hesitated, a line forming between her brows. For a moment Ivy wondered why she looked unhappy—then she realized, and felt a stir of pity. "It's all right," she said. "I'm not going to run off without saying goodbye. I'll meet you in the barn."

Molly's face relaxed. She hurried to the window and slid the pane open, then flashed Ivy a smile and slipped away.

"I've got your clothes," said Molly when she came into the barn. "I had to work fast to keep my mum from seeing them, but I don't think she suspects anything. Still... phew!" She wiped her brow dramatically, and thrust a cloth sack at Ivy. "They're still damp, though. Keep my clothes on for now."

Ivy slung the bag over her shoulder. "I'm grateful for all your help," she said. "I wish I knew how to repay you."

"I'll tell you how," replied Molly. "You're going to let me come with you and help you find your mother. And don't say I can't," she went on before Ivy could protest, "because I looked up dance schools in Truro and there was only one that did dance *and* theater, so I know exactly which one it is. If we get on the next bus, we can be there in about an hour. And my mum already said I could go, so there's no reason for you not to let me."

"But what if Richard comes back, and you're not here to—"

"He's not coming back," Molly interrupted. "I know he isn't. Because he did the same thing to me, last time." Her mouth twisted bitterly, but then she raised her chin again. "Are we going or not? Because the bus will be here in ten minutes."

Until now, Ivy had thought she'd be better going alone. But though flying to Truro might be quicker, it would be pointless if she ended up lost the moment she got there. She needed a guide who knew the city, understood the human world, and could help her find her way.

Maybe that was what Richard had intended, by leaving her and Molly together. Not only so Ivy could get the help she needed, but so that Molly would get what she wanted, too.

"All right," Ivy said. "It's a bargain."

By the time the two girls had run up the hill to the bus stop Ivy was flushed and short of breath, but not nearly as winded as usual. Perhaps the sunlight and fresh air was doing her some good. "Do I look human enough?" Ivy asked Molly as the bus rumbled toward them. "You don't think anyone will notice?"

"I'm sure they won't," Molly assured her. "You're the proper size for a human, and you're wearing my clothes." She pulled a handful of coins out of her pocket and began counting them. "I don't even know why I made such a fuss when my mum drove in. I could have introduced you as a friend from school, and she'd never have known the difference."

The bus slowed to a stop, its door hissing open. Molly galloped up the steps and Ivy followed, trying to imitate her confidence. They dropped into their seats and the bus started off again, bumping along the hedge-lined road.

At first they passed only scattered farmhouses and the occasional abandoned mine, but soon the houses grew taller and closer together, and a few bigger buildings crept between them. The lane broadened to a roadway teeming with vehicles, and for a time Ivy was mesmerized by the different shapes and colors speeding past. Then they circled through a turn and the route narrowed again, buildings of stone and plaster closing in on both sides. Some of them bore signs with names that Ivy was still trying to decipher—what was an *Optician*, for instance?—when Molly said triumphantly, "See, we're nearly there. Told you it wouldn't take long."

Ivy's hand curled tight around the metal bar beside her. Soon she would look into her mother's face for the first time in six years. Would she see the gentle, loving woman she remembered, or a cold-eyed stranger? Had Marigold summoned Ivy to apologize, or only to justify herself?

Ivy still hoped everything would make sense once she'd heard her mother's story. But though Richard had said it was no secret, Ivy couldn't imagine what Marigold was doing at a dance school. Perhaps she was tidying up the place by night in exchange for food and lodging, as piskeys of old had done for humans who showed them courtesy. But that didn't explain why her mother had left the Delve in the first place, or stayed away for years without a word.

"Here we are," announced Molly, jumping up as the bus came to a stop. Breathing deeply to calm her jangling nerves, Ivy followed. They stepped off into an open, stone-paved area surrounded by buildings, where humans sat on benches or strolled along carrying brightly colored bags. In the near distance three pointed towers rose above the rooftops, gray against the cloud-feathered sky. Some kind of fortress, perhaps?

"This way," said Molly. She set off at a brisk pace, and Ivy hurried after her. At any other time she would have paused to gaze at all the new things around her—this was her first visit to a human city, after all. But right now Ivy's every step whispered *Mother, Mother, Mother*, and she could think of nothing else.

They turned left at the next corner, onto a street lined with handsome gray stone buildings and vehicles parked along both sides. They walked along the gently rising pavement for some time before they reached another corner. There Molly led her across the road to a doorway tucked between two shops, with a sign that read RISING STAR DANCE & THEATER ACADEMY. Music floated down to them from an upstairs window—a lively, hard-drumming tune that made Ivy's feet itch to dance. Molly opened the door, and they went in.

They walked into a narrow entry room papered in cream and purple, with a desk along the right side and a staircase rising steeply to the left. The woman at the desk looked up and smiled. "Hello, girls," she said. "What can I do for you?"

Ivy stood paralyzed, not knowing what to say. How could she explain that she was here to look for a missing piskey who might or might not call herself Marigold? But Molly stepped in quickly to rescue her. "We're interested in your dance classes," she said. "Could we go upstairs and have a look?"

The woman hesitated, her eyes flicking past Ivy and Molly as though searching for a parent behind them. But when Molly clasped her hands beneath her chin and gave her an imploring look, her expression softened. "Go on, then," she said. "As long as you don't disturb the class. And if you've got any questions, come and talk to me."

Ivy's legs felt shaky and her pulse beat raggedly in her throat, but she couldn't wait any longer. Eyes on the staircase, she stepped past Molly and began to climb. Three, four, five steps she rose, and with every one the music became louder. Soon she could hear the thumps and creaks as the students moved across the floor.

"Five, six, seven, eight!" called a clear voice. "Kick, and *turn*—well done, Meg, you've got it now!"

On the fifteenth step the staircase ended, opening onto a room lined with mirrors on one side and windows on the other. Music boomed from boxes set high in each corner, and in the middle of the floor a group of girls were dancing. But Ivy had only an instant to take it all in before her gaze fell on the woman leading the class, and her mind went blank with shock.

It was her mother.

Marigold wore fitted black clothing and soft slippers, her brown-gold hair tied up with a scarf around her head. Her wings had vanished—hidden by glamour maybe, or perhaps they'd disappeared when she grew to human size. She was still slender, but there was a strength in her limbs and a rosy glow to her skin that Ivy had never seen before. And though six years had gone by, she looked younger than ever—no older than Molly's mother in fact, though Ivy knew enough of Marigold's history to guess that she must be at least fifty. How could that be?

"Go on, Ivy," Molly whispered, poking her. "You're blocking the steps. Ivy!"

The music was so loud, it seemed impossible that anyone could hear her. But Marigold turned—and froze, her wide eyes fixed on Ivy. For a timeless moment the two of them stared at one another, as the students faltered and stopped dancing in confusion. Then Marigold shook herself as though waking from a dream, stepped quickly to the oldest, and whispered a few words in her ear. At once the girl moved to the front of the class, calling her fellow students to attention—and as they went back to dancing, Marigold hurried over and seized Ivy's hand.

"Come," she whispered.

Blood pounding in her ears, Ivy obeyed. She was dimly aware of Molly giving her a thumbs-up as Marigold led her into an adjoining room. She shut the door, turned swiftly—and at last Ivy was where she'd longed to be, in her mother's arms.

"My brave, beautiful girl," Marigold murmured, stroking her hair. "I can't believe you're here. What you must have gone through, to come all this way... and how big you've grown!"

Ivy pressed her face against her mother's shoulder, breathing the scent of her skin. She had always smelled sweet, like the sachets of dried herbs and petals she scattered among her clothes. But now her fragrance was richer and more subtle, like a living plant instead of a dead one.

"I thought the spriggans had taken you," Ivy said, thick with emotion. "I thought I'd never see you again."

"I know," said Marigold, clasping her tighter, as though afraid Ivy would vanish if she let go. "And I am so sorry, my darling."

Grief ached in Ivy's chest, and she pulled back. "Then why did you do it?" she asked, searching her mother's face. "How could you run away, leave us all thinking you were dead, for... this?"

"You think I left the Delve so I could teach human girls to dance?" Marigold's brow creased in dismay. "Oh, no, no, dearest. I would never have done that to you. I came here because I had nowhere else to go."

"How could that be?" asked Ivy. "You had the Delve. You had us."

Marigold sighed. She drew up a chair for Ivy, and sat down across from her on the sofa. "I was ill when I lived in the Delve," she said. "More ill than I ever allowed you or anyone else to see. So I couldn't have stayed much longer, even if—" She swallowed, touching her throat as though it hurt her. "Even if other things hadn't happened."

Ivy could guess what those other things might be, but it didn't make her feel any better. "You mean the fight between you and Dad."

Marigold recoiled. "How do you know about that? You should never—" Then she stopped and went on more calmly, "Flint told you, I suppose."

"Mica overheard it," said Ivy. "He told me you wanted to take me and Cicely with you, but Dad said no."

The tension went out of Marigold's face. "Ah," she said softly. "I should have guessed. Poor Mica." She bowed her head. "Yes, your father and I fought, and we parted on unhappy terms. I couldn't convince him to leave the Delve with me, and he wouldn't let any of you children go either. But he knew that I had to leave, and there was nothing he could do to save me."

"Why? If you were sick, then Yarrow could have—"

"I was dying," Marigold interrupted. "I was coughing up blood, and Yarrow had done as much as she could for me already." She closed her eyes. "I was terrified of being caught by the spriggans, and I knew nothing about the outside world. But I had to get away from the Delve."

"Why?" Ivy asked, baffled. "What was so bad about the Delve?"

"So many things," Marigold murmured. "More than I ever guessed until it was too late. I'd seen Betony's only child die stillborn, and it took so long for me to have children at all... I think part of me knew all along that something wasn't right. But when you were born without wings, so weak and tiny, and I saw you struggling to breathe... I couldn't deny the truth any more."

She still wasn't making sense to Ivy. "You mean there's a curse on the mine, or on our people? Something the spriggans did?"

"Not magic," Marigold said soberly. "Poison."

Ivy caught her breath. "But how? Who would—"

"It could be in the air, or the water, or perhaps in the rock itself; I don't know enough about such things to tell, and I never had the chance to search it out. But every piskey in the Delve is dying, whether they realize it or not." Her lips thinned. "I tried to warn them—your father first, and then Betony. But they refused to believe."

Poison. Ivy could hardly fathom it, and yet she couldn't

deny it either. It would explain why Richard had found it so difficult to heal her, and why she felt stronger now than she ever had living underground. And when she remembered her father's coughing, his yellowed teeth and shaking hands—surely that was no ordinary sickness.

Yet she could understand why Aunt Betony had been skeptical. There were parts of Marigold's story that didn't seem to add up. "But why would you be sicker than anyone else?" Ivy asked. "Why not the knockers, who work in the mine every day?"

"The knockers have some immunity," Marigold replied, "built up from centuries of working underground. And they and the hunters can go outside whenever they please, which helps to strengthen their resistance. But the women are more vulnerable. Especially the faery-born ones... like me."

Ivy's stomach turned cold. Her mother, a faery? "That's not possible. You were born in the Delve—you've lived there all your life—"

"I know. I found it hard to believe at first, too." Marigold gave her a sad smile, her eyes turning distant. "My mother died giving birth to me, and I never knew her. I only knew that the other children in the Delve were brown and sturdy, where I was pale and thin and found it hard to breathe. Aster, the healer before Yarrow, made potions to help me grow stronger, and I learned to use glamour to make my faery wings look like a piskey's should. But I never understood why I was different, until I left the Delve."

She took Ivy's hand, folding it between her own. "One of the first strangers to show me kindness was a faery who had survived the destruction of Thistledown Wyld, my parents' old home. She'd seen my father killed in battle, and my mother taken prisoner with the rest of the women. Her captors didn't realize that she was already expecting a child."

"The spriggans, you mean," said Ivy a little wildly. Surely

only spriggans could do such a terrible thing. "They attacked your village, and then our people rescued you—"

"Spriggans!" Marigold gave a bitter laugh. "There haven't been spriggans in Kernow for decades, or at least not enough of them to matter." She shook her head. "No, Ivy. It was piskeys who destroyed my home and took my mother captive. And if they hadn't hidden underground where no one could reach them..." Her expression turned hard. "Then my people—my *true* people—would have wiped them out long ago."

12

"No!" Ivy pulled away from her mother and scrambled to her feet. "That's a lie! Our ancestors fought the faeries, but only to stop them invading our land. If we went around attacking peaceful folk and stealing their wives and daughters—if we were no better than spriggans—how could we live with ourselves? How could we forget something as horrible as that?"

"I don't know," said Marigold, sounding weary. "Like you, I only know the legends as they are, not how they came to be. But I know I was not the only faery woman to be captured and taken to the Delve. Just one of the few who survived." She looked down at her pale, ringless fingers. "There are many kinds of deception, Ivy. Sometimes the most powerful lies are the ones we tell ourselves because the truth is too ugly to bear."

Ivy covered her face with her hands. She wanted to deny what her mother was saying, but how could she? If Mica was right, she'd done that very thing herself. In her grief over losing her mother, she'd blocked out the memory of her parents' fight so completely that she couldn't recall it even now.

"No wonder you never came back," she said hollowly.

"Why are you telling me this? Why did you ask me to come, if you don't want anything to do with us any more?"

"Oh, my darling, *no,*" said Marigold, rising to grip Ivy's shoulders. "Discovering that I was a faery changed many things, but it never changed my love for you. That's why I sent for you, so we could be together—"

"What about Mica and Cicely? They're your children too!"

"Yes, of course," said Marigold soothingly. "But they take after their father, and his knocker blood makes them strong. They may live a hundred years in the Delve and never guess that they could have, *should* have, lived longer. But you..." She tucked a curl tenderly behind Ivy's ear. "You are more faery than either of them, and you have been suffering since the day you were born. How could I abandon you?"

"And yet you did," Ivy said, backing away from her. "You left me there for six years, never knowing if you were dead or alive. Where were you all that time? Why didn't you send a message? *Why didn't you come back?"*

Marigold sighed. "For many reasons," she said. "But the worst mistake was mine. I trusted someone I should not have trusted. And because of that, I was captured and taken to London, where I spent the next five years as a slave."

London. Ivy had heard the name once or twice in the droll-teller's stories—the greatest city in England, unimaginably huge and far away. "Whose slave?" she asked, hushed.

"She called herself the Empress," said Marigold. "She was old, cruel and very powerful, and her plan was to conquer the whole faery realm before she died. I managed to escape from her once, but her servants caught me before I even reached the border of Kernow. And the horrors I witnessed after that, when she sent me and her other slaves into battle..." She passed a hand over her eyes as though to wipe away the memory. "I longed to send you a message, but I feared even to try in case it was intercepted. If the Empress knew about the Delve, she would have tried to conquer it as well."

"But you got away from her in the end," said Ivy, "or you wouldn't be here. So why didn't you send a message then?" It was a struggle to pull her turbulent thoughts together, but she had to know the truth. If her mother was a faery, if she'd been the pawn of someone so evil, could Ivy trust her anymore?

"I wanted to," said Marigold. "But even once the war ended and the Empress was dead, it was some time before I could return to Kernow. And even then there were... obstacles. I had to wait for the right opportunity, and a messenger I could trust." She glanced at the door, as though remembering for the first time that Ivy had not come alone. "Where is Iago? I must tell him how grateful I am for bringing you to me."

She must mean Richard. How many different names could one faery have? "He left," Ivy said. "I don't know where he went."

"Ah." Marigold sounded wistful, but not surprised. "Well, at least he kept his word."

"Is that really his name? Iago?"

"He had another name once, when we were both slaves of the Empress. But I know why he prefers not to use it." Marigold gave a rueful smile. "He has made some powerful enemies, and I took a great risk by helping him. But I also knew it would put him in my debt, and that he would do anything to be rid of that burden."

So that was all Ivy had been to Richard—a burden. It wasn't really a surprise, but it was surprising how much it hurt. She swallowed.

"Do you understand now?" asked Marigold softly, touching Ivy's face. "I know I've made some terrible mistakes. But we're together now, and I want to make things right. Can you forgive me? Can we start again?"

Ivy hesitated. All her emotions pulled toward her mother,

yearning for her approval and love. Only the part of her that feared being tricked or betrayed warned her not to trust too quickly. But she'd listened to those fears with Richard, and what had it gained her?

Besides, this wasn't just about Ivy's feelings any more. There was something far more important at stake.

"I want to," she said. "But first, I need your help." She took a deep breath. "Cicely's gone missing."

Marigold looked shocked, then increasingly distressed as Ivy told how her little sister had disappeared three nights ago, and even Betony's magic and Mica's best efforts had failed to find her. Soon her mother's eyes were brimming with tears, and Ivy no longer doubted that she cared about Cicely's fate.

But Ivy didn't tell her everything. She wasn't sure what Marigold would think of her shape-changing, and she was ashamed to admit it was her fault Cicely had gone to the surface. All she said was that Cicely had vanished without a trace, like Keeve before her.

"I thought she'd been taken by the spriggans," Ivy said, lowering her voice as the music in the adjoining room stopped. "Especially after Gem and Feldspar saw that stranger by the Engine House. But if there aren't any spriggans–"

"Mrs. Flint?" The door opened and a girl with long brown hair leaned inside. "We've finished the lesson."

"Excellent, Claire. I'll be right with you." Marigold wiped her eyes hastily, then touched Ivy's arm and whispered, "Don't worry. We'll find her," before following the human girl out.

When she had gone, Ivy blew out a long breath. Hard as it had been to tell her mother about Cicely, it was a huge relief to know she no longer had to search for her alone. But as she listened to Marigold apologizing to her students and praising their hard work, Ivy felt a twist of misgiving. Her mother sounded so human, so at ease in this strange new world. Even if they did find Cicely, it seemed Marigold had no intention of returning to the Delve. So how could they ever be a whole family again?

Chattering voices filled the dance studio, followed by the sounds of multiple feet galloping down the stairs. The commotion had barely subsided when Marigold opened the door and said to Ivy, "There's someone here to see you."

"Ivy!" exclaimed Molly, popping up behind Marigold and waving a handful of papers. "I had a brilliant talk with the receptionist downstairs. She says I might be able to get into one of their advanced classes, if I can talk my mum into letting me audition."

"That's wonderful," said Ivy, and turned to her mother. "This is Molly—she's a friend of Richard's. She was the one who brought me here today."

"It's all right," Molly said in a confiding tone before Marigold could speak. "I know you and Ivy are faeries. But I won't tell anyone."

She'd said *faeries* and not *piskeys,* but Marigold didn't correct her, even for Ivy's sake. "How extraordinary," she said faintly. "And you're interested in our school?"

"Oh, yes," said Molly. "I want to be an actress more than anything."

Oddly, that seemed to put Marigold at ease. The color returned to her face, and she smiled. "Now I see where Richard comes in. Well, I'm not involved in the theater part of our program, but I'd be glad to put in a good word for you with Trix, our drama teacher. I can't tell you how grateful I am to you for bringing Ivy to me."

Molly blushed. "It was really nothing," she said. She folded up the papers and stuffed them into her pocket, then turned to Ivy with a shy smile. "Thanks for letting me come with you."

And there was that *thanks* again, so casual it was almost meaningless. But Molly obviously meant well, so Ivy smiled back. "I won't forget your kindness," she said. "I hope we'll see each other again."

"Me, too," said Molly. She looked from Ivy to Marigold, her expression wistful and a little envious. "Good luck." She scampered down the stairs and went out.

Marigold laid a hand on Ivy's shoulder. "I know a spell that may help us find Cicely," she said. "But we can't do it here. Let me look after a few things, and then I'll take you home."

When Ivy and her mother left the dance school, the air was misty with rain. As they walked down the hill Marigold spoke to her in an undertone, drawing her attention to all the strange sights around them and comparing them to things Ivy would know from the Delve. She pointed out shops and restaurants, galleries and museums, and showed Ivy how to safely cross the street.

"I was terrified when I first came to Truro," she said, tucking her arm into Ivy's. "I don't want you to feel that way. It's a lovely city, and now that we're together there's nothing to fear."

Before long they had made their way back to the open, cobblestoned place where Ivy and Molly had climbed off the bus. But now they were facing the other way, Ivy realized that half the square was filled with cloth-draped booths, much like the Market Cavern at home. The smells of hot food wafted toward her, savory and sweet, and beads clattered as a merchant woman rearranged the necklaces hanging in her stall. Nearby a boy in short trousers juggled four balls at once, while a crowder with pink hair played a lively jig on her fiddle. They passed a booth draped with scarves in a jewel-box of colors, another full of wooden puppets that danced on strings, and a third selling animals made of woolly yarn. They were coming to the end of the row when a brightly painted sign caught Ivy's eye. It read: CORNISH PISKEYS - FOR GOOD LUCK! And beneath in smaller letters, *Handcrafted in Kernow by local artisans.*

Beneath the sign stood a table crowded with brown clay statues. They were almost the proper height for piskeys, but their bodies were squat and their features grotesque. Was this really how humans imagined her people? Ivy picked one up, surprised at its lightness, and turned it over. The inside was hollow.

"Like those, do you?" said the seller, a weathered human with wild gray hair. "They're special, they are. Make a nice gift, or a souvenir."

They looked hideous to Ivy, but she didn't want to insult him by saying so. "Do you make them?" Ivy asked, but the man shook his head.

"I just sell 'em, lass. Eight pounds each. Or ten for Joan the Wad, she's the luckiest of all, see?" He lifted up a figure of a bristle-haired piskey hugging her knees, but Ivy had never seen anything that looked less like Betony, or anything she cared less to own. She lowered the statue she was holding, about to excuse herself and walk away.

But she couldn't put the thing down. It stuck to her hands, as though glued there. A buzzing sensation filled Ivy's palms, and she looked at the seller in alarm. But he only beamed and said, "Good choice. I'm fond of that little fellow myself. Want me to box him up for you?"

Ivy shook her head. "Mum!" she cried out, and Marigold hurried over. She seized the piskey in both hands and twisted it out of Ivy's grip. "Not today," she said to the man, and set it back on the table.

Ivy's hands stung and her legs felt shaky as Marigold pulled her away. The last thing she saw was the old piskey-seller waving cheerfully at her, before he retreated into the shadows and disappeared.

"I've never felt anything like that," said Ivy, taking the teacup her mother handed her. They were sitting in the kitchen of the place where Marigold lived—she called it a *flat* for some reason, even though they'd had to climb a flight of stairs to get there. "It was like some kind of spell, but... humans can't use magic, can they?"

Marigold poured her own cup and sat down. The rain was falling hard now, pattering against the glass like tiny fists knocking to be let in. "No," she said. "But there are old powers in the earth of Kernow, and not all of those powers are good ones. The piskeys and the faeries fought some terrible battles here, and the spells they used against each other still linger in the soil... and beneath it."

"Do you think he knew that? The man who was selling them?"

"I doubt it," said Marigold. "But I'd stay away from those statues, if you see them again. I've learned to be cautious of things made from Cornish earth."

"But you touched it, when you were helping me," said Ivy. "Didn't it pull at you too?"

Marigold shook her head. "I could never sense things in the rock and soil, not the way your father and the other piskeys could. But then, faeries were not made to live underground. I had no idea how weak my magic was, or how much stronger it could be, until I came out of the Delve."

She took Ivy's hand, stroking her thumb across it. "You'll

see for yourself, when you've been here a little longer. There is so much faery in you, and you've been trapped in the earth so long... you've barely even begun to come into your power."

Her tone was soothing, but Ivy felt more uneasy than ever. She felt sure her mother was right about the Delve—why else would Ivy feel so much better outside of the mine than she ever had living in it? Yet she didn't like the eager, almost hungry way her mother looked when she spoke about power. Or the way she'd said *when you've been here a little longer,* as though she felt sure that Ivy would never leave Truro again.

"What about Cicely?" Ivy asked. "You said you had a spell to help us find her."

"Yes," said Marigold, taking Ivy's other hand. "A faery spell for searching, stronger than the one Betony tried back in the Delve. Close your eyes, and I'll show you."

The searching charm should be able to locate any faeries within fifty miles, or so Marigold said. Since Cicely was half faery, it ought to be able to find her—and it would show her where to find them, as well. Ivy concentrated on doing as her mother told her, linking her power with Marigold's as they searched for the telltale flare of Cicely's magic. But though she pushed her magical strength to the limit, she felt nothing.

"It's not working," she said, dropping Marigold's hands in frustration. Was her magic too weak? Was her sister too far away?

Or had the worst happened, and Cicely was already dead?

Marigold touched her cheek tenderly. "You're tired," she said, "and so am I. Don't lose hope. We'll try again tomorrow." She rose and began clearing away the dishes.

Ivy didn't want to wait. She wanted to keep searching, even if it took all night. But Marigold's magic was clearly more powerful than hers, and if they couldn't find Cicely together, what hope did Ivy have of finding her alone? She slumped in her chair, picking at the too-soft wood of the tabletop, and looked around.

Her mother's flat was far smaller than the cavern she had left behind, and painfully bare of decoration. The furnishings looked flimsy, all wood and cloth, and the white-painted walls and gauzy curtains gave the place a washed-out, ghostly feeling. Even her mother no longer wore the topaz pendant that Ivy's father had given her, only a thin twist of hemp with a few glass beads and shells strung upon it. How could she be happy living in such meager surroundings, all alone?

"What if we could get rid of the poison in the Delve?" Ivy asked. "Would you come back then?"

"It's not as easy as that," said Marigold, her eyes on the dishtowel she was folding. "Betony never thought I was good enough to marry her brother. And she hated me even more for having children, since she and Gossan never could. When I told her about the poison—" She put a hand to her throat, and for a long moment she was silent. Then she said, "I can't go back, even if I wanted to. And I can't leave Serita."

Ivy frowned. "Who is Serita?"

"She started the Rising Star Academy with Trix, six years ago. When I came to Truro for the first time, weak and sick and not knowing where to turn, she was kind to me. She invited me to one of her performances, and when I watched her dance..." Her eyes grew faraway. "I'd never seen anything so wonderful, or so free."

"But there was plenty of dancing in the Delve," Ivy said.

"Not like this," said Marigold, with a shake of her head. "In the Delve it was always the same steps, the same dances, over and over. Never anything new." She sat down across from Ivy again, her gaze intent. "Don't you understand, Ivy? There's a price we pay for our magic, faeries and piskeys alike. We can do many things that humans can't, but they have something we lack—creativity. That's why we need them, even more than they need us."

"That doesn't make sense," Ivy said, a little resentfully. "Most of the women in the Delve have never seen a human, but they still create all kinds of things."

"Perhaps," Marigold said, "but the methods they use to make them haven't changed since the day they went underground. Every now and then you might see a piskey-woman with a new clothing pattern or a new recipe, if her husband or son brought it back from the surface. But that doesn't happen often—you know how men are." Her tone became bitter. "As long as their beds are warm and their bellies full, they hardly notice what we women do."

There was some truth to that, Ivy had to admit: she'd been annoyed by Mica's selfishness too many times to think otherwise. But she also couldn't forget how shattered Flint had been by his wife's disappearance, the emptiness she'd left inside him that no amount of good food, or even the love of his children, could fill.

And Marigold hadn't even asked how he was doing.

"But when magical folk and humans work together," Ivy's mother continued more brightly, "everyone benefits. We gain new ideas and skills from our human friends, while our presence makes their creativity stronger. The more time a faery spends with a human, the greater that shared creativity becomes. That was what happened with me and Serita." She gave a reminiscent smile. "Once I got up the courage to try the new dances she showed me, it wasn't long before I could do them as well as she could."

"Did she know you were a... faery?" asked Ivy. It was still hard to get used to the idea that her mother had no piskey blood in her at all.

"No," said Marigold. "And when I was captured by the Empress, I thought Serita would never forgive me. I'd left her without even saying goodbye. But when I returned to Truro she welcomed me, even though I couldn't tell her where I'd been. Then she told me she was ill, and that she wouldn't be able to teach for several months. She asked if I would take her place at the school until she was better again."

Which explained why Marigold had sent Richard to deliver her message, instead of coming herself. She'd made a promise to Serita, and like a true faery she was determined to keep it. But the knowledge brought Ivy no comfort. She could understand her mother not wanting to come back to the Delve. She could even understand her being afraid of Betony. But she'd made it sound as though Serita was more important to her than her own husband and children.

"Yet I never forgot about you," said Marigold softly, no doubt reading Ivy's thoughts in her face. "I missed you every day. And I'm so glad you came to me. I feared you'd choose to stay in the Delve, and I couldn't have borne it if—"

She plucked a white cloth from the box on the table and dabbed her eyes. Then she went on in a firmer tone, "But you're safe now, and that's all that matters. Once we find Cicely, we'll send a message to your father and brother. Then everything will be all right."

Ivy slept fitfully that night, and woke with the first rays of dawn. It wasn't that she'd been uncomfortable on the sofa—Marigold had offered her the bed and she'd declined it, knowing she'd feel more secure with a wall at her back. But she couldn't stop thinking about Cicely.

When her mother emerged from her tiny bedroom, Ivy got up at once. "Could we cast that searching spell again now?"

"Yes, of course," said her mother, taking Ivy's hands in her own.

They stood with eyes closed and heads bent, their shared magic rippling out across the city into the countryside beyond. Marigold had been right in urging her to rest, thought Ivy; her mind felt clearer, her power stronger than before. Hope rose inside her, and she concentrated with all her might. Surely they'd find Cicely now.

But though they sent out one call after another, there was no answer—not even the tiniest spark. "I'm sorry," said Marigold heavily, letting her go. "It's no good."

"But we can't give up," said Ivy. "We have to keep trying!"

"We can cast the spell again tonight," her mother said. "But I don't know what more to do. I fear..." She looked up sharply. "Where are you going?"

"Out," said Ivy. "I need to—" Then her eyes started to burn, and she couldn't speak any more. She hurtled out of the flat, slamming the door behind her.

Ivy returned to the flat late that evening, weak with exhaustion and misery. She'd flown from one end of Cornwall to the other, stopping every few miles to cast the searching spell. But only once did she sense the glow of faery magic, and as soon as she did it vanished, as though whoever it was didn't want to be found. It might have been Richard, but it certainly wasn't Cicely.

When Marigold opened the door, she didn't ask Ivy what had happened. She threw her arms around her, and Ivy closed her eyes and stood motionless, swallowing back a sob.

Then she came inside and ate the dinner her mother had saved for her.

Yet later that night, when the flat was quiet, Ivy's grief welled up again. She wept into her pillow until she had no tears left and then fell into exhausted sleep, her dreams haunted by a truth she could no longer deny.

Her little sister was dead, and it was her fault. Her mother was a faery, who'd left the Delve by her own choice and had no intention of ever returning. Ivy had destroyed her family and betrayed her people, all for nothing.

And now she could never go home.

13

Over the next few days Ivy became used to her new life in Truro, though she still felt restless and discontented. Marigold bought her new clothes and introduced Ivy to her human friends—including the ailing Serita and Trix, the academy's drama teacher. But she didn't offer to cast the searching spell again, and Ivy didn't ask her to.

Ivy had been in the city for nearly than a week, and had lost hope of seeing anyone from her past life again, when she made a discovery that changed everything. She was walking the streets around the cathedral one afternoon when she felt an itch at the back of her mind—a nagging sensation as though she'd forgotten something, or as though some soundless voice were calling her name.

It was impossible to ignore the feeling, even if she'd wanted to. Ivy followed it down the pavement, step by step, until she found herself in front of a shop that sold books and art supplies—and her gaze fell to a grinning piskey statue in the window.

Not again, she thought in disgust, and tried to walk away. But the tug inside her was too strong, and before she could stop herself she put her hand on the latch and pushed the creaking door open. A bell jangled, and the shopkeeper sang out, "Be with you dreckly!"

"It's all right," Ivy called back—she'd learned a few things from shopping with her mother. "I'm only looking."

"Right then," came the reply, and Ivy was left alone with a line of bookcases stretching away on both sides, and the window display in front of her. The piskey sat just within reach.

Ivy's hands tingled, blood rushing to the surface of her skin. She didn't want to touch the figure, yet she needed to—as though it were some missing part of herself, and without it she'd never be whole again. She fought the impulse, shutting her eyes tight and backing away. But her head and her heart throbbed in protest, and the piskey's call was too urgent to ignore. Reluctantly she bent and lifted the piskey statue from its place.

It was as ugly as the ones she'd seen in the market, a little man in a pointed cap and short jacket. But this one didn't stick to her hands, and it felt heavy compared to the one she'd held before. She turned it toward her, wondering what made it different—and nearly dropped the statue in shock.

For an instant, so quick she nearly missed it, the piskey's eyes had flashed silver.

Ivy gripped the statue convulsively. *What are you?* she thought, and a faint voice echoed in her mind: *Help... me.*

But not just any voice. A voice she had heard before.

It was Richard.

"How much for this?" Ivy asked, dashing to the back of the shop and brandishing the statue at the startled owner. Whether Richard was trapped inside the figure or whether he'd only been using it to speak to her, Ivy didn't know. But she couldn't leave the shop without it.

"It's not for sale," the man said, looking baffled. "It's just for show—"

"I'll pay you twice what it's worth," said Ivy, reaching into her purse. "Where did you get it? And when?"

"A couple of days ago, in the Pannier Market," he said. "But look, if you want it that badly, I won't cheat you. Nine pounds'll do it. Want it boxed up?"

Ivy cradled the statue protectively. "No, that's all right," she said. "I'll carry it with me."

"...And that's when I heard Richard's voice," Ivy explained to her mother as they sat at the table with the clay piskey between them. "But I've been trying all day to get it—him—to talk again, and nothing seems to work."

Marigold rubbed her forehead, as though the news pained her. She'd just returned to the flat after teaching her last class and she looked tired and disheveled, her hair windblown and her clothes spattered with rain. "Ivy, are you sure? It might just have been an echo. A shadow, a memory, of some piskey or faery who died calling for help a long time ago."

"It was Richard," Ivy insisted. "I know it was. We have to help him."

Reluctantly Marigold laid a hand on the statue and closed her eyes. But after a moment she shook her head. "I can't feel anything," she said. "I don't see how he could be in there, Ivy."

Ivy looked into the clay figure's dull brown eyes. It definitely felt heavier than the other statues she had handled, and the base was solid, not hollow. Did she dare to smash it and see if Richard was trapped inside? But what if he was part of the statue now, and she ended up killing him?

"I don't like this," said Marigold. "We should get rid of it." She reached for the figure, but Ivy pulled it away.

"I owe Richard my life," she said. "I can't give up on him."

Her mother's lips thinned, and she gave the statue a resentful look. But she must have known it was fruitless to argue with Ivy, because she sighed and leaned back.

"Molly rang the school today," she said, unwinding the knot of her hair and running her fingers through it. "She's going to audition for Trix tomorrow."

And just like that, she'd changed the subject. Did she really not believe that Richard was in danger? Was she so wrapped up in her own concerns that she didn't care? Or was there something else going on—something Ivy's mother didn't want to tell her?

Whatever the reason, the message was clear enough. If Ivy wanted to help Richard, she'd have to do it on her own.

She sat by the window long after her mother had gone to bed, waiting for the clouds to part so she could try some spells on the piskey statue by moonlight. But the sky remained closed, and the rain kept falling. At last, discouraged, Ivy set the clay figure on the tea-table and lay down on the sofa beside it.

"I'm sorry, Richard," she mumbled, her fingers tracing the statue's homely features—so unlike the sharp, fine-boned face she remembered. "I wish I knew how to help you."

The clay piskey didn't answer, or give any sign of hearing. But there was something forlorn about it despite its comic grin, and it seemed cruel to leave it sitting there all alone. What if Marigold got up and took it away in the night? Ivy picked up the statue and tucked it in beside her—and immediately felt better, as though that was what she should have done all along.

"Good night," she whispered, and closed her eyes.

That night Ivy had strange dreams, each more vivid than the next. She flew over the rooftops of a great city, where buildings of glass and steel rose like armored giants into the sky. She held a pebble that became a silver knife, its blade sharp enough to kill. She saw the faces of people she'd never met before—an older woman with blunt gray hair and a wry expression, a cheerful-looking man who winked at her before disappearing behind a curtain, and a richly dressed faery with blonde curls and a sweetly vicious smile. One moment she was in the midst of a group of skinny boys all fighting like wild animals; the next she was sprinting through a moonlit garden with smoke billowing around her and lights exploding on every side. But none of the dreams seemed to connect to one another, or make any sense.

Then all went black, and for a dreadful moment Ivy could see nothing at all. She might have thought herself dead, if not for the searing pain in her ankle. But when the darkness grayed into rosy twilight and a girl with tousled black hair dropped to the ground before her, Ivy realized with a shock that she was looking at herself.

These weren't her dreams. They were Richard's memories.

Where are you? she cried out silently. *Who did this to you? How can I set you free?*

More images flashed in her mind, confusing as the ones that had come before. A wounded swift spiraling toward the ground. Molly looking shocked, then furious. Marigold in a half-crouch, eyes narrowed and hands blazing with magical power. But just as Ivy despaired of making sense of it, she heard Richard's voice again.

Don't trust... Mother...

Ivy's heart gave a hard thump. Did he mean that the way it sounded?

Trapped me... Keeve is... Cicely...

Cicely! Was he saying she and Keeve were still alive, and together? Could they be trapped inside the piskey statues too?

Find... Richard whispered, and then more faintly, *Molly... your blood... save...*

She was losing him, and she couldn't bear it. Not when she

understood so little of what he was trying to say. *I want to save you!* Ivy shouted. *But you have to tell me how. Richard!*

There was no answer. Then a shadow loomed up behind her, and Ivy sensed she was in danger. She tried to run, but her feet were stuck in place, and all at once she couldn't move, couldn't speak, couldn't even breathe—

With a strangled cry, Ivy bolted awake. She was lying on the sofa with the blanket tangled around her legs, and through the nearby window the first light of dawn was glowing. Beside her the piskey statue beamed its foolish grin, its gaze empty as ever.

Yet it hadn't just been a nightmare. Richard had spoken to her, and she'd seen the past through his eyes. Ivy stared into the distance, her throat burning. She had to remember everything he'd said to her, before—

"Ivy?" Marigold came out of the bedroom, clutching a robe about her. "Are you all right?"

In that moment she looked exactly like the woman who had tucked Ivy into bed on the night before her first Lighting. And yet Ivy couldn't forget how she'd appeared in Richard's memory, with cold eyes and power crackling around her fingertips.

Don't trust... Mother...

Ivy pushed the piskey statue under the blanket. "I had a bad dream," she said. "But it's over now."

The Pannier Market was a busy place, full of indoor shops and booths selling merchandise of every kind. Ivy made her way past lighted cabinets full of fresh meats and cheeses, shelves of books and antiques, and a gorgeous display of fresh-cut flowers, until she found the stall she was looking for.

"Well, good morning," said the gray-haired vendor, folding his newspaper and getting up to greet her. "Thought I might see you again. Looking for these?" He gestured to the clay piskeys standing on one side of the table, next to a set of tiny porcelain faeries cupping flowers in their outstretched palms. "Only got three at the moment, but I'll be getting more soon. Collect the lot!"

Ivy shifted the weight of the bag on her shoulder, conscious of Richard's weight inside. "Where do they come from?"

The man scratched his ear. "D'you know, I can't quite remember. Can't be far, though, or I couldn't sell them as local. St. Austell, maybe?" He squinted as though trying to bring back the memory, then shook his head. "Sorry. Mind's not what it used to be. It's all a bit—" He waved a hand vaguely.

An unpleasant suspicion crept into Ivy's mind, though she didn't want to believe it yet. "Then tell me everything you know, please," she said, pushing a little magic into her request. She couldn't afford to waste time on half-truths and evasions, not when there were lives at stake. "Who brought them to you the first time? And when?"

"It was about a fortnight ago, I know that much. But..." The merchant frowned. "Can't recall what she looked like, or even how old she was. Isn't that odd."

She. Ivy clutched her bag tighter, waiting for him to finish.

"Anyway, she gave me one of these piskeys, said she made them herself. Told me to keep it in my stall for the week-end, and see if it didn't bring me good luck." His face brightened. "And didn't it! Got a head full of ideas all of a sudden, and knew just how to show off my wares. Never sold so much in two days in all my life. I was sorry to see that little fellow go, I can tell you. But she said she'd bring more when they were ready... and she did." He picked up one of the piskeys and contemplated it. "Can't say these ones seem as lucky, though. Not sure why."

Ivy knew why—she could see that the statue he held was hollow, with no living piskey or faery inside it. And it wasn't hard to guess that the *little fellow* he was talking about, the one who'd brought him such good fortune, had been Keeve.

So the piskey-maker was a woman—a woman who knew that Cornish clay had strange powers, and that contact with magical folk enhanced human creativity. She despised piskeys enough to make a mockery of them, and sell them in the market as slaves. And as if that weren't proof enough, she'd erased the man's memories so he wouldn't be able to identify her...

The same way she'd erased Ivy's memory, the night before she ran away.

What if Marigold no longer cared about the piskeys of the Delve, not even her own husband and son? What if she'd come to hate them for having destroyed her home, killed her father, and taken her mother underground to die? What if she'd decided that a slow death by poison wasn't good enough, and come up with a more fitting revenge—a spell that could capture piskeys and trap them in clay prisons for the rest of their lives? Keeve could have been her first victim, and then—if only by accident—Cicely. Finally Richard had found out the truth and confronted her, and she'd had to get rid of him too...

Ivy had missed her mother so much, these past six years. She'd been willing to take any risk, brave any danger, to see her again. But she was no longer the woman Ivy remembered. She might still care about Ivy—*you are more faery than any of them,* she'd said. But anyone with piskey blood would find her a ruthless and implacable enemy.

And now Marigold had a plan to destroy the Delve.

A plan that Ivy had to stop.

For the next few hours Ivy wandered the streets of Truro, brain working feverishly as she tried to decide what to do next. But with every corner she turned, she found herself more at a loss than before.

Her first thought was to confront her mother, and demand that she release the piskeys she'd taken prisoner. But though Ivy's magic was growing stronger by the day, she was still no match for Marigold's faery powers. If she acted too hastily, she might end up as a statue herself.

Then she thought of flying to the Delve, and warning Betony of the danger. But how could she prove that her suspicion was true, let alone tell the Joan what to do about it? She hadn't found Cicely or Keeve yet, and she had no proof that Marigold was behind their disappearance. All Ivy had was a foolish-looking statue, and the person trapped inside it wasn't even a piskey.

She needed to find out more about the spell that had trapped the piskeys, and whether there was any way to break it. Maybe then she'd figure out a way to stop Marigold before anyone else got hurt...

"Ivy!"

Startled, she turned as Molly bounded up to her, a shopping bag in each hand. "You look so... I mean, you look great!" the human girl exclaimed. "Are you having a good time with your mum?"

She looked so delighted to see Ivy, so full of hope and life and innocence, that Ivy couldn't bear to discourage her. "I'm glad to see you, too," she said. "Are you here by yourself?"

"Oh, no," Molly said. "My mum's in there, trying on clothes."

She pointed to a shop across the road. "But she's coming to my audition this afternoon, and—" She bit her lip. "I'm really nervous."

Ivy had forgotten about Molly's audition; she'd been too wrapped up in her own worries. But she'd seen Molly in Richard's dream-message, and heard him say her name. What if the human girl was more important than Ivy had thought?

"I tried about twenty different speeches," Molly went on fretfully, "and my mum helped me pick the best one, but I don't know." She toed the cobbles. "I wish Richard was here."

He was, if only Molly had known it. But if Ivy showed her the statue and told her what had happened, she'd probably be too upset to audition.

Yet theater was Richard's passion, as dance had become Marigold's. Surely he'd want to help Molly do her best, even if he couldn't see it. "Would it help if we—if I came with you?" Ivy asked.

"*Would* you?" Molly's doleful expression vanished, and her eyes shone. "That would be brilliant."

The only problem was that Marigold would be there as well, but Ivy had to face her mother sometime. "What about your mum, though?" Ivy asked. "Do you think she'll mind me being there?"

Molly waved this aside. "Oh, I've told her all about you. I mean, not *everything*, obviously, but I told her I had a friend whose mum was a teacher at the school, and that seemed to make her feel better about the whole thing. She's looking forward to meeting you." She swung one of her shopping bags to the other hand, and hooked her arm through Ivy's. "Why don't you join us for lunch?"

Until now Ivy had been too busy worrying to even think of food. But now, as she looked into Molly's eager face, she began to feel better—and hungry.

"All right," she said. "I will."

Mrs. Menadue looked dauntingly perfect in a sleek gray dress and sandals, her hair unruffled by the summer breeze. She smelled of the same musky perfume as before, which made Ivy's nose wrinkle. But she spoke graciously enough when Molly introduced them—and she even insisted on paying for Ivy's lunch, though she seemed preoccupied and let the two girls do most of the talking.

Once the meal was finished they walked to the Rising Star Academy, where Trix was waiting for them. "Well, hello!" she said warmly, clasping Mrs. Menadue's hand. "You must be Gillian. I'm Beatrix Little." She shook Molly's hand with equal warmth, and gestured to the stairs. "Come up to the studio and we'll have a chat. Ivy, are you looking for your mum? She's in the office."

"I came to see Molly's audition," Ivy said. "But I can wait here if you like."

"Do that, there's a love," said Trix. "I'll call you when we're ready."

Ivy sat down on the bottom stair, but even so she could hear most of the conversation taking place above. Gillian Menadue seemed concerned about how much it would cost to send Molly to the school, and Molly was insisting she could pay for some of the lessons herself, while Trix was suggesting ways they might make it easier to afford.

None of that was Ivy's business, so she did her best to ignore it. But it made her realize something she hadn't thought about before. Life in a human city was expensive compared to the simplicity of life in the Delve, and judging by the tiny size of her flat, Marigold didn't have much money to spare.

Yet she'd bought new clothes for Ivy, and they'd been eating regular meals together. Could that be why she'd been selling the piskey statues—so she could afford to keep Ivy with her? The idea was revolting, and yet...

"Ivy!" Trix called down to her. "We're finished now. Come on up."

Tucking Richard's bag under her arm, Ivy hurried upstairs to find Molly standing against the mirrored wall, fidgeting as she waited for her audition to begin. Gillian sat with folded arms, her face impassive, but Trix gave Molly an encouraging smile.

"Go ahead," she told her. "And don't worry too much—you're not auditioning for a role, it's just to help me decide which of our classes you belong in."

Molly nodded. Her eyes sought Ivy's and held them a moment, then she drew herself up and began to speak.

"Oh, misery, misery!" she declared. *"Again comes on me the terrible labor of true prophecy, dizzying prelude."* Her face twisted and her voice cracked with anguish as she went on: *"Do you see these who sit before the house, children, like the shapes of dreams? Children who seem to have been killed by their kinsfolk, filling their hands with meat, flesh of themselves..."*

Trix blinked, but Gillian remained unmoved. Ivy gripped Richard's cloth-wrapped statue, unsettled as much by Molly's harsh expression as the gruesome words she recited. Surely she couldn't think that this was the kind of speech Trix wanted to hear? She cast a pleading look at the human girl, hoping she would stop and try a different piece instead. But Molly didn't seem to notice.

"...For this I declare, someone is plotting vengeance," she finished huskily, and let the words hang in the air a moment. Then she bounced upright, her old self again. "How was that?"

"Er," said Trix, looking flustered. "I can't say I expected a fourteen-year-old to choose that particular reading. But you delivered it quite... convincingly." She turned to Mrs. Menadue. "Your daughter has talent. I think she could go far given the proper training, and I'd be glad to put her in one of our advanced classes."

Gillian looked resigned. "Well, I'll have to discuss it with my husband. But I suppose we might be able to work something out."

"Oh, *thanks,* Mum!" Molly exclaimed, and threw her arms around her mother's neck. For an instant Gillian's face pinched with distaste, but then she relaxed and patted Molly's shoulder.

"All right," she said. "I should have known you were meant for the theater, dramatic thing that you are. Just like your father."

The door to the office opened and Marigold emerged, smiling. "I heard your speech," she said to Molly. "That was very—" Then her gaze focused on Gillian and she stopped dead, the color draining from her face.

Mrs. Menadue detached herself from her daughter and stood up. "Marigold," she said, a note of triumph in her voice. "So this is where you've been."

14

"What's going on?" whispered Molly, tugging Ivy's arm as their mothers stared at each other. "Did you know my mum knew yours?"

Ivy shook her head. "I had no idea." But judging by the expression on Marigold's face, she wasn't nearly as glad to see Gillian as the human woman was to see her.

Trix must have sensed the tension in the air, because she turned to Mrs. Menadue and said brightly, "You'll give us a ring then, when you decide? Our advanced class is quite popular, and it would be a shame if I had to put Molly on the wait list."

"Yes, of course," Gillian replied. But she didn't move, or take her eyes off Marigold.

"So..." Trix tried again, turning to Ivy's mother. "Everything all right?"

"You can go now," Marigold told her. "I'll look after everything. Have a good night." She watched Trix until she disappeared down the stairs, then swung back to Gillian. She looked determined and a little fierce, as she had in Richard's memory. "What do you want?"

"Only to talk to you," said Gillian. "Is that wrong? I've—"

Her voice faltered, and for a moment she sounded as young as Molly. "I thought we were friends."

Marigold studied her coldly. Then she said, "Ivy, would you and Molly leave us for a little while?"

Molly looked uncertain, but Gillian waved her off. "We'll be fine here," she said. "Go and buy yourselves some ice cream." She walked toward the office, and Marigold stepped aside to let her in. The door closed behind them.

"Well," said Molly, but Ivy shushed her with a gesture. Silently she slipped across the room and leaned against the office door, listening.

"*No*, Ivy," said Marigold from inside, and Ivy knew she was beaten. She might not like leaving her mother alone with Gillian, but there seemed no reason Marigold would do the human woman harm. Reluctantly she turned away, and followed Molly down the stairs to the street.

"I can't figure it out," said Molly, as the two of them walked through Lemon Quay a few minutes later. "Your mum's a faery, and my mum's, well, my mum. How would they know each other?"

Ivy shook her head, equally at a loss. Perhaps Gillian had been one of the humans who helped Marigold after she'd first left the Delve, and they'd lost touch when Ivy's mother was captured by the Empress? But Gillian hadn't seemed shocked to see Marigold, only disappointed at her unfriendly manner. As though the two of them had been on good terms until lately, but then Marigold had started avoiding Gillian without telling her why...

"It's not like she *knows* your mum's a faery," Molly added, gazing into the distance. "She doesn't believe in that stuff. My dad's never minded me being mad about faeries, but my mum's always got so annoyed when I talked about seeing them, or wanting a faery of my own."

Ivy tightened her grip on her bag. "What do you mean, *of my own?*" she said.

"I mean to be a real friend, and stay with me always," Molly said defensively, reddening. "Not someone who goes away with no warning, and won't even tell me where..."

All at once she caught her breath, as though she'd been struck by an epiphany. "Wait. Your mum's *a faery.*" She whirled to face Ivy, a wild light in her eyes. "What if my mum can see faeries too, like I can? What if she met your mum years ago and they got to be friends, like Mar—I mean Richard—and me?"

Ivy was startled. She'd never considered that possibility. Richard and Molly had an obvious connection in their mutual love of theater, but Gillian wasn't a dancer, and the only human Marigold seemed to have that kind of bond with was Serita. "I don't see how—" she began, but Molly kept talking rapidly, as though she hadn't heard.

"But then your mum went away, or stopped talking to her, or—or something. And my mum was hurt, just like I was." She broke into a smile. "Don't you see? *That's* why my mum was trying to keep me away from faeries! It wasn't because she thought I was stupid for believing in them, it was because she was trying to protect me!"

To Ivy it sounded as though Molly were making her own story into Gillian's, and telling herself what she wanted to hear. But what if the human girl was right? Perhaps Gillian and Ivy's mother had been close at first, but then Marigold had been captured and forced to serve the Empress. And when she came back, she'd been so wrapped up in helping Serita and carrying out her revenge on the piskeys that she didn't have time for Gillian any more.

"It makes sense of everything," Molly said softly. Then a determined look came over her face and she pushed past Ivy, heading back the way they had come.

"Wait," called Ivy. She wasn't exactly afraid of Marigold—her mother had no reason yet to suspect Ivy of turning against her. But they'd only been gone a few minutes, and she doubted that either of the women would be pleased if Molly barged in. "It's too soon."

But Molly didn't slow down. Ivy had no choice but to run after her.

"Back already?" asked the woman at the school's front desk, but Molly ignored her. She sprinted up the stairs, and with an apologetic glance at the secretary, Ivy followed.

When they reached the upper level Molly started toward the office, but Ivy was quicker. She darted in front of the other girl and pressed her ear to the door. Molly did likewise. There was no sound.

The two girls exchanged looks, and Ivy eased the door open. Two chairs faced each other across the desk, and the computer spun a web of colored light in one corner. The window stood open, curtains rippling on the breeze. But the room was empty.

"They must have gone out," said Ivy. She backed into the studio and called to the secretary, "Did my mum say where she was going?"

"What do you mean?" asked the woman, appearing at the foot of the stairs. "She's in the office."

So the secretary hadn't seen them leave. Perhaps she'd merely been distracted, but Ivy feared otherwise. What if Marigold had left the school by magic, and taken Gillian with her?

Yet why would she? What use could Molly's mother be in her plans to destroy the Delve?

"Come on," Ivy said to Molly, telling herself not to panic. Nothing terrible had happened yet. "Let's walk about a bit. Maybe they'll turn up."

For half an hour Ivy and Molly wandered the streets in search of Gillian and Marigold, but without success. They were on their way back to the school, and Ivy was wondering if she ought to cast a searching spell, when she caught the cloying, familiar scent of Gillian's perfume. Relieved, she turned to follow it—and saw Molly's mother stumbling around the corner. All her poise had vanished: she was ashen and shuddering, clothes rumpled and hair in disarray. And Marigold was nowhere in sight.

"Mum!" exclaimed Molly, rushing to her. "What happened?"

"I'm all right," she murmured, gripping Molly's shoulder. "I'm just—I've had a bit of a shock."

"Where's my mother?" Ivy asked sharply.

Gillian blinked, as though the question puzzled her. "We were talking," she said. "Something about a plan, and fixing past mistakes..." She put a hand to her forehead. "How long was I gone?"

Queasiness rose inside Ivy. She sounded like the vendor

in the Pannier Market—as though her memories had been deliberately tampered with.

"It's okay, Mum," said Molly. She glanced at Ivy, and for once there was no warmth in her eyes. "I know about Marigold being a faery."

Gillian's shoulders sagged. "I should have told you," she said. "But I kept hoping you'd grow out of seeing faeries, or at least you'd stop wanting to get close to them... I didn't want you to be hurt."

"What did my mother do to you?" Ivy asked.

"She asked me to help her," Gillian replied. "Something to do with clay... But I said no, and then—" Her forehead furrowed, as though she were struggling to remember. "She was angry. She raised her hand, and everything turned so bright..."

Ivy turned away, feeling sick. It had hurt when she first suspected her mother was responsible for turning Keeve, Cicely and Richard into statues, but part of Ivy had clung to the hope that she might be wrong. After this, though, how could she doubt it any longer?

It was obvious what had happened. Marigold had tried to convince Gillian to help her carry out her revenge, but the human woman had refused, and paid the price for it. It was a mercy that Ivy's mother hadn't turned Gillian into a statue as well... though if Marigold hadn't spared her own daughter, it was hard to imagine why. Unless the spell only worked on magical folk?

"Did she hurt you, Mum?" Molly asked anxiously.

"No," said Gillian. "But she's gone now. And I don't think she's coming back."

Ivy paced the floor of Marigold's flat, hugging Richard's statue for comfort. Even now that she knew her mother was evil, she couldn't quite believe she'd run away. Why bother sending Richard to bring Ivy to Truro, only to abandon her at the first sign of trouble?

But when she looked for something to eat and found nothing in the refrigerator but a few apples and a half-empty container of yogurt, it was hard to believe anything else. Perhaps Marigold had just forgotten to buy more food, but more likely she'd known she'd be leaving soon, and hadn't thought shopping worth the trouble.

Yet even now that Ivy was sure her mother was guilty, she had no way to prove it. Perhaps Marigold had found a way of using the magic-soaked Cornish earth to turn the piskeys into statues, but her traps couldn't be easy to spot or Keeve and Cicely wouldn't have fallen into them. Ivy could turn herself into a swift and fly to the Delve this very minute, but what use would it be if no one believed her when she got there?

The other problem was that Ivy had no idea where her mother had gone, let alone how to stop her. She could cast a searching spell, but that would also warn Marigold that Ivy was coming—and in that case she might as well stay here for all the good it would do.

Ivy rubbed her eyes and let out a shaky breath. She was still fighting tears of rage at her own powerlessness when the telephone rang.

It couldn't possibly be for her. But she couldn't ignore it, either. Ivy picked up the receiver awkwardly and said, "Hello?"

"Ivy?" said the voice on the other end. "It's Gillian Menadue."

When she'd last seen Gillian, the human woman was still upset by her fight with Marigold. Molly had urged her to see a doctor, but she'd said all she wanted was to go home. The two of them got into their car and drove off, and Ivy had felt miserably certain that she'd never see either one of them again.

Apparently she'd been wrong. "Oh," said Ivy. "Hello."

"Has your mother returned?" Mrs. Menadue asked. She sounded calm now, more like her usual self. "Is anyone looking after you?"

"No," Ivy said.

"I was afraid of that." Gillian sighed. "Well, Molly and I have been discussing it, and we don't like to think of you being all alone. Would you like to stay with us, at least for tonight? We can make up a bed for you in the study."

Ivy was quiet, considering the offer. It seemed unlikely that Marigold would return, and she couldn't forget that Richard had mentioned Molly in his dream-message. Maybe it was time to tell the human girl what had happened to him, and make use of that creativity Marigold had mentioned. If Molly could figure out a way to free Richard, maybe he could help Ivy stop her mother...

"Yes, please," Ivy said, picking up Richard's statue and stuffing it in her bag. "I'll be glad to come."

When Ivy got off the bus, Molly was waiting for her. "I can't believe my mum invited you," she said as they walked down the hill in the evening cool, midges swarming from the hedge beside them. "It's like she's a different person." She broke into a smile, then sobered and added, "I'm sorry about your mum, though. I hope she's not... I mean, maybe it was just a misunderstanding."

Ivy nodded, not trusting herself to speak. Soon they reached the Menadues' house, snug and welcoming in the twilight with its softly lit windows and open door. "I need to finish up in the barn," Molly said. "Why don't you go in? My mum's got supper for you, if you're hungry."

Ivy would have preferred to stay with Molly, but her stomach betrayed her with a rumble. "All right," she said, and crossed the yard to the front step of the house, where Mrs. Menadue stood waiting. Her perfume hung heavy in the air as she led Ivy to the kitchen, and sat her down with a bowl of soup and some crusty bread.

"This must be hard for you," she said, taking the chair across from Ivy. "I'm sorry."

Ivy had disliked Molly's mother at first, but now she felt ashamed of herself for judging the woman so harshly. "I'm sorry for what my mum did to you," she replied.

Gillian gave a faint smile. "It could have been worse," she said. "It was my mistake to try and reason with her, and convince her to let go of the past." She poured herself a cup of tea and sipped it. "I should have realized how impossible that would be, after she'd spent so many years trapped in the Delve."

Ivy nearly inhaled her soup. "You know about the Delve?"

"Oh, yes," said Gillian. "Not that your mother ever told me exactly where it was. Only that she'd been living in an old tin mine somewhere between here and Redruth." Her gaze became distant. "She was weak and exhausted when I found her, and so unhappy. When I recognized her as a faery and offered to help, she seemed so grateful. I thought we'd be friends forever."

"Did she say anything to you about her plan?" Ivy asked. "I know you don't remember much, but—"

"I remember some things," Molly's mother said. "Like the conversation we had in the beginning, when she discovered the truth about her past. Something about how if she wanted to avenge her family and rescue the women of the Delve, she'd have to get rid of all the men first. Once the hunters and foragers were gone, the other piskeys would have to come up to the surface."

Ivy's heart was galloping now. "Did she say how she planned to get rid of them?" she asked, but Gillian shook her head.

Still, the pieces were coming together in Ivy's mind now, and she could imagine what her mother had done. It must have taken years for Marigold to find the magical earth she needed, and figure out how to turn the piskeys into statues. But as soon as her spell was ready, she'd sneaked back to the Delve and set a couple of traps on the hillside to test it out. Then she'd sent Richard to fetch Ivy, not wanting her half-faery daughter to get caught up in her revenge.

Catching Keeve would have pleased Marigold, but it must have been a nasty shock when Cicely fell into her trap. So why hadn't she released Ivy's sister right away? Perhaps she didn't know how to undo the spell, or—more likely—she'd been afraid to release Cicely in case she interfered. So she'd hidden her somewhere safe, while she used the clay-bound Keeve to win over the vendor in the Pannier Market. Then she gave the man some empty statues to keep him busy and make a little money, until she had more of the real piskeys to sell.

It was hard to imagine how Richard had ended up as a statue, though. Perhaps he'd flown back to the Delve to investigate Cicely's disappearance, and caught Marigold setting another trap? He'd confronted her, and she'd cast the spell on him to keep him from talking...

Molly's mother touched her hand, calling her back to the present. "Ivy," she said seriously, "I know you're worried. But your mother must have wanted to protect you, or she wouldn't have gone to the trouble of fetching you out of the Delve. So you mustn't chase after her. You'll only get hurt."

Ivy knew she was right. Yet she couldn't shake the feeling that time was running out for the piskeys of the Delve, and if she didn't act soon it would be too late. Marigold knew all the mine's entrances and exits; in minutes she could lay traps in front of every one. If she found a way to lure all the males out onto the surface...

The thought was more than Ivy could bear. How could she sit idle while her brother, Mattock, and all the other piskey-men she cared about were turned into statues and sold off as good-luck charms? Even Flint... her father might be safe for a few days in the depths of the mine, but once all the other men were gone and the women were crying out for food, surely he'd have to come out too.

"I know it could be dangerous," she said to Gillian. "But I have to try. I just don't know how yet."

Mrs. Menadue sighed. She got up and put her teacup in the sink, while Ivy stared at her soup as though she might find the answer floating in its surface. But the scattered vegetables and bits of meat refused to give her any ideas, and it seemed that Molly's mother didn't have any either.

Or did she? There must be a reason Ivy's mother had wiped Gillian's memory and disappeared. Perhaps something about their conversation had forced Marigold's hand, and convinced her she had to act quickly?

And if Ivy could figure out what her mother was afraid of, perhaps she'd know how to stop her.

"Do you remember anything else she said today?" she asked Mrs. Menadue. "Or what you said to her, when you were alone?"

Gillian looked exasperated. "Enough," she said, taking the bowl from Ivy. "Time you went to bed—the study's the first door on the right. We can discuss it in the morning."

Which was so maddeningly *human* of her, and so like a mother as well. As though Ivy were the one being unreasonable, and if she went to sleep like a good girl the problem would go away.

"I need to know now," insisted Ivy. She didn't want to have to use magic, especially since her mother had meddled with Gillian's mind already. But she'd never forgive herself if she got to the Delve too late. She stretched out her thoughts–

Mrs. Menadue gave her a stern look. "Not in my house, you won't," she said. "And if you try using magic on me again, I'll throw you out."

Richard had told her the house was protected, but Ivy hadn't realized the charm would work that way. Shame hunched her shoulders, and she left the table without another word.

The study was dark and quiet, and the foldaway cot Mrs. Menadue had made up for Ivy was as comfortable as the sofa at her mother's flat, or more so. She'd said goodnight to Molly under Gillian's watching eye, then discreetly slipped Richard's statue out of her bag and laid it beside her, in case he found the strength to send her another dream-message. But that had been over an hour ago, and no matter how hard Ivy tried to quiet her restless thoughts, she couldn't sleep.

If this were the Delve, she would have gone for a walk. But the air outside was fresh, and more likely to wake her up than make her sleepy. Besides, Ivy's mind was the problem, not her body.

Perhaps she should try reading. There weren't many books in the Delve, except a few dry accounts in the Joan's library; stories were the droll-teller's business, not something to be put on paper. But Ivy knew her letters well enough, and it wouldn't hurt to try.

There was no need to turn on a lamp, not when she carried her own light with her. Glowing softly, Ivy slid out of bed and crept to the bookcase. But to her disappointment, most of the volumes seemed to be about fixing mechanical things like cars and motorcycles—subjects that would probably have fascinated Mica or even Cicely, but held little appeal for Ivy.

She had picked her way through the shelves without finding anything of interest when she spotted a worn, ring-bound volume called a *Road Atlas.* Curious, Ivy opened it and found it was a book of maps, showing only Cornwall but other parts of England as well. But as she turned the pages, a square of folded paper dropped out. Another map?

Carefully Ivy opened the page and smoothed it. It showed far more detail than any other map she'd seen—even individual farmsteads were marked and named, along with a great many places starting with "Wheal" that Ivy recognized as the locations of old tin and copper mines. In fact the Delve had been called Wheal Felicity, back when humans worked there. Could it be on the map too?

It took a little searching, but eventually she found Wheal Felicity in the top left corner, with the neighboring wood to the east. But someone had marked an X next to it—no, two X's, one to the northwest and another between the Delve and the wood. And when Ivy looked more closely, she could see cross-marks beside several other mines in the vicinity as well. As though the map's owner had been visiting one location after another, and marking off their progress...

Not that your mother ever told me exactly where it was, Gillian had said. *Only that she had been living in an old mine somewhere between here and Redruth.*

With shaking hands Ivy folded the map and tucked it back in its hiding place. Hurriedly she dressed in her old waistcoat and breeches, pushed Richard's statue into her bag and slung it over her shoulder. Then she turned herself invisible and slipped out.

The mischievous-looking piskey she'd seen on Molly's shelf, the first time she came to the house... could it be? It hadn't looked anything like Richard's statue, or the other clay figures she'd seen. But if there was even a chance that it might be Keeve, Ivy couldn't run away and leave him. Steeling her courage, she tiptoed down the hall to Molly's bedroom.

The curtains were drawn, and a thin slice of moonlight glimmered between them. Easing herself past the bed where the human girl lay sleeping, Ivy moved to the shelf and picked up the little piskey.

No wonder it had reminded her of Keeve. It *was* him. Every detail of his face was perfect, though he was half the size of the crude figures the vendor in Truro was selling; in fact he could have fit inside one, and probably had.

But how had he come to Molly? Ivy looked back at the girl beneath the faery-printed coverlet. Her hair snaked across the pillow, and she was drooling a little in her sleep. Did Ivy dare to wake her?

It might be a mistake—even a fatal one. But she needed to know. Ivy crouched next to the bed and whispered, "Molly."

She held her hand ready to clap over the girl's mouth if she cried out, but Molly only rolled over. "What?" she mumbled.

"I need to know about this piskey," Ivy said, holding Keeve up for her to see. "Where did you get him?"

Molly struggled up onto her elbows. Ivy watched for any hint of fear or guilt, but the girl only looked bemused. "That? My dad gave it to me."

"Your *dad?*" exclaimed Ivy, before remembering to lower her voice. "But hasn't he been away?"

"Yeah, but... he buys me presents sometimes, before he goes. And then he leaves them for me to find while he's gone, so I know he's thinking of me."

She reached for the figure, but Ivy held it away from her. "Are you sure it came from your father? Not your mother?"

Molly wrinkled her nose. "Why would my mum give me a piskey statue?"

That was all the answer Ivy needed. Molly didn't know, she'd assumed. And judging by her reaction, she had no idea there was anything sinister about the statue, either.

"Never mind," Ivy said, with a furtive glance at the door. "Just one more thing. When we first met, you said your mum was a teacher. What does she teach?"

Molly sighed. "Can't we talk about this tomorrow?"

"Please," said Ivy. "It's important."

"I teach a beginners' art course," said Gillian Menadue mildly from the doorway. "We do sketching, painting... and sculpting with clay."

Ivy's heart collided with her ribs and dropped into her stomach. How could the human woman have crept up on her unnoticed? She backed toward the window, trembling with the urge to fly. But the glass panes were shut.

"Mum?" asked Molly. "What's going on?"

"Nothing you need to worry about," Gillian replied. "Go to sleep."

It was not a suggestion, it was a command. Molly blinked, and a bewildered look came over her face. She opened her mouth to protest—then her eyes closed and she slumped, unconscious.

Ivy turned to Gillian in shock, unable to believe a human could wield such power. But then she caught the woman's natural scent, a sweet herbal fragrance utterly unlike the false perfume she'd worn before...

"You're not human," Ivy said, hoarse with disbelief. "You're a faery."

Gillian smiled.

15

"You can't fly," said Gillian softly as she and Ivy faced each other, with the sleeping Molly between them. "And you won't run, either. Not when I have your sister... and now your mother as well."

She was right, but Ivy hated her for it. She stood rigid, cursing herself for not seeing through Gillian's deception sooner. Until a few minutes ago she'd believed that Gillian had been fortunate to escape from Marigold. Now she knew that her mother had been the unlucky one.

"Where are they?" Ivy demanded. "What have you done to them?"

"I can show you, if you like. They're still alive, though not very happy at the moment. But you could change that. Come with me."

"And be turned into a statue? I don't think so."

"If I wanted to do that to you," Molly's mother replied, "I would have done it by now. Do you want to see your family or not? Trust me, you'll never find them on your own."

Ivy hesitated, studying Gillian's face for signs of treachery. Then she stepped around Molly's bed and walked to join her.

The faery woman smiled. With all the grace of a hostess she ushered Ivy through the house and out into the cobbled yard, where the moon glowed like a lantern among the pin-pricked stars.

"I'll saddle Duchess," she said to Ivy, opening the barn door. "We'll get there faster on horseback."

Ivy's brows crooked together. "You're going to leave Molly here alone?"

"No harm will come to her in this house," Gillian replied airily as she walked into the barn. "Not with all the protective charms I've laid around it. She'll sleep peacefully until morning."

As though it didn't even matter to her how Molly would feel when she realized what her mother had done. A suspicion surfaced in Ivy's mind, and she spoke it aloud: "Is she even yours? Or did you kill Molly's real mother, and take her place?"

That got Gillian's attention; she stopped and turned. "What an unpleasant idea," she said. "Of course Molly is my daughter. Where do you think her faery blood comes from?"

"Well," said Ivy, "you seem to have come up with a few unpleasant ideas of your own. Like turning piskeys into statues, for instance." She gripped the strap of her bag, where the figures of Richard and Keeve were hidden. "Did you turn my mother into a statue too?"

"Of course not," Gillian replied, taking Duchess's bridle off its hook. "The Claybane only works on piskeys or spriggans, and your mother's lineage is as pure faery as my own."

"So is Richard's," said Ivy. "But that didn't keep you from turning him into a statue."

"You mean that weasel-faced boy your mother sent to find you?" Gillian looked surprised, then amused. "So he managed to make contact with you, even while trapped in the Claybane. I wouldn't have thought that possible, unless the two of you had a *very* strong connection..." Her brows rose in mock dismay. "Dear me. Does your mother know?"

"Yes, that's who I mean," said Ivy, refusing to take the bait.

It made sense that she and Richard had some sort of bond after all the magic he'd put into healing her, but that was none of Gillian's business. "Why punish him? What did he ever do to you?"

"He arrived at a very inconvenient time," said Gillian as she opened the door to Duchess's box and slipped the bridle on. The gray mare snorted and tossed her bony head, but she held the reins until the horse subsided. "I'd almost convinced your mother to tell me where the Delve was located, so I could go and fetch you out before you died of the poison. But when your Richard turned up, she decided to send him instead."

So that was what the map had been about, with all the crossed-off marks. Gillian hadn't known which mine the piskeys lived in, so she'd been visiting each one in turn, leaving a trap or two at each one to see if any piskeys fell into it. But there were hundreds of abandoned mines in this part of Cornwall, so the search could have taken months—or years.

"Though he did turn out to be useful, when I tracked him to the Delve," Gillian continued, dropping the saddle onto Duchess's back. "I caught my first piskey that night. And after that I no longer needed your Richard, so I left a few clues to help your people find him, and I thought that would be the end of it."

No wonder Mica and Mattock had caught the so-called spriggan so easily. Richard could never have guessed he'd been followed, much less betrayed. "But it didn't work," Ivy said. "He escaped. And then what? He came back to the Delve one night looking for my sister, and found you setting more of your traps?"

Gillian gave a little shrug as she crouched to pull the girth tight. "It was remarkably poor timing," she said. "One might even say bad luck. But more so for him than for me, in the end."

"So you sold him to the dealer in the Pannier Market, and left him to die."

"Die?" Gillian straightened up, looking offended. "Certainly not. Only the first piskey I caught died, and that was an accident."

Ivy had already guessed that Keeve might be dead, but it still hurt to hear it. The lump of clay in her purse was all that was left of that black-eyed, mischievous boy who'd left so many bottles of cream at her door, and now he'd never milk a cow or play a prank again.

"Why are you doing this?" she asked, hoarse with emotion. "Keeve had nothing to do with what happened at Thistledown Wyld—that was fifty years ago! My mother wasn't born yet, and you can't have been more than a child yourself—"

"Cleverly guessed," Gillian said. "But you're only half right." She seized Duchess's bridle as the mare danced sideways. "You're also half piskey, as I recall. Do something about this beast."

"Shh," said Ivy, reaching to stroke the horse's shivering neck. "I won't let her hurt you." Duchess bowed her head meekly, and Ivy led her into the yard.

"Good," said Gillian, swinging herself into the saddle and reaching a hand down to Ivy. "Now get up behind me, and I'll take you to your mother."

Ivy had longed to ride a horse since she was a child, learning her animals from the mosaic on the walls of the Upper Rise. She'd heard the droll-teller describe how piskeys of old used to borrow horses from their human neighbors simply for the pleasure of riding them around the countryside, and it had been a cruel disappointment when she realized she'd never be allowed to do the same.

Now she had her wish after all, but it brought Ivy no pleasure. Bumping along on the back of a leather saddle while Gillian held the reins, forced to cling to the faery woman's waist for support, was far from the joyous romp she'd envisioned. Especially once they came down the slope into the wood below, where the branches arched thickly over the darkened path. Only the light-spell Gillian had conjured kept Duchess from stumbling off course.

"The first time I saw a piskey," Gillian said as they trotted along, "I was six years old. They came to our wyld, armed and armored, and demanded we pay them tribute. But our queen refused, saying that we had lived there in peace for a hundred years, and that the land was ours as much as theirs. So they left, but that night they returned in force. My father was killed in the fighting, and my mother and sister taken captive. I was the only one who escaped."

"I know about Thistledown Wyld," said Ivy. "My mother told me. But—"

"You know nothing," said Gillian curtly. "The wyld where Marigold's parents lived was my *second* home, where I found refuge after the first was destroyed. When the piskeys came to Thistledown I was a grown woman, and this time it was my husband they killed." Her hands tightened on the reins. "I escaped again, but at bitter cost—I lost the child I was carrying, and nearly died myself. And as I lay in the ruins of my home with the bodies of my people around me, I swore on my own lifeblood that I would hunt down the piskey-men of Kernow and punish them as their cruelty deserved."

Ivy looked down, swallowing. It nauseated her to hear that her ancestors had been so ruthless, and she would never look at some of the old uncles in the Delve the same way again. Yet Gillian's story didn't explain everything she'd done, much less justify it. "But my people don't fight any more," Ivy said. "Now they're the ones hiding, and living in fear."

"The *women* live in fear," Gillian retorted. "I learned that much from your mother. Your men may be wary of other magical folk, but it doesn't keep them from hunting and foraging, and trading with the humans as they please. What kind of justice is that after all the evil they've done?"

"It's not like—" began Ivy, but Gillian cut her off.

"Don't tell me they're risking themselves for your protection. Haven't you noticed that the men of the Delve live longer than the women, that they show fewer signs of age, that their injuries heal more easily and that they're less prone to sickness? Can't you see they're deliberately keeping you weak, so they can control you—the daughters and granddaughters and great-granddaughters of the faery women they stole from wylds like mine?"

"But the Joan is the most powerful piskey in the Delve," Ivy protested. "And she's the one who decides how we should live. Why would she keep us underground if she didn't believe it was for the best?"

Yet even as she said it, Ivy remembered that Betony could go outside whenever she liked, and often did. She had to maintain the spells that protected the Delve from intruders, after all—and with her ability to conjure fire, no one would dare to tell the Joan it was too dangerous.

"I've never met your Joan," Gillian replied, "but she wouldn't be the first female to put her own interests ahead of anyone else's. Perhaps she fears that if she lets the other piskey women go above, one of them may grow powerful enough to challenge her for the throne. Or perhaps she's afraid the males will overthrow her if she does anything to threaten their privilege and power." She leaned sideways to avoid a jutting branch, then continued, "But she can't truly believe that you're safer underground, even if a thousand spriggans were waiting on the surface. Surely your mother told you about the poison in the mine? If you'd seen how ill Marigold was when she came to me, you'd agree that death itself could hardly be more cruel."

"So that's why you decided to turn the men into clay statues," said Ivy, "and let the women go free?"

"Not exactly," Gillian said. "Even after meeting Marigold and hearing her story, I still meant to kill every male in the Delve if I could. But I was only one faery, and I knew that even if I could convince your mother to join me, we would not have enough power between us to kill more than a few. I discovered the Claybane later, after Marigold had disappeared."

"After you betrayed her, you mean," Ivy said coldly. Now she knew what her mother had meant when she said, *I trusted someone I should not have trusted...*

"The Empress's servants found her without any help from me," Gillian retorted. "She was careless, and too unskilled at hiding. I was sorry to see her taken away, but what good would it have done me to interfere? I had been living as a human for a long time while I planned my revenge, and I had no intention of throwing away my disguise to fight some fool of a so-called Empress."

Her indifference made Ivy furious. "So that's all Molly was to you? Part of your disguise?"

"Hardly," replied Gillian. "Faeries may be more reserved than piskeys, but that doesn't make us heartless. Still, I was glad when I heard that the Empress was dead, and I no longer needed to stay so close to my human family. By that time I had located the site of an ancient battle between the piskeys and my ancestors, and found a book which told of spells my people had used against their enemies—including the magical clay that would trap any piskey who touched it, but leave faeries and humans unharmed."

She kicked Duchess into a canter as they crossed a roadway, then settled back into a walking gait on the other side. "When Marigold returned to Truro I sought her out and apologized, hoping to rebuild our friendship. I knew she was anxious about your welfare, so I urged her to send you a message, and offered to deliver it to the Delve myself. But Marigold's time with the Empress had changed her, and she was no longer so quick to trust. She began to avoid me, and when I saw her talking to your Richard, I knew she had grown suspicious of my motives."

"Why didn't you let her go, then? If you knew she wasn't going to help—"

"I would have," Gillian replied, "if not for your sister... and you. When I found Cicely trapped in the Claybane I had no idea who she was, but it troubled me. I had thought that only male piskeys and the Joan ever went out of the Delve. I wanted to talk to your mother and make sure I hadn't misunderstood, but she was still keeping her distance. It wasn't until Molly came home with her pamphlets from the school, and I saw Marigold's name on one of them, that I found my chance to talk with her again."

And by that time Ivy's mother had seen the clay piskeys, and knew that Ivy believed Richard to be trapped inside one. She knew that Cicely was missing, as well—so once Gillian showed up, it wouldn't have taken Marigold long to realize that her old friend had become the piskeys' deadliest enemy.

"She fought you, didn't she?" asked Ivy.

"Yes," said Gillian. "Though I tried to reason with her. I offered to free Cicely if she would help me—or at least promise not to interfere. But she refused, and I was forced to restrain her." She sighed. "That was when I decided to approach you, and hope you might be more sensible."

"Sensible?" asked Ivy. "You killed a boy I grew up with. And now you're talking about turning my brother and my father and—and all the men I care about into statues for the rest of their lives. How am I supposed to be *sensible* about that?"

"You know the way you were forced to live in the Delve

was unjust," Gillian said. "You know you were deceived, or at least misled, about the dangers of going up to the surface. You know your Joan refuses to believe that the mine is unsafe to live in, even though you were born crippled and your mother nearly died. Doesn't that make you angry, Ivy? Don't you agree that something has to change?"

"Yes, but–"

"Don't answer yet," Gillian told her. "Just think about it. When we reach the place where your mother and sister are waiting, we'll talk again."

A few minutes later, Gillian brought Duchess to a halt and nudged Ivy to dismount. Beside the path, scarcely visible through the surrounding shrubbery and the vines snaking over its surface, stood a low stone building that looked like it had once been part of a mine.

"Here we are," Molly's mother said, securing Duchess's reins to an overhanging branch and leaving the mare to graze. She raised a hand and the plants recoiled, revealing a stout and surprisingly modern-looking door. With a spark from her fingertips she unlocked it, and pushed it wide. "My workshop. Mind the step."

Willing her skin to glow brighter, Ivy stepped cautiously over the threshold onto the floor below. The building consisted of a single bare room, damp and musty-smelling. She glimpsed shelves along one wall and an old plastic feed bucket in the corner, but apart from that the place looked empty.

Ivy rounded on Gillian, ready to demand where she'd hidden her mother. But before she could speak, the faery woman waved her hand. The shadows parted, and Ivy could see—

"Mum!" Ivy cried, rushing to her. Marigold slumped against the wall, her brown hair hanging over her face. Her chest rose and fell, but she didn't move even when Ivy shook her. "What have you done to her?"

"No more than it seems," Gillian replied. "She's asleep—but she won't wake unless I allow it. As for your sister, she too is safe, and in good company."

Ivy looked up, and her heart flipped over. The whole bottom shelf was filled with ugly grinning piskey statues, empty and waiting. And on the shelf above them stood a row of the real piskeys, frozen in mid-struggle. She saw Gem there, twisted back on himself as he tried to wrench one foot free. She recognized Feldspar, his hands uplifted and his eyes bulging in shock. And at the end of the row stood a terrified-looking piskey girl with two braids hanging over her shoulders.

"Cicely!" Ivy snatched the little figure from the shelf and cradled it. Like the statue of Keeve in her bag it was perfect in every detail, her sister's mouth still frozen open in her last, wordless scream. No wonder Gillian had crafted those jolly-looking shells to hide her victims; what human would want to buy a statue that looked like this?

"I would have freed her if I could," said Gillian. "I had no wish to harm a child, especially a girl. But the spell to release her requires not only my blood but the blood of a close relative, so there was nothing I could do for her until today."

Richard had said something about blood in his dream-message, too. "Why does it have to be a relative?"

"My ancestors created the Claybane as a way of taking hostages," Gillian replied. "It was designed to hold enemies captive without need for prison or guard, until someone from their tribe came to make an offer of peace. If no one came within seven days, the piskey or spriggan trapped in the Claybane would die."

So that was what had happened to Keeve. His time had run out, and there'd been no one to save him. Ivy clutched Cicely's statue's tighter. "Then the others will die too, if they aren't released?"

"No," said Gillian. "I altered the spell, once I realized my mistake. They will live indefinitely... if you can call it living."

So there was still a chance to free Cicely. But there was nothing she could do for Gem and Feldspar... or for Richard, either. Grief aching in her chest, Ivy let her bag sink to the floor.

"You can't save the men of the Delve," Gillian told her. "With or without you, I will have my revenge. But you can save your sister and your mother, and the other women as well, if you help me."

Ivy looked down at Cicely's tiny, pleading face. How could she let her sister go on suffering when she had a chance to rescue her? It was Ivy's fault that Cicely had fallen into Gillian's trap; now it was Ivy's responsibility to get her out of it.

"What do you want me to do?" she asked quietly.

"I know where to find the Delve," said Gillian, "but not its entrances and exits, or the footpaths that your hunters use. Your Joan's protective glamours are too strong." She moved closer to Ivy. "I could carry on setting traps all over the hillside, but it will be more effective if you show me where to put them."

Ivy felt as though an iron band had clamped about her throat. "And if I don't?" she managed to ask.

"Then your sister will remain trapped," Gillian said. "Your mother will sleep until she dies. And you will stay here with them, a helpless prisoner, while I carry out my plan." She walked around Ivy, fingers trailing over her wingless shoulders. "But you won't make me do that, will you, Ivy?

Your father and brother may believe their lives are worth more than yours, but surely you know better?"

Revulsion shivered up Ivy's spine, but she didn't move. She found herself thinking of Mica—how arrogant and selfish he'd become in the wake of their mother's disappearance, and how little he seemed to care about anything Ivy did. How she'd been ready to share her deepest secret with him, only to be shamed into silence by his bigotry. The shattering pain she'd felt when his stone struck her in mid-flight, and nearly killed her.

And her father, too. What had Flint done for her, since her mother went away? How many times had she looked to him for comfort and met nothing but stony indifference? He might as well be a statue already, for all the life that was in him. Why should Ivy risk her own life, let alone Marigold and Cicely's, for his sake?

"Don't think of it as a betrayal," Gillian urged softly. "Think of it as justice for all the faeries your piskey ancestors killed—those faeries were your ancestors, too. And think what you'll be doing for the women of the Delve. They may not understand at first, but once they learn the truth, they'll be grateful to you for delivering them."

Ivy choked out a laugh. "After I've helped turn their husbands and sons into statues? I don't think so."

"Of course they will. Don't you see, Ivy? Once the present Joan is gone and the women of the Delve are free, they'll need a leader who knows the ways of the upper world. They'll have no choice but to look to you for guidance, and once they see how much stronger and healthier and happier they are living on the surface, they'll realize how wrong they were to listen to someone like Betony."

The moonlight slanted through the door as she spoke, haloing Gillian's auburn hair and limning her body with silver. For a moment she was as beautiful as the faeries of legend, and Ivy could almost see the world she was describing. A world where the women of the Delve would be free to walk in the sunshine, and gaze at the stars whenever they pleased. A world where sickness was rare instead of commonplace, and piskeys could live for centuries without growing wrinkled and feeble, or losing their wits with age. A world where her people could live in peace with faeries as well as humans, and their creativity could blossom unhindered.

Yet when Ivy looked into Gillian's face, the vision died away. She had seen that same false innocence on Keeve's face right before he pulled off a prank, and it reminded her that Gillian didn't really care about saving the women of the Delve, only about taking revenge on the men she hated. It also reminded her that Molly had got her theatrical gift from somewhere, and it might not have been from her father's side...

For this I declare, whispered Molly in her memory, *someone is plotting vengeance.*

Ivy raised her chin defiantly. "No. I'm not helping you. If you want to destroy the Delve, you'll have to do it by yourself."

Fury twisted Gillian's features, but she soon regained her composure. "So you'd rather stay here with your mother and sister, and die?"

"I'd rather take my chances with them than trust you," said Ivy. "I don't know if you can lie, but I can tell you're hiding something. I'm not going anywhere."

Gillian took a little pouch from her pocket. "You're as stubborn as your mother," she said. "I only hope your sister can forgive you for it." And she flicked a pinch of sparkling dust on the ground at Ivy's feet.

Ivy tried to take swift-shape, but it was too late. The dirt had turned to a slimy puddle of clay, gluing her feet to the floor. She threw her weight from one side to the other, but she was already frozen to mid-calf, and the muck was spiraling higher every second.

"I'm sorry it came to this," Gillian said, plucking Cicely's statue from Ivy's hand. "I would have preferred not to use a child—they can be so unreliable. However..." She took out a pocketknife, flicked it open and pricked Marigold's finger. "I've waited too many years to be patient any longer."

The clay crept up toward Ivy's hips, and her whole lower body felt numb. Ivy fought the spell, hurling all her magic into the effort, but the Claybane kept rising.

Yet Cicely had only screamed once before she was trapped, and the others looked as though they hadn't had time to cry out at all. If the clay hadn't engulfed Ivy already, perhaps her faery blood was strong enough to keep it at bay until she could escape.

If Gillian noticed the Claybane's slowness, it didn't appear to trouble her. She held Marigold's hand over Cicely's statue and squeezed a drop of blood onto the clay; then she pierced her own finger and smeared it across the figure's feet.

Fissures spread over the statue, rapidly growing wider. All at once the clay crumbled and Ivy's little sister staggered out, tiny but alive.

"Cicely!" Ivy shouted, as the Claybane slithered past her waist. "Don't listen to her! Don't do anything she says!" But Cicely seemed too dazed to hear.

Gillian stooped and lifted Cicely from the ground. "Don't worry," she said, slipping the piskey girl into her coat pocket. "I'll tell her everything she needs to know. Perhaps she'll prove more sensible than you and your mother. I would hope so, if I were you."

Then she walked out, and shut the door behind her.

"Cicely!" Ivy screamed, but it was no use. Alone in the growing darkness, she thrashed her arms and hurled herself against the Claybane, teeth grinding with the effort to break free. She had to save her sister—had to warn Betony and the other piskeys about Gillian's plan—

But as the clay inched up over her ribs, Ivy knew it was hopeless. Her mother was asleep, Richard trapped inside his statue, and no one but Gillian knew that Ivy was here, or had the power to free her.

She'd risked everything to save her mother and sister. But she'd failed them both, and now Ivy couldn't even save herself.

16

By the time the clay reached Ivy's shoulders, she no longer had any strength left to fight it. Desperately she shouted, "Mum! Marigold! Please wake up!"

But her mother didn't stir. The only sound was a scraping of branches and a distant whinny that must have been Duchess, protesting as Gillian rode her away.

Ivy drew a sobbing breath. "Please," she begged, not even knowing with whom she was pleading. "It can't end like this. Please, if there's anyone who can hear—" Then she threw her head back and screamed with all her might, "HELP ME!"

Her words dropped like stones into the silence, and for a few heartbeats all was still. Then the door creaked open, and she heard the last voice she'd ever expected to hear. "Ivy?"

If she hadn't been encased in hard clay up to her neck, Ivy would have collapsed with shock. "Molly?"

The younger girl stooped through the doorway. The beam of her flashlight fell on Ivy, and she exclaimed aloud. "What happened to you?"

"No time," Ivy wheezed as the Claybane crept up her jaw. In a few seconds she wouldn't be able to speak at all. "Only blood can break the spell—my mother's blood on my head, your mother's on my feet—has to be a close relative—"

She'd barely gasped out the words when the clay covered her mouth, cutting off her breath. Ivy's eyes rolled wildly as the slime crawled over her cheeks, and then everything went black.

No sight, no sound, no feeling. Total darkness surrounded her, without even the tiniest pinprick of light. Her lungs refused to fill, and even her heart had stopped beating. Ivy knew she ought to be dead... and yet in some way that only magic could explain, she wasn't. She was alive, and worse, she was *aware.*

And yet there was nothing to do or see, no reason for living. She felt no pain, but as the minutes dragged on, her numbness became an agony in itself. She would have welcomed the slash of a knife or an arrow piercing her side, if only it meant she could feel anything at all.

Now she knew how Richard must have felt when he woke from the beating Mica had given him, and found himself chained up in a cell black as death. No wonder he'd been half-crazed when Ivy found him; no wonder he'd started babbling Shakespeare to break the unbearable silence. She'd tormented him without knowing it, giving him a taste of the light he longed for and then taking it away. It had never occurred to her to care how he must feel. Why should she? He was only a spriggan...

Just as to Gillian Menadue, Ivy was only a piskey.

Despair pressed in on Ivy, crushing her spirits. She was never going to get out of here. Even if Molly begged her mother to show mercy, even if Cicely betrayed the whole Delve to try and free her, Gillian would never let Ivy go. She'd spend the rest of her days in this horrible nothingness, knowing all the while that Richard and so many others were suffering the same fate—and that her failure had put them there.

Ivy wanted to scream, weep, pound her fists against the darkness until it shattered and let her go. But she couldn't do any of those things. She could only stand helpless while the endless seconds ticked by—and the worst was knowing she still had a lifetime of imprisonment ahead of her.

But just as Ivy felt she could endure it no longer, that she would go mad with the sheer pointlessness of it all, *something* happened. The tiniest feather-touch on her forehead, so light that at first she thought she'd imagined it. But then a tickle ran over her scalp, as though some buzzing insect had landed in her hair—and the itch kept growing, spidering across her forehead until she was half-wild with the need to scratch it.

Then suddenly—oh, glory—the shell over her face cracked apart, and she could breathe again. Ivy let out a moan, and opened her eyes.

"It's okay, don't be scared," blurted Molly, sounding as frantic as Ivy felt. She was scratching at the Claybane that covered Ivy's neck and shoulders, tearing off fragments as fast as she could go. "I couldn't find my mum, so I tried my blood and your mum's instead, and I didn't think it was going to work but then it did—"

Ivy's mouth was dry, and her tongue felt thick and heavy. In a slurred whisper she asked, "How... find me? Thought you... sleeping."

"No, I wasn't," said Molly, pulling a chunk of Claybane off Ivy's upper arm and flinging it away. "I was only pretending. I got dressed as soon as you and Mum left the house, and when I saw the two of you ride off on Duchess I followed you. But I couldn't get too close in case she spotted me, and then I lost the trail for a bit, so by the time I got here—*oh!*"

All at once the spell broke, and the last of the clay dissolved into powder. Ivy almost collapsed before Molly caught her, lowering her to the dusty floor. "Are you all right?" she asked anxiously. "You look like you're going to be sick."

Ivy waved a hand in what she hoped was a reassuring gesture. It was like a gift to feel her chest expanding with each breath, her heart beating in a steady rhythm she'd never take for granted again. But her wits, like her muscles, were weak with shock. "Molly," she gasped, fumbling for the other girl's blood-smeared hand. "You saved me. I owe you my life."

Molly squeezed back, but Ivy could feel her fingers trembling. "My mum... she's a faery. And that makes me..."

"Half faery," said Ivy. "That's how you broke her spells."

"But I've lived with her my whole life. How could I never have noticed—never guessed...?"

Ivy tried to get up, but her legs were too shaky. She sighed and leaned against the wall. "She fooled a lot of people, Molly. Other faeries, even. Don't blame yourself."

"But why did my mum put you in that clay stuff? What is she trying to do?"

Ivy explained the situation to Molly as briefly as she could. Then she finished, "I have to stop her, Molly. She's got my sister. And if I don't get to the Delve right away, she'll turn my father and brother into clay piskeys and sell them in the market, like she did to Richard."

"Richard!" Molly sat up, her eyes wide. "You found him? Where is he?"

Ivy pulled her bag across the floor and opened it to show Molly the statue. "He's trapped in this," she said. "Your mother turned him small, and sealed him inside."

Molly picked up the fat, smiling piskey and stared at it, her nose wrinkled in revulsion. "Can we...is there any way to get him out?"

"The shell's hollow," said Ivy. "We could try breaking it, I suppose—"

Without waiting for her to finish, Molly slammed the statue

against the wall. Its head shattered, and as she wrenched the shell apart, a tiny figure dropped out. She caught it and raised it to the light.

Even in the half-darkness the despair on Richard's face was clearly visible, and Ivy's insides twisted with shame. How could she have misjudged him so badly? He hadn't flown off and abandoned her, as she'd assumed—he'd been trying to help her find Cicely, and this had been his reward.

"It's no use," she said miserably. "Even if your blood does work as a substitute for your mother's, we can't free him without finding one of his relatives as well."

"I don't care," retorted Molly. "I'm going to try anyway." She squeezed her cut thumb until the blood welled up again, and smeared a scarlet line across Richard's feet. "Your turn."

"Molly, there's no point—"

"I don't care!" Molly shouted, eyes brimming with tears. "I thought he flew away because he didn't care, but he was stuck in that stupid ugly statue all the time, and it wasn't his fault, and we're all the family he's got!" She snatched up one of the pottery fragments and thrust it at Ivy. "We have to try!"

She was right. Ivy set her teeth, stabbed the shard into her thumb, and wiped a streak of blood across the statue's brow.

"Please," whispered Molly, clasping her hands together and rocking back and forth. "Please, God, let it work."

But though they held their breath and waited, no cracks appeared in the figure's surface. "I'm sorry," Ivy said quietly at last. "There's nothing else we can do."

Molly picked up the statue and hugged it, her shoulders shaking. Ivy reached to comfort her, and found that she could move freely again. She let her hand rest on Molly's shoulder a moment, then pushed herself to her feet.

"Look after him," Ivy said as she limped to the door. "And my mother, too. I'll be back soon—I hope."

Then she flung herself into swift-form, and flashed away.

Ivy had never flown so hard or so fast, not even when the other swifts were chasing her. She didn't know how far she was from the Delve, but her instincts told her unerringly which direction to go, and she was determined to get there before Gillian could carry out her plan.

She zoomed over winding river valleys, rocky hills and strips of woodland, the open-pit scar of a modern mine and the ruins of several old ones. Once she glimpsed a falcon—perhaps even a hobby—wheeling overhead. But Ivy had no time for any fears but one, and she kept flying.

Soon she began to spot landmarks she'd noticed on previous flights, and knew she must be nearing the Delve. Yet she saw no sign of Gillian and Duchess, let alone Cicely. Perhaps the faery woman had turned them all invisible, so they could ride to the Delve without being noticed?

Or more likely she hadn't bothered bringing the mare at all, and transported herself and Cicely to the Delve by magic instead. In which case Cicely could be showing Gillian the Delve's entrances at this very minute, and Ivy might already be too late...

Seconds later the familiar broken chimney and slanting walls of the Engine House rose up before her, black against the night sky. Ivy circled the capped entrance to the Great Shaft, then dove straight between the bars, plunging into the darkness below.

But in bird form her skin didn't glow, as it did when she was in piskey shape. The blackness inside the shaft was too dense for even a swift's night vision to penetrate, and panic jolted Ivy as she realized she was flying blind. Fluttering wildly to slow her descent, she scrabbled with her short feet until her claws found an outcropping and then hung there, breathing fast.

Now what? She had to get down to an adjoining tunnel somehow. But if she changed back to piskey shape here, she could lose her grip and fall. And if the drop didn't kill her the landing would, because the flooded part of the shaft went down for fathoms and Ivy had never learned to swim.

Yet she couldn't cling here forever. Her swift's heart drumming, Ivy dug her claws deeper into the crack and willed her body to change.

As her form shifted, so did her balance. Her fingers slipped, and she started to fall—but then her skin-glow kindled into brightness, lighting up every cranny of the rock, and she jammed her hands into a bigger crack just in time. Hanging by her fingertips, Ivy groped with her feet until she found a toehold. Then she inched her way across the rock to the nearby tunnel, swung herself past the iron railing, and dropped to the ground below.

She had made it. She was inside the Delve.

Dawn was coming, and soon the younger men would head right into Gillian's traps. Should Ivy warn Mica and Mattock? Or should she go to the Joan first? She wavered, but only for an instant. By the time she convinced Betony to listen, it might be too late. Ivy sprinted down the tunnel, heading for her home cavern.

As she skidded around the corner Mattock stepped out of the doorway ahead, yawning and scratching sleepily at his ear. But he was fully clothed, with his hunter's knife at his side, and Ivy knew he must be heading to the surface.

"Matt!" she called to him. "Don't go!"

He turned toward her, blank with astonishment. Urgently Ivy went on, "You can't go out of the Delve. It's not—"

Mattock lunged at her and snatched her off the ground, whirling her in an exuberant embrace. "Ivy! You're alive!"

Crushed to his chest, Ivy could hardly breathe. Yet it was so good to see Mattock's broad honest face that she couldn't help hugging him back.

"I missed you too," she said, but then she wriggled out of his hold and backed away. "Mattock, listen. There's a powerful faery up above who wants to capture all the men in the Delve. If you go outside, you'll fall right into her trap."

Mattock looked baffled, but he didn't interrupt her. He kept his mouth shut—he'd always been good at that, unlike Mica—and gave Ivy all the time she needed to explain. And by the time she'd finished telling him about Gillian and the Claybane, his expression was so grim that Ivy knew he'd believed every word.

"You tell the Joan," he said. "I'll get up to the Earthenbore and stop anyone who tries to come through."

She'd meant to warn Mica and the other hunters herself, but having Mattock do it would be even better. She squeezed his arm. "I won't forget this, Matt. You'll be a hero to the whole Delve, when all this is done."

"I'll settle for being yours," he said, and covered Ivy's hand with his own. Then, before she could think of a reply, he flashed her a lopsided smile and dashed away.

"...And she's up there with Cicely this very moment," Ivy said, pacing around the Joan's stateroom. It had driven her nearly wild to have to wait until her aunt was ready to receive her, and she was desperate to make up for lost time. "Soon she'll have sprinkled Claybane around all the exits, and if anyone touches it they'll be trapped. You have to tell the hunters to stay inside, or—"

"Do not presume," Betony interrupted, "to tell me what I have to do." She slammed her palms on the arms of the chair and rose, wings bristling with irritation. "For a hundred years the Delve has been our refuge. I will not allow some upstart faery to turn it into a prison." She turned to her consort. "Gossan, how long will it take your knockers to open a passage to Wheal Diligence?"

That was the nearest mine to the Delve, its shafts and adits far enough away that Gillian probably wouldn't waste time trapping them, even if she guessed they were there. A grudging admiration roused in Ivy at her aunt's foresight, and she began to think they might be able to stop Molly's mother after all.

But Gossan shook his head. "It's below the waterline," he said. "Even with all our knockers working together, it'd take days to pump it dry."

"No chance of sending up a war party and taking her by surprise, then." Betony tapped a finger against her lips, eyes narrowed as she thought. "Very well, there's only one thing to do. I shall fly out and confront this Gillian myself."

"But that's exactly what she wants you to do!" said Ivy protested, as Betony strode forward. "The Claybane works on all piskeys, not just males. If you step—"

"I said *fly,*" retorted Betony. "I understand why that would not have occurred to you, given your own weakness. But a trap on the ground is no threat to anyone with wings." She stopped in the doorway and turned to add, "Gossan, have the knockers dig a new passage to the surface, and warn the other men to remain underground until I give the word. Nettle, send a runner to tell the women and children to remain in their caverns. I will call a meeting in the Market Cavern when I return."

"My sister's still out there," said Ivy. "I'm coming with you."

"Cicely has already suffered enough because of your

foolishness," Betony replied icily. "You are far too reckless to be useful, even if I thought I could trust you. Stay here."

Ivy turned pleading eyes to Gossan, hoping he would intervene. But he didn't even look at her. He walked to the doorway and took Betony's face in his hands. "Be careful, my love," he said, and kissed her. Then he went out.

Betony tightened her belt and smoothed her hair, a high color in her cheeks. "I will return," she announced, "with this so-called Gillian Menadue as my prisoner. She will regret that she ever dared threaten my Delve." And she too walked out, slamming the door behind her.

"Don't take it to heart," said Nettle to Ivy, once the Joan was gone. "She's worried, and that always makes her sharpish." She reached for the cord of the message bell by the door and gave it a tug, sending a metallic jangle echoing down the corridor. "But never you fear. Our Joan's more than a match for that Gillyflower."

"Gillian," said Ivy dully. She sank into a chair by the fire, wondering why she felt so cheated. Surely she ought to be grateful that Betony had taken over? Surely she didn't imagine that she, a mere piskey-girl with no authority and no great share of magic, could protect the Delve better than the powerful Joan the Wad herself?

Yet Ivy couldn't shake the feeling that stopping Gillian wouldn't be that easy. True, the faery woman couldn't have guessed that Molly would resist her sleeping spell, much less rescue Ivy from the Claybane. But even so, Ivy feared Gillian had more than one plan in mind, and that if her first attack on the Delve failed, it wouldn't take her long to launch another.

Either way, Ivy couldn't sit idle when Cicely was in danger. She had to do something to help her sister, or at least find out what had happened to her. But how could she get away from Nettle without the old woman getting suspicious?

Her thoughts were interrupted by a rap on the door.

"Reporting for duty," chirped a boy's voice as Nettle opened it. "What's the message?"

It was Quartz, Jenny's little brother and the fastest runner in the Delve. And just like that, Ivy knew how to get where she needed to be. She rose quickly and put a hand on Nettle's shoulder. "There's no time to lose," she said. "I'll go with him, and tell him everything."

The old woman gave her a shrewd look, and Ivy feared she would refuse. But then she nodded.

Ivy grabbed Quartz's arm and pulled him into the Silverlode. "Come on," she said, and they ran down the corridor together.

As they headed for the main staircase, Ivy explained to Quartz that there was an enemy faery threatening the Delve, the Joan had gone out to deal with her, and the surface was off-limits to all piskeys until further notice. At first the boy only gaped at her, so astonished that he barely seemed to hear the message. But Ivy kept repeating it until she was sure he understood, and then urged him to run off and spread the word.

"Don't waste time telling them I'm back, either," she said. "Just pass on the Joan's orders and keep moving. My story can wait."

Quartz looked ready to explode with curiosity, but his runner's training won out; he thumped a fist against his heart and sprinted off, trilling the high-pitched call that would bring the other piskeys out to hear his message. Ivy headed the opposite way, resolutely ignoring her weariness as she darted up a side tunnel and took the stairs two at a time. She'd have to climb up the Great Shaft before she could turn into a swift again, but–

"Mattock? Matt! Hey, you down there–have you seen Mattock?"

Ivy stiffened, gripping the rail. Of all the bad luck, it was Mica. He must have wakened on his own, and wondered why

Mattock hadn't come to fetch him. And he'd already seen Ivy's glow, so it was too late for her to turn invisible, or run away.

"He's up by the Earthenbore," she called, dimming her light and trying to sound raspy and old so he wouldn't recognize her.

"No, he isn't. I was up there a few minutes ago." His voice hardened with suspicion. "Who's that?"

She couldn't deal with Mica, not right now. First he'd demand to know where Ivy had been all this time, and then he'd try to stop her from leaving the Delve. And if Mattock wasn't in the Earthenbore, something was badly wrong—she had to find him. Ivy stepped backward, then whirled and dashed the way she had come.

"Hey!" Mica pounded down the stairs after her. "Stop!"

This was a disaster. She couldn't let him chase her all over the Delve; she was still tired from battling the Claybane, and she needed to save her strength for climbing. But he was close now, and there was nowhere to hide...

"Ivy?" asked Mica, faint with disbelief, and then louder, "Ivy! It *is* you!"

She spun to face him. "I don't have time to explain, Mica! The Delve's in danger, and there's nobody to keep the hunters from going outside. Cicely's alive but I have to rescue her, so whatever you want from me, it's going to have to wait!"

Mica gazed at her, his eyes deep-set and haunted. Ivy readied herself to flee—but then her brother said quietly, "All right. What can I do?"

"Mattock told me he was going to guard the Earthenbore,"

Ivy panted at Mica as they raced through the tunnels together. "Are you certain he isn't up there?"

"I went halfway up the Hunter's Stair and yelled his name," said Mica. "There's no way he wouldn't have heard me."

A shiver ran through Ivy. Something had definitely gone wrong. Mattock would never be foolish enough to go outside, not after she'd warned him of the danger—and especially not when he knew Ivy was counting on him. She put on another burst of speed and turned into the Narrows, shouting "Mattock!"

"I told you," Mica said irritably from behind her, "he's not up there."

Ivy didn't bother to argue. She dodged down the corridor and up the steps, made a sharp turn—and stopped, grabbing the wall for support. In the middle of the Earthenbore, only a few paces from the top of the stair, stood the clay-covered form of Mattock.

"What the—" Mica caught Ivy as she stumbled back. "What *is* that?"

"Something terrible," whispered Ivy. Her legs were shaking, but she grabbed Mica's shoulders and pulled herself upright. "Aunt Betony. Did you see her, when you were looking for Matt? Where was she going?"

"I—yes. She was heading for the Great Shaft. But—"

Not waiting to hear more, Ivy took off running. Every footstep sent a jolt of terror through her body, knowing she might hit a patch of Claybane at any moment. Yet she and Mica had already covered this ground, so she had to trust the path was still safe.

"Keep your distance!" she shouted to Mica as he ran after her. "Stay back!" She reached the junction, turned down the tunnel to the Great Shaft...

And her foot skidded out from under her.

It was too late to catch herself, and impossible to stop. Ivy shrieked, windmilled, and sat down hard, right in a newly laid patch of Claybane.

But she wasn't the only one. Ahead of her, frozen mid-stride, stood a perfectly formed statue of Betony.

17

Mica started toward her, but Ivy flung up her clay-smeared hands in warning. "Don't!" she cried. "Stay where you are!" She could barely speak, her throat was so choked with terror. Soon the Claybane would come slithering up her body and she'd be trapped again, this time with no hope of ever getting out. "Find Gossan. Tell him..."

But the words failed her, because what was there to say? Even if Mica warned the Jack that the enemy was inside the Delve, there was nothing either of them could do about it. With Cicely as her guide the whole mine was open to Gillian, so her traps could be anywhere. And the Claybane dust was invisible until the spell took hold, so Ivy couldn't even tell her fellow piskeys what to look for...

"Tell him what?" asked Mica, puzzled. "Why don't you get up?"

Was he really so stupid he couldn't see what was happening? "Because I'm stuck in the Claybane!" Ivy shouted. "And any minute now I'm going to end up like—"

Then it dawned on her that she *hadn't* ended up like Betony, after all. Her hands and legs were wet with slime, but the Claybane hadn't moved, even though she ought to have been half covered in it by now. Bewildered, Ivy climbed to her feet and stepped backward. There was no resistance.

"It's not working," she murmured, gazing at her muddy palms. "But why?"

"Why indeed?" asked a cool voice from the shadows. "How did you manage to escape my Claybane the first time, for that matter? Apparently the faery part of you is stronger than I'd thought. How irksome."

Wary, Ivy dropped to a crouch as the far end of the tunnel lit up and Gillian Menadue stepped out, no longer invisible. She'd made herself smaller to fit into the Delve, and for the first time Ivy saw her wings, translucent and brittle-looking as a wasp's. Yet there was nothing delicate in the way Gillian held them. They rose from her shoulders at a menacing angle, like blades that might come slashing down at any moment.

"Mica," said Ivy, not taking her eyes off the faery woman, "get out of here."

"But you—"

"I can look after myself!" Ivy shouted. "Just *go!*"

And for a wonder, he did. As his hurried footsteps faded, Gillian tipped her head to one side and gave Ivy a curious smile. "Was that your brother? Handsome boy. But he'll never make it. There must be Claybane all over the Delve by now."

"Enough," said Ivy tightly. "What have you done with my sister?"

"Cicely? She's well enough." Gillian waved a hand at the statue of Betony, and it shrank to the same tiny size as the figures Ivy had seen in the workshop. She nudged it aside with her foot. "She's just busy at the moment. I told her that unless she carried out my instructions you would die, and since then she's proved quite useful... for a child."

"So you sent her to spread Claybane around the tunnels for you, while you waited here to catch Betony," Ivy said, barely suppressing her fury. Cicely must have been terrified, to obey

Gillian without resistance. "That's why you came down here, wasn't it?"

"I was prepared for a battle, if your Joan proved difficult. But she walked straight into my trap." The faery woman's smile deepened, lips parting over her white teeth. "I knew you piskeys had grown careless living underground, but I never knew destroying you would be *this* easy."

She spoke with confidence, and Ivy's heart sank. Yet if Gillian was so certain she'd succeeded, why was she still here? There must be something she had left to do, or she would have gone back to the surface already...

So maybe it wasn't too late to stop her.

"And when Cicely's done her part," Ivy asked, "what then? Are you planning to sit here and wait for everyone to turn into statues? That could take a while."

"Oh, I have an idea of how to speed things up," said Gillian. "A little something I was working on before I found the Claybane. But it may not be necessary, once the news spreads and your people start to panic. We'll see."

Ivy glanced over her shoulder. Did she dare to turn herself into a swift and make a break for it? But the day-lamps were out, and she wouldn't get far without light. She could make herself invisible and grope her way along, but that wouldn't hide her from an enemy as powerful as Gillian. Her best hope was to keep the conversation going until she could distract the faery woman and escape.

"I warned the other piskeys about the Claybane," Ivy said. Though half the people she'd told were already trapped, but Gillian didn't need to know that. "They know how it works."

"Of course you did," Gillian said mildly. "But as I'm sure you've noticed, it's hard to avoid a trap you can't even see. The only way to get safely out of the Delve now is to fly, and only females can do that. Or at least," she added with a patronizing smile, "*most* females."

Once Ivy would have bristled at the taunt, but now she ignored it. Let Gillian go on thinking her weak—she'd find out how wrong she was soon enough. She sneaked a look at the light-spell Gillian had conjured, hovering by the roof of the tunnel. Could she snuff it out and extinguish her own skin-glow at the same time? Maybe—but she'd have to wait for the right moment to do it.

"We'll find our way out," Ivy told her, trying to sound bold. "My people may not have the same kind of magic you do, but we know the earth and we're stronger than you think. Besides, even if you do capture all the men, what makes you think the women won't come after you instead?"

"I doubt that, considering how little they know of the surface," Gillian replied. "I suspect they'll be far too busy trying to find food and shelter to think about revenge. On the other hand..." She gave a little shrug. "I haven't cared much for the piskey women I've met so far, faery blood or not. Perhaps I'll leave you all to the Claybane and save myself the trouble."

Inwardly Ivy cursed herself; that wasn't the conclusion she'd wanted Gillian to come to at all. But there was no taking her words back now. "How is that any different from the way my ancestors thought about faeries?" she demanded. "That one is as good—or bad—as another? You're no better than they were, for all your talk about justice."

Molly's mother looked at her nails, feigning indifference. But Ivy went on with growing passion, "Can't you see how backward this revenge of yours has become? You've spent your whole life brooding over faeries who died a long time ago, and hating piskeys who don't even know you exist. What about Molly and her father? They're still alive, and they care about you. And you treat them like they're worthless."

That struck a nerve. Gillian held up a warning finger, power crackling at its tip. "Hold your tongue," she said, "or I'll burn it out. You know nothing about my family."

"I know Molly," Ivy replied, edging closer to the woman as an idea began to crystalize in her mind. "She's bright and talented and kind, and she deserves a mother who cares for her, not just her own selfish plans. How are you going to look her in the face, when she confronts you with the evil you've done?"

"Molly doesn't know anything about it," Gillian said flatly. "She's sleeping."

"No, she's not," said Ivy. "She's back in your workshop, crying because of what you did to Richard. Her faery godfather."

"Impossible," Gillian said. But she sounded uncertain, and silently Ivy rejoiced. Her plan was working! If she could only keep the woman distracted a little longer...

"All her life Molly's longed to get close to faeries." Ivy walked casually past Gillian and turned, her back to the Great Shaft. "No wonder, since she's half faery herself. But you kept her from that part of her heritage, kept yourself at a distance, so you could carry out your twisted revenge. Do you think she's going to forgive you for that? Especially now that she knows what you did to Richard, and to me?"

As Ivy spoke, she laid a hand on the railing. An icy tingle ran up her arm, but she made herself hold steady. If Gillian didn't realize that Ivy could touch iron, then maybe...

"Ivy?" said a small, trembling voice, and Ivy's breath caught. She turned to see Cicely at the entrance of the tunnel, the empty sack of Claybane dangling from her hand.

She would have run to Cicely, but Gillian was too quick. She stepped between them, holding out her hands as though in benediction—but the look she gave Ivy warned that bad things would happen if she dared to interfere.

"Well done," the faery woman told Cicely. "You have saved your family. Come and join us."

But Cicely backed away. "You lied to me," she said. "You

said Ivy was trapped, and that you were the only one who could free her. But she's here. And you made me—" She gave a little sob, and flung the Claybane sack onto the floor. "You *lied!*"

Gillian's face hardened, and Ivy knew the faery woman was about to do something terrible. "Cicely, run!" she shouted, but Gillian's gaze had already locked onto her sister's. Cicely's shoulders went slack, hands dropping to her sides, and her face turned blank as a doll's.

"Walk to me," commanded Gillian, and without hesitation Ivy's sister stepped forward—right onto the patch of Claybane.

"No!" Ivy shouted, but her cry died out as Cicely continued walking straight through it. Molly's mother looked startled, but she seized Cicely's wrist and pulled her to her side.

"Well," she said. "It appears the Claybane only works once, so now you're *both* immune. Which means I can't let either one of you out of my sight."

Muffled shouts and screams echoed up the shaft from the lower tunnels, piskeys starting to panic as the Claybane did its work. In the corridors doors opened and slammed, footsteps pounded and were suddenly cut short, and a child wailed in wordless terror.

"Listen to that," said Ivy, slapping the rail so hard the iron shuddered. "You hate my people for what they did to yours. Do you think the children of the Delve aren't going to hate you just as much for what you've done here today? Your own daughter already does!"

Gillian's hand clenched on Cicely's shoulder. "Never," she said. "Molly is *mine*."

"She was until you started treating her like a nuisance," Ivy retorted. "Not to mention deceiving her, and hurting her friends, and using magic on her against her will. But she broke your spell, and she got me out of the Claybane, too. She'll never trust you again."

The faery woman stood immobile. Deep lines formed about

her mouth, and for a moment she looked as old as Nettle. But then she shook herself and straightened up. "It makes no difference," she said. "It's done now. And I'm about to—"

A thunderous *crack* shook the tunnel, and loose rocks showered down. Ivy backed against the wall, flinging her arms over her head, and Cicely let out a scream. But when the dust cleared, the faery woman still stood with Cicely, encased in a shimmering bubble of magic. Rocks had fallen around them, but none had broken through.

Still, if it was Mica swinging that thunder-axe, he hadn't struck in vain. The confusion had broken Gillian's mental hold, and now Cicely was struggling like a wild thing. Gillian gripped her wrists, trying to twist her into submission, but the piskey girl lunged forward and bit her arm.

With a shriek Gillian let go, and as Cicely hurtled away Ivy knew her opportunity had come. She extinguished her glow, willed herself into swift-shape, and flung herself at Gillian.

Nothing happened.

Arms outspread in a futile mockery of wings, Ivy crashed to the floor of the tunnel. Breath whooshed out of her lungs, and her chin hit the ground so hard she tasted blood. Gasping, she scrambled back and clutched the railing to pull herself up. But the iron stung her hands, and she snatched them away.

What a fool she'd been! How could she have forgotten what had happened in Molly's barn, when that loose nail had canceled her invisibility spell? Either being away from the Delve had strengthened the faery part of her nature, or Richard's healing had brought it to the fore. But Ivy was no longer immune to the effects of iron. She'd hoped to trick Gillian into touching the rail, but instead she'd only crippled herself.

The ceiling rumbled again, and more rocks slid down. But the cave-in was going to kill Ivy long before it hurt Gillian, whose magical shield clung to her like a second, impenetrable skin. She fired off a spell at Cicely that sent her tumbling, then stooped over Ivy and seized the back of her neck.

"Try to attack me, will you?" she spat. "Little fool. You're not fit to lead your people—you're not even fit to live." She picked Ivy up as though she were weightless, and flung her against the railing.

The metal groaned as Ivy slammed into it, and she felt her ribs crack. For a sickening moment she hung over the rail, the dark shaft yawning below her. Then with a desperate effort she shoved herself back and collapsed to the rock-strewn floor.

She'd failed completely. Her whole plan had depended on being able to transform into a swift—her secret triumph, her greatest pride—but now even that was denied her. Panting, Ivy clutched her cracked ribs and waited for the killing blow.

But it didn't come. Gillian stared at Ivy, then at her own hands. For the first time, she looked shaken. Could she be realizing she'd gone too far?

"You can stop this," Ivy croaked. Every breath felt like someone was knifing her, but she managed to struggle upright. "It's not too late. Molly will—"

Gillian shook her head. "Molly has betrayed me," she said harshly. "There's nothing for me to go back to. It's over—and so are you."

She pressed her hands together and pulled them slowly apart. A swirling, smoky globe coalesced between her palms, swelling outward until it was the size of Ivy's head. Balancing the spell-sphere on her fingertips, Gillian walked to the railing—but to Ivy's frustration, she didn't touch it. She reached out over the Great Shaft and let the spell drop.

A few seconds passed in silence. Then a muffled explosion sounded, far below. "What..." Ivy gasped. "What have you done?"

Gillian gave a short laugh. "You'll find out," she said. "Goodbye, Ivy." She took a step back, her form shredding into mist...

Only to reappear, solid again. Her transportation spell had failed.

Disbelief flashed across the faery woman's face, and she gathered herself for another try. But the next time was no better. Whether it was the presence of the iron railing, or something in the rock itself, Gillian couldn't leap away.

For one spiteful moment Ivy was glad. Gillian was trapped now, like the rest of them. Whatever nasty spell she'd just dropped down the shaft, she'd have to suffer it too. But Gillian only shrugged. "Well," she said, "I said it myself, didn't I? There's only one way out of the Delve." And her wings began to beat, lifting her into the air.

Another crack spread across the ceiling, and more rocks tumbled down. Any minute the tunnel would collapse, and Ivy and Cicely would be crushed to death. Gillian would escape, leaving Marigold to die, and the piskeys of the Delve would be trapped in clay forever.

No. Ivy couldn't let that happen. If she died trying to stop Gillian, so be it... but for the sake of the people she loved, she had to try.

Pain stabbed her chest as Ivy sucked in her breath. Then as Gillian glided past her she leaped up and grabbed the faery woman's leg.

She nearly missed. But she caught Gillian's ankle at the last second, fingers skittering down the soft fabric of her trousers, then clamping tight around flesh and bone. Dragged into the air by the faery's fast-beating wings, Ivy crashed against the railing—but this time, she was ready. She hooked her feet between the bars and hung on with all her might.

Gillian kicked out savagely, and Ivy's head snapped sideways as the woman's heel smashed into her cheekbone. Stars filled her vision, but she refused to let go.

The railing creaked, and a shower of gravel fell from the bolts that anchored it. Gillian fought to free herself, wings buzzing as she fired off one spell after another. But Ivy was right behind her, too small to easily hit. And as Ivy held on, putting all her weight into the effort, she was dimly surprised at her own strength. Perhaps being half faery was good for something after all.

But she had to end this quickly, or Gillian would escape. For Cicely's sake and Marigold's, for Mica and Flint, for Mattock and Jenny and all the others, Ivy had to give everything she had. Though her face throbbed and her side shrieked with agony, she grabbed Gillian's free leg and yanked as hard as she could.

Even Gillian's wings couldn't counteract that sudden jerk. As she shot backward, her flailing hand clutched the rail—and the iron lit up in a sizzling flash. She screamed and collapsed, her whole weight dropping onto the railing as her wings went limp.

Weak with relief, Ivy let her go. But then the anchor bolts broke free of the crumbling stone around them and the railing teetered forward, taking the unconscious faery with it. *Molly,* thought Ivy wildly, and flung out a hand, but too late. Bouncing off the shaft walls with one hideous clang after another, the iron railing and its passenger fell through the fathomless dark. There was a distant splash, and then silence.

Ivy pressed her face to the stone, sick with horror. She'd only meant to knock Gillian unconscious, not kill her. But another rumble shook the rocks around her, and she had no time for regret. Ivy heaved herself upright, staggered up the tunnel, and dragged her unconscious sister to safety in the passage beyond.

She was about to collapse when she remembered Betony. Ivy hurled herself back into the tunnel, snatched up her aunt and dived for safety—just as a great slab of the ceiling smashed down, and the entrance to the Great Shaft disappeared behind a heap of granite.

For a moment Ivy could only lie next to Cicely, coughing feebly as clouds of stone dust rolled over her. Then she heard the clomp of approaching boots, and gentle hands helped her to her feet. She turned to her rescuer—and found with dim astonishment that it wasn't Mica.

It was her father.

Of course. Only a skilled knocker would know how to wield his thunder-axe so effectively, or how to collapse a single tunnel without bringing down half the Delve. He'd taken an enormous risk, but he'd been trying to save them—and that meant he cared. Ivy seized him by the shoulders and kissed him on both cheeks.

"How did you know we were here?" she asked. "Did Mica tell you?"

Flint nodded. He looked more gray and weary than ever, but as he stroked Ivy's hair there was a tenderness in his eyes she hadn't seen since she was a child. "I'm sorry," he rasped.

There was so much Ivy wanted to tell him, so many questions she wanted to ask. He'd known Marigold was leaving the Delve, heard her warning about the poison; why hadn't he gone with her, or believed her story until it was too late? When he found her shawl tangled in a gorse-bush, with the blood she'd coughed up fresh upon it, had he truly thought spriggans had taken her, or did it only make him realize how ill she'd been? Had losing her finally convinced him the Delve was dangerous, and made him determined to find the source of the poison even if it killed him?

Ivy longed to know, but that conversation would have to wait. She still didn't know what spell Gillian had dropped down the shaft, and she couldn't assume the danger was past. She gave her father a last grateful squeeze and said, "Stay here and look after Cicely, please? I've got to find the others."

Ivy limped through the corridors, clutching her aching ribs. Her cheekbone stung where Gillian had kicked her, and all her bones felt out of joint. If only Richard were here to heal her—but no, she couldn't let herself think about him right now, or stop to mourn the piskeys who stood mute and frozen along her way. Not only males but wild-eyed matrons, a child caught in mid-wail, and even the skinny form of Quartz, who'd barely made it halfway up Tinners' Row with his message.

By the time Ivy reached Silverlode Passage, her vision was so clouded with tears that she could hardly see. Impatient, she tried to rub the blurriness away, but it only swirled before her eyes like smoke—because, Ivy realized with a start, it was smoke. And now she could smell it, too: an acrid, nose-wrinkling stench like old urine on straw.

It must be from the spell that Gillian had dropped down the Great Shaft. How dangerous was it? It couldn't be potent enough to kill, surely, or she wouldn't have bothered creating the Claybane. But it *smelled* poisonous, and the further Ivy went down the passage the more unbearably pungent it became. Soon Ivy was coughing with both hands wrapped around her middle, and her lungs felt as though they were on fire.

Her fellow piskeys would never be able to endure it. As soon as the smoke started creeping into their caverns, they'd panic and dash for the surface—exactly as Gillian had planned. Somehow, Ivy had to get them safely out of the Delve.

"Gossan!" she shouted, peering in all directions. She paused to check the Market Cavern, but it was empty. "My lord Jack! Where are you?"

At the other end of the corridor, the door to the Joan's

stateroom opened. Nettle stood there alone, looking smaller and more wizened than ever in the flickering torchlight. "He's gone," she said. "Just like my lady. And neither one of them's come back."

Which meant that Gossan too must be a statue, trapped in some side corridor. But if so, there was no point searching for him. Statues didn't breathe, as Ivy and Nettle did—though it was getting more difficult by the moment. Steeling herself not to panic, Ivy slipped out of her shoes and kicked them aside. With bare feet she'd be better able to feel the Claybane when she stepped into it, and tell Nettle when she needed to fly.

"Come with me," she said. "We've got to get everyone out of here."

By the time Ivy and Nettle reached the upper levels, there was a small crowd of frightened piskeys shuffling after them. No one had collapsed yet, but Ivy's head was beginning to reel, and she feared it was only a matter of time.

"There's a patch here," she shouted, as they came up to a statue of two piskey-boys clutching each other. One of the women sobbed and reached toward it, but her companions pulled her back. Ivy shuffled over the Claybane-coated floor, toes groping for dry rock. "All right," she said, "it's safe on this side."

At once the female piskeys spread their wings and began ferrying the men and boys over the trap. Their first few rescue attempts had been awkward, and they'd lost one stout knocker when the women who were carrying him let go. But they were getting better at it now, and soon all were safe on the other side.

Still, it was slow progress, especially with more piskeys joining them at every door they passed. The journey up to the Earthenbore seemed impossibly long, and Ivy wished there was a quicker way—but since both the upper and lower tunnels to the Great Shaft were blocked and the shaft itself was full of choking fumes, she couldn't think of one.

Fortunately, Ivy's people knew how to work together. Soon two of the younger hunters had stationed themselves at the back of the group and cast a shielding charm to keep back the smoke, while others gathered rolled-up mats and blankets to drop over each patch of Claybane they passed, so that they'd know where the traps were when they returned. That showed more creativity than Ivy had expected, and she wasn't surprised to find that the hunters who'd thought of it were the ones who'd had the most contact with humans.

When they climbed the stairs to the second level, Cicely was waiting with Flint behind her. Her face was dirty and there was a bloody scrape across her forehead, but her eyes were clear.

"I want to help," she told Ivy. "What can I do?"

Ivy explained about the spell Gillian had dropped down the Great Shaft, and the need to get all the piskeys up to fresh air. "Can you collect everyone on this level?" she asked. "Tell them to bring plenty of rugs to mark the patches of Claybane once you've found them—they can't stop the traps working, but they'll keep people from walking into them by accident. Then use the women to fly the men across—that's what we've been doing."

Cicely nodded. "I'll tell Mica." And she dashed off so fast her feet scarcely touched the ground. Flint shouldered his thunder-axe and moved to the rear of Ivy's group, giving her a long, searching look as he passed. But Ivy couldn't pause to ask what was on her father's mind; the smoke was getting thicker every moment. "Come on," she said to the others. "We've got to hurry."

They'd made it as far as Long Way, and Ivy was feeling out the edges of a particularly large patch of Claybane, when someone gasped. She turned back to see that Nettle had stumbled, and Jenny and Teasel were helping the old woman up again—but the dark smear of mud across Nettle's hand and cheek made plain that it was already too late.

"Move aside, everyone," Ivy said. She hated to leave Nettle without company in her last moments, but she couldn't risk any of the others getting caught in the Claybane's spell. "You'll have to go around her. Nettle, I'm sorry. We'll come back for you when the air's cleared."

"Aye," said Nettle in a tremulous voice, shuffling to the edge of the tunnel. "I'll be well enough."

They all glided past her, many with sorrowful looks and murmurs of sympathy, but Nettle didn't move. She looked so small and drab that she might have been made of clay already. Ivy was about to call the rest of the crowd to move on when the old woman called out:

"Eh then, young Flint, where are you off to?"

Startled, Ivy turned. Nettle was still standing by the side of the tunnel, looking back into the hazy darkness—and to Ivy's astonishment, the Claybane didn't seem to have affected her.

"Wait," Ivy told the others, and ran to join her. "Are you a faery?" she asked Nettle in a low voice. "No piskey blood at all?"

"Ayes, but what of it?" retorted the other woman. "Your father's just decided to run off and play the hero—or the fool. What good's he going to do going back into that mess?"

Alarm stabbed into Ivy. Surely Flint didn't think he could destroy Gillian's spell with nothing more than his thunder-axe? She ran a few steps into the darkness and glowed as bright as she could, calling his name. But the light only reflected off the thickening haze, and her father did not reply.

"Ivy!" Jenny shouted to her. "My mum's fainting—we have to go!"

For a final moment Ivy wavered, torn between grief and duty. Then she wiped her eyes, took Nettle by the arm, and hurried to rejoin the others.

Minutes later, they had made it safely up the Hunter's Stair and were turning into the Earthenbore when a tremor shook the tunnel behind them. Ivy looked back to see Cicely and Mica sprinting up the Narrows with their own crowd of piskeys, the glow of their skins lighting up the tunnel like noonday—but they too stopped short as the rumbling grew louder.

"What is that?" Cicely shouted up to her, but Ivy shook her head.

"Don't stop!" she called. "Keep running!"

The women who could still fly seized the men at the front of the crowd and began carrying them along, not even waiting for Ivy to tell them where the Claybane ended and safer ground began. Ivy ducked past them and ran along the Earthenbore. "We're almost out!" she yelled as she turned up a side tunnel. "Follow me!"

She dashed through a final patch of Claybane, turned to snatch a rolled-up rug from Hew's hands and flung it down. "Go!" she commanded, and the piskeys flew, leaped, or scrambled across the walls to avoid the trap, then hurtled out the exit to freedom.

"That's the lot," Mica panted, dropping down from the roots he'd used to swing himself along the ceiling. "Let's—"

A billow of gray-green smoke blasted up the tunnel toward them. "Go!" he shouted, shoving Ivy out onto the hillside. Ivy seized his arm, dragging him after her, and the two of them tumbled into the heather—as Gillian's spell exploded out of all the exits of the Delve at once.

For a moment the whole hillside was blanketed in foul smog, and the piskeys pressed their faces to the ground. But soon the smoke cleared, and when Ivy raised her head there was nothing left but a few wisps of vapor. The sky was the color of tin, a gentle rain pattering on the leaves. And to the east the sun glowed softly through the clouds, like a promise that all would be well.

"It's all right," Ivy called to the others, wincing as she climbed to her feet. "We're safe now."

18

It took hours for the smoke in the Delve to clear. The piskeys made camp in the valley, hidden by the strongest glamours the women could cast—but the spot was far from comfortable, and when Ivy came up from exploring the tunnels and announced that the air was fit to breathe again, no one complained about having to leave it. Still, she caught Jenny looking wistfully over her shoulder as they all filed underground, and Ivy knew it would be a long while before the women of the Delve forgot their time in the sunlight.

Nettle gathered a small group of the oldest and most magically talented piskeys to investigate the Claybane, and soon they'd worked up a spell to turn it to harmless dust. But that did nothing to free the ones who were already trapped. It was a grim business finding all the statues scattered around the Delve and carrying them down to the Market Cavern, and only the news that Gillian's body had been found gave Ivy any hope that their efforts would not be wasted.

It was an even darker moment when the knockers clambered out of the passage that had once led to Richard's cell, carrying two bodies on stretchers. First came Flint, his hands crossed over his chest and his face peaceful as a sleeping child's. Then a dripping form with a blanket draped over it, which only Nettle dared to lift as the carriers lowered the stretcher to the floor.

"Oh, little sister," she whispered, a tear sliding down her wizened cheek. "My poor Gillyflower. Who was the slave then, you or me?"

She'd called her *Gillyflower* before, Ivy remembered with a start. She'd even mentioned that she'd had a sister by that name, right after Cicely disappeared. But Ivy had never thought to connect Nettle to Gillian until now.

"Why didn't you say anything?" she asked, crouching beside Nettle. "You must have known who she was, when I came to warn Betony and Gossan."

Nettle wiped her eyes on her sleeve. "I couldn't let her see me like this, all gray and wrinkled. I knew she'd never understand."

"Understand what?" asked Ivy.

"That I loved the Delve, and I didn't want to leave it," Nettle said. "Oh, I was frightened at first, but I married a good knocker, and he was kind to me. And the Joan—the old Joan, before Betony—she treated me like a daughter, after my own mother died." She drew the blanket gently over Gillian's bruised face. "I might've been born faery, but I'm a piskey now. And what's good enough for the others is good enough for me."

There didn't seem to be much Ivy could say to that. She touched Nettle's shoulder in silent sympathy, and backed away.

"Ivy?" whispered Cicely, creeping under her arm. "Is Dad... is he really... gone?"

Yarrow had bandaged Ivy's ribs and dosed her with willow bark, but the thought of Flint made her chest hurt all over again. He'd given his life for the mine he loved, sacrificing himself to destroy Gillian's smoke-spell with one last, mighty blow of his thunder-axe. But the poison that was killing the piskeys of the Delve, weakening their magic and ageing them before their time, was still there. Her father would be honored as a hero, and yet he hadn't really saved anyone in the end.

"I'm afraid so," Ivy said, leaning her head against her sister's. "But Mum's still alive, and maybe she'll wake up soon." Yet even as she spoke, she feared it was too much to hope. If Gillian's death hadn't undone the Claybane, why should it undo any of the other spells she'd cast?

Mica stood on Ivy's other side, watching in silence as the knockers carried their father's body away. He hadn't spoken to Ivy since she'd told him that she'd left the Delve to look for Cicely and find their mother; he hadn't even reacted to the news Marigold was alive. For a time they'd worked together as a team, and he'd seemed willing to listen to her; but now that the crisis that had united them was over, he'd gone back to his old stubborn ways again. Did he blame Ivy for Flint's death? Or was there some other grudge he was holding against her?

Ivy didn't know, and she was too tired to think about it. So when Mica stalked away without looking at her, Ivy let him go.

Gillian's stretcher lay to one side of the tunnel. Yarrow was stooping over the body with bowl and knife in hand, ready to collect the blood that would set the trapped piskeys free. Cicely started forward, but Ivy held her back.

"You don't want to see this," she said. "Go and find Jenny in the Market Cavern. I'll come in a minute."

With obvious reluctance, Cicely obeyed. Ivy watched the healer work, her heart leaden with sorrow. She hadn't meant to kill Gillian, but how could she explain that to Molly?

Yarrow rose, holding out the bowl. "There isn't much," she said. "We'd better try it here first and make sure it works. Did you bring the Joan?"

In answer, Ivy reached into her bag and drew out the tiny statue of Betony. She bit open the cut on her forefinger and squeezed a drop onto the figure's head, then held it out to the healer, who dipped a cloth into the bowl and wiped blood across its feet. Ivy held her breath.

But though they waited for several seconds, then minutes, not a single crack appeared. "I was afraid of that," said Yarrow. "The spell needs the blood of the living, not the dead."

Ivy nodded soberly. There was only one hope left for the piskeys now. But when Molly found out what had happened to her mother, would she be willing to help them?

In all the misery and confusion, with most of the piskeys still gathered in the Market Cavern, it wasn't hard for Ivy to slip out. Moving gingerly to spare her bandaged ribs, she made her way through the twisting passages to the surface. Then she changed shape—it was easy now the effects of the iron had worn off, though she still felt bruised all over—and flew off into the afternoon sky.

Like all piskeys Ivy had a good sense of direction, but in bird form it was keener than ever. Soon she spotted Gillian's workshop, and swooped down to land before the door on her own piskey feet. It was too much to expect that Molly would still be waiting for her, but at least she could see her mother one last time.

Yet when Ivy tore back the covering vines and pushed the door open, she found the building deserted. Gem and Feldspar's statues still stood forlornly upon the shelf, but there was no sign of Marigold—or Richard. All that remained was an overturned bucket of Claybane dust, and a few shards of broken pottery.

Troubled, Ivy took to the air again and wheeled eastward, toward Molly's house. She landed in the yard, changed to human size and ran up the steps to hammer on the door. "Molly! Are you all right? Are you there?"

For a moment no answer came. Then a soft voice said, "Ivy?" Locks clicked, and latches rattled. The door flew open—and with a laugh like a sob, Ivy fell into her mother's arms.

"She woke up after I yelled at her and shook her a few times," Molly said proudly, when Marigold had stopped embracing Ivy long enough to show her inside. The sunlight lay in golden wedges on the carpet, the curtains danced on the breeze, and the sitting room looked as bright and cheerful as Molly herself. "I guess it was like when I got you out of the Claybane—being only half faery I didn't have enough power to break my mum's spell right away, but it worked out in the end." She peered at Ivy's bruised face. "You look awful. What happened?"

This was the moment Ivy had dreaded. "Molly," she said quietly, "your mum is dead."

Molly's cheeks turned ashen. She backed up until her legs bumped the armchair, and then sat down hard. "How?" she asked in a whisper.

"She fell down the Great Shaft," Ivy said. "She was trying to get away, and I was trying to stop her, and the railing broke." She covered her face with her hands. "I'm so sorry."

Molly leaped up and ran from the room. Her door slammed, but even at the other end of the corridor Ivy could hear the human girl weeping. She stood numbly, sure she'd just ruined any chance of Molly ever helping the piskeys of the Delve, until she felt Marigold's arm circle her shoulders.

"Come and sit down," her mother said. "Tell me everything."

It took a long time for Ivy to explain all that had happened, and by the time she finished her throat was raw and her chest ached with unshed tears. "I couldn't stop Dad from going down there," she said. "It was like he *wanted* to die, and it was such a waste—I never even got to tell him you were alive—"

Marigold touched the place where her wedding pendant had once rested, the lines around her mouth deepening with sorrow. "Oh, my love," she whispered, as though Flint could hear her. "We made so many mistakes, you and I."

"I made a lot of mistakes too," said Ivy. "When I talked to the man in the market and found out that someone had erased his memory the way you did mine, I thought..." She faltered at her mother's sharp inhale, and raised pleading eyes to hers. "I know. It wasn't you selling the piskeys, it was Gillian. But... I was right about what you did to me, wasn't I?"

Marigold closed her eyes. "I didn't know what else to do," she said. "When I came out from the bedroom that night and you asked me why I was crying, I couldn't lie. I thought perhaps if I told you a little of the truth it would be all right, and you'd understand why I had to go. But you guessed too much—things too dangerous for you to know—"

"What things?" asked Ivy, but Marigold shook her head.

"I can't tell you," she said. "But... when you realized what was happening, you wanted to come with me. I told you that the surface world wasn't safe, that there were spriggans and faeries and all kinds of danger, and that I didn't even know if I would survive. But you said you'd follow me anyway. And I—I couldn't let you do that." Tears glimmered in her lashes. "I'm sorry. Please forgive me."

Ivy's thoughts were in turmoil, and she didn't know what to say. But when Marigold reached out to her, she didn't resist. They clung to each other for a long time, and when Ivy raised her head Molly was standing in front of them, her eyes swollen but no longer wet. How long had she been listening? Ivy was afraid to ask, but then Molly spoke:

"I'm sorry about your dad," she said. "And I'm sorry about what my mum did, too." Her lips quivered, but she pressed them together and went on in a rush, "If you think my blood can help the other piskeys, the way it helped you—then I'll come."

Gratitude warmed Ivy's chest. Awkwardly she rose and hugged Molly as hard as her bandaged ribs would allow. "Thank you," she whispered, knowing what she said and meaning it—that her debt to the human girl was greater than she could ever repay. "Thank you, Molly."

Molly had never been to the Delve before, so Marigold couldn't take the two girls there by magic—and none of them knew how to drive Gillian's car, either. But Molly had ridden Duchess back from the workshop that morning, and now that Dodger's leg had healed there was no reason they couldn't take him along as well. It seemed that Ivy would get a proper ride of her own after all, especially since they still had to pick up Gem and Feldspar on the way—though with all her aches and pains, she feared she wouldn't get much pleasure out of it.

"Come with us," said Ivy to Marigold, as Molly led the newly saddled horses into the yard. "Please."

But Marigold only gave a sad smile. "I'm afraid not," she said. "Tell Mica and Cicely that I love them, and that if they can find it in their hearts to forgive me, my door will always be open. But I can never return to the Delve."

"Why not?" asked Ivy. "Surely it's not going to kill you

to come back for a few minutes? Betony's trapped in the Claybane—she's not going to make any problems for you."

"You don't understand. I—" She put a hand to her throat. "I can't."

Bitterness welled up in Ivy. She turned her face against Dodger's warm, quivering neck and said, "All right."

"But don't forget what I told you about the poison," Marigold urged, as Ivy climbed stiffly onto the horse's back. "Don't throw your life away. Please, get away from that place as soon as you can, and come back to me."

With her brown eyes brimming with anxiety and her hands clasped against her heart, she was the very picture of a concerned mother. Yet she wouldn't return to the Delve even to see her other children... and she hadn't offered to heal Ivy's injuries, either. Was healing like shape-changing—something that only male faeries did? Or was it a hint to Ivy, that she couldn't expect any favors unless she did as Marigold wanted?

If so, Ivy was having none of it. She was sick of faery half-truths and manipulations. She'd managed without her mother before; there was no reason she couldn't do it again.

"The Delve is my home," Ivy said, straightening up in the saddle. "And Cicely and Mica need someone to look after them. Maybe you couldn't convince Aunt Betony to listen to you, but I'm not going to give up until I do. Goodbye."

Then she touched her heels to Dodger's sides and they trotted after Molly and Duchess, leaving Marigold behind.

It had been more than a century since any human set foot in the Delve, and not even the most curious explorer had ever seen the tunnels the piskeys had dug for themselves. But Ivy had used her magic to turn Molly piskey-size, and now she followed Ivy through the passages in hushed awe, once or twice lifting a hand to touch the mosaics and semi-precious stones that adorned the walls.

They reached the lower levels of the Delve unnoticed. But when the two of them walked into the Market and the piskeys caught sight of the stranger in human clothing, shocked exclamations rose from every side. As Ivy set Gem and Feldspar's statues down and hurried to Betony's, she could feel Mica's glare boring into her from the other side of the cavern. But before he could march up and demand an explanation, she held out her hand to the prick of Molly's pocketknife, and they stooped to wipe their blood across the trapped Joan's brow and feet.

A tense moment passed, and Ivy began to fear her kinship with the Joan might not be close enough after all. But at last the clay began to crack, then crumble, and in a shower of dust Betony burst free, transforming to her proper piskey size.

"The Joan!" shouted Hew, leaping up and waving his cap in the air. "Our Joan's come alive again!"

And with that the cavern erupted into chaos, as everyone came running to see the miracle. Ivy nearly shouted herself hoarse before she could quiet the crowd and explain. But once the piskeys realized who Molly was and why she had come here, they started hushing one another and chivvying themselves into order. Soon each family had lined up beside the statues of their loved ones, while Yarrow bent over Molly's arm with a lancet.

"Molly, is it?" said Nettle, when the healer had finished the bloodletting and carried the bowl away. "Bless your brave soul, lass. I can't tell you what Gillyflower would have said, but as your aunt, I'm that proud of you." Then she patted Molly's cheek and limped off, leaving the human girl blinking with astonishment.

"How can she be my aunt?" she asked Ivy. "She's a piskey. And she's *old.*"

Too old, thought Ivy. She must be unusually tough to have survived even this long underground, and she probably wouldn't live many years longer. But that was more than Molly needed to know at the moment. So she kept her eyes on the bandage she was tying around Molly's arm and said only, "She was your mother's older sister. Faeries live a long time."

Meanwhile Yarrow hurried about the cavern with bowl and rag in hand, touching each of the statues' feet. Gossan was the next to break free of the Claybane, and in seconds he and Betony were embracing. One by one the trapped piskeys emerged from their shells, and the cavern echoed with shouts of joy.

"We did it," Molly said. But her smile was wan, and so was Ivy's. They'd saved the Delve together, but it would be a long time before either one of them felt happy again.

"Come on," Ivy told her, holding out her hand to the girl. "I'll take you home."

As soon as they returned to the house, Molly rang her father and the local police to tell them that Gillian had disappeared while exploring the site of an old mine. Ivy stayed with her as long as she could—after all the noisy jubilation of the Market Cavern, the Menadues' house was almost unbearably quiet, and it seemed cruel to leave Molly there alone. But as soon as the first car turned up the lane, Ivy hugged the girl goodbye and flew back to the Delve.

As she walked the tunnels, one piskey after another rushed up to embrace her or pump her hand in gratitude. Many wanted to know where she'd been for so long, and what she meant to do now—especially Mattock, who gazed down at her with an admiration that bordered on worship, and went on holding her hand long after he'd stopped shaking it. But though Ivy was glad to see all of them, she didn't like being the focus of so much attention. She excused herself, telling them she was too tired to talk about it at the moment, and hurried on.

Ivy had never meant to be a hero, and it bothered her to find herself treated as one. Especially since she wondered whether the Delve would ever have been in danger at all, if not for her. Yes, Gillian could still have found the right mine by process of elimination—that was what the map in the Menadues' study had been about, after all. But she couldn't have set her traps half so effectively without Cicely's help. And she would never have got her hands on Cicely if not for Ivy.

Fortunately, Cicely seemed to have forgiven her mistakes, or at least she hadn't thrown them in Ivy's face yet. But Ivy wasn't so sure about Mica. He had taken Flint's death harder than any of them, and judging by the stony look he'd given Ivy when she and Molly left the Market Cavern, he wasn't nearly as impressed with her accomplishments as Mattock...

Lost in thought, Ivy turned the corner into Long Way—and froze. The door to her family cavern was open, the day-lamps spilling light into the corridor. And standing outside the doorway, her arms folded and her broad mouth set with disapproval, was Betony.

Ivy's muscles locked up, and every instinct screamed at her to fly. But she was done with running and hiding. Mica and Cicely needed to hear the truth about Marigold's disappearance and the poison in the mine, and so did Betony, whether she chose to do anything about it or not.

Squaring her shoulders, Ivy stepped forward. "My Joan," she said. "How can I serve you?"

It was nerve-wracking—and humiliating—to have to stand before her aunt like a criminal and give account of herself, with Cicely and Mica looking on. Especially once it became clear that Betony had already questioned Cicely, and learned that Ivy had been sneaking out of the Delve on a regular basis. She'd also searched the cavern and found the rope Ivy had used to climb up and down the shaft to Richard's cell.

After that, it was no use hoping that her aunt wouldn't make the connection between Ivy's nighttime absences and the "spriggan" who had so mysteriously escaped from her dungeon. And when Betony demanded to know whether Ivy had set the prisoner free, she had no choice but to admit it.

"But it was all a mistake," Ivy insisted. "He had nothing to do with Keeve disappearing—that was Gillian's fault. And if you'd left him to starve—"

"It would have been no more than he deserved," said Betony coldly. "Do you think I didn't recognize what he was the moment I saw him? Spriggan or not, he was a servant of the Empress, come to spy out our defenses. If I had let him go, he would have returned with more of his kind, and turned us all into her slaves."

Ivy was startled. "You know about the Empress?"

"The old Joan warned me against her, when she passed on her power to me. The Empress has been a threat to our people for decades, and part of the oath I swore when I became the Joan was that I would do my utmost to keep even one piskey from falling into her hands." Her chin lifted proudly. "So I made sure that Gossan taught every hunter and forager to avoid faeries at all cost, and never go more than a few miles from the Delve. And I encouraged the old legends about spriggans and faeries to be retold at every Lighting, so that my people would never forget how dangerous the outside world could be."

And naturally, the women and children who'd heard those legends had assumed the spriggans to be the real danger. Even the men who knew better wouldn't be likely to correct them, since they wanted to keep their families safe just as much as the Joan did. Not a direct lie, just an omission... and done with the best of intentions, however unfortunate the result.

Still, it was high time the truth came out. "The Empress is dead," Ivy told her. "We don't have to hide any longer."

"Dead!" Betony's brows shot up, but then her eyes narrowed again. "Is that what *he* told you? What makes you so sure he wasn't deceiving you, so as to betray you to his mistress?"

Ivy wasn't sure of anything, where Richard was concerned. He'd provoked her and bargained with her, puzzled and frustrated her, and nearly everything about his past was still a mystery, including his proper name. And when she asked Molly where his statue had gone, the human girl had seemed just as baffled to find him missing as Ivy had been.

But wherever he'd come from, whomever he'd once served, she owed him too much to deny him now. "He wasn't working for the Empress, he was working for my mother," she said, watching Betony for her reaction. "But it doesn't matter. Gillian turned him into a statue, and we couldn't turn him back."

If Betony was surprised to hear Marigold was alive, she didn't show it. "I see," said the Joan, and her mouth relaxed. "Then we have one less threat to worry about. So you set the prisoner free, believing he could take you to your mother?"

"Yes," said Ivy. "And he did. I met her a few days later, alive and well. That's when I found out she was a faery, and she told me—"

Betony cut her off. "I am not interested in what Marigold had to say. She was strange and unnatural from the first, and I should have known she wasn't a true piskey. She has no business meddling in the affairs of the Delve."

"No business?" Ivy could barely speak for outrage. "She has a husband and three children here!" But then she saw apprehension flicker in Betony's eyes, and all at once she understood. "You knew why my mother left, didn't you? You knew because you *made* her leave. Banishing her was the only way you could stop her talking about the poison in the Delve."

"Poison?" exclaimed Cicely, sitting up. "You mean the spell that Dad—"

"Not that poison," said Ivy. "I mean the one that's been killing our people for years." She turned to her sister. "Haven't you ever wondered why our people age and die so quickly, when other magical folk live far longer? Why I was born without wings, and Mum started coughing blood, and Dad got sicker every day he worked in the diggings?" In fact that might well have been the reason Flint had started working so hard once Marigold was gone—because he'd realized that the only way to prove the mine was dangerous was to poison himself. "We can't keep living like this. We have to change our ways, or—"

"How dare you talk as though *you* know what's best for our people!" snapped Betony. "You're as treacherous as your mother, and if you don't hold your tongue, I'll stop it for you."

Ivy opened her mouth—and another realization hit her. The reason for Marigold's abrupt silences and vague explanations, her refusal to return to the Delve. The way she'd choked and touched her throat whenever she said too much ...

"You made her swear not to tell anyone what you did to her," she said to Betony, hoarse with disbelief. "You made her promise never to go near the Delve again."

Color rose to Betony's cheeks, but her haughty expression

didn't alter. "She agreed to those terms in exchange for her life. And it was a fairer bargain than she deserved."

Once again, Ivy had misjudged her mother because of someone else's deceit. Rage welled inside her, and her fingers stiffened into claws—but no, she couldn't fly at Betony now, it would ruin everything. She had to think of Cicely and Mica, too.

"Well, you can threaten me all you like," she said defiantly, "but I'm not my mother, and you can't frighten me into making the bargain she did. I know this mine is poisoned—I'm living proof—and I'm going to stay here until you do something about it."

The Joan stalked up to Ivy, robes billowing. "You know *nothing,*" she spat. "You were born wingless because your mother's blood was weak, and for no other reason. You crave sunlight because she did, but that has nothing to do with the rest of us. The only danger in the Delve was the enemy *you* brought here by your carelessness, and the only poison that has ever threatened us was the spell your father gave his life to destroy."

"That's not true!" Ivy shouted at her. "How can you be so blind? The piskeys of the Delve are your responsibility, and most of them have faery as well as piskey blood, just like I do. They need you to give them their freedom, not sit there and watch them die so you can stay in power!"

Betony slapped her across the face.

Cicely shrank back, and Mica started halfway to his feet as Ivy and her aunt stared at each other, both of them breathing hard. Then with deadly softness the Joan spoke. "For generations we piskeys have poured our lives into this mine. We have made it a place of beauty and strength, our people's greatest pride. It protected us from the spriggans while they lived, and since then it has hidden us from the Empress and her servants. It is safe, it is secure—and most of all, it is secret. That is how our people have survived.

"But when this faery, this stranger, appeared in our midst, you forgot all of that. You disobeyed my order to stay away from the prisoner, and allowed him to seduce you into setting him free. What did he offer you, to make you believe you could trust him? Did he tell you he would shower you with treasure, and make you his queen?"

Nausea gripped Ivy's throat. "No. What makes you think I would want—*no.*"

"Then what?"

She couldn't lie, much as she wanted to. "He said he would teach me to fly."

Betony regarded her in astonishment, then threw back her head and laughed. "And you believed him?"

But horror was dawning on Mica's face, and Ivy knew he'd finally put the pieces together: their conversation about shape-changing, the swift he'd marked out as an impostor and felled with one deadly stone, the way Ivy had vanished when he and Flint needed her most.

Don't say it, Ivy begged him silently. *If you ever loved me at all, don't tell her that I can change shape.*

For one last moment Mica held her gaze. Then abruptly he got up and walked to the other side of the cavern. He braced his hands against the wall and bent his head between them, and he did not look back.

"Your brother is ashamed of you," said Betony. "As he should be." She raised her voice, pronouncing each word distinctly as she went on. "You have admitted to consorting with a servant of the Empress, and releasing him against my orders. You left the Delve on several occasions without permission, and enticed an innocent child to follow your example. You revealed your piskey nature to a human girl—whom you then brought into the Delve. Any one of those crimes would be worthy of severe punishment, but all together, there can be no question that you deserve to die."

Cicely whimpered. Mica turned, but he didn't speak. Ivy stood unmoving, staring straight ahead as the Joan continued:

"But you are my brother's daughter, and you and Mica and Cicely are the last of our family line. For the sake of Flint's memory, and because of what you did to destroy the faery Gillian and undo her spells, I will not have you executed. But it is clear you have little respect for my authority, and that if I allow you to remain you will spread sedition among my subjects. So..." She drew herself up. "I banish you from the Delve, now and forever. Go where you wish and call yourself what you will, but you are no longer a piskey."

"No!" cried Cicely, leaping off the sofa and throwing her arms around Ivy. "You can't! She didn't mean me to follow her out of the Delve, she was trying to find our mother! And she saved your life! All our lives!"

"Cicely, get away from her," said Mica, striding over. "Don't be a fool."

"No!" Cicely shouted at him. "You can stay here and poison yourself to death if you want, but I won't!" She turned pleading eyes up to Ivy. "Take me away with you. Please. I want to see Mum again."

Ivy looked at the Joan, whose face might have been chiseled out of granite. "Let me take Cicely," Ivy said, "and I won't fight you. We'll leave the Delve together, and you can tell everyone we went to live with Marigold."

"Very well," said Betony. "But you'll go at once, without speaking to anyone. And you'll take nothing with you." She turned to Mica. "If you wish to prove your loyalty, son of Flint, you'll see to that." Then she stalked out the door and slammed it behind her, the day-lamps flickering in her wake.

Cicely hid her face against Ivy and burst into tears. Mica

stood awkwardly for a moment, then put out a hand and patted his little sister's hair.

"You'll look out for them, won't you?" Ivy asked him. "Mattock and Jenny and the others." Even if Mica was too disgusted to even look at Ivy any more, even if he was determined to stay in the Delve at any cost, he must know that their mother hadn't been lying about the poison in the mine. He was the only one who could help the piskeys now.

But Mica didn't reply. He walked to the door and held it open. "You'd better get moving," he said gruffly. "You've got a long way to go."

EPILOGUE

Sunlight warmed the treetops, and the sky was untroubled by cloud. Ivy glided over the countryside, swift-wings outstretched on the breeze. She and Cicely had been staying with Marigold for three days now, and though Ivy hadn't minded looking after her sister and showing her the sights of Truro, she'd been longing all the while to fly again.

She hadn't told either of them about her shape-changing. Male faeries might be accustomed to transforming themselves into birds or animals, but it seemed that females had a different approach to magic, and she feared that even Marigold wouldn't be pleased to find that her daughter could become a swift.

So what was Ivy now—a piskey, or a faery, or neither? Would she ever find a place she belonged? Ivy didn't know, and it troubled her. Especially since it had already become clear that a one-bedroom flat was too small for three, and that feeding two growing daughters was straining Marigold's income to the limit.

But Ivy was still too young to live on her own, even if she'd felt confident enough posing as a human to try. And she couldn't ask Molly for help, not when she and her father were still grieving...

A crow flapped overhead, and with a flick of her wingtips

Ivy increased speed, leaving the bigger bird behind. It posed no threat, but part of her would scarcely have minded if it had. At least that would have given her a challenge to surmount, an enemy that she could defeat. At least that might have made her feel not quite so useless.

Soon another bird rose up on her left side—only a small one, but Ivy had no desire for company. She angled away, catching an updraft so she could be alone again. But the newcomer followed, easily matching her speed. She was about to shriek a warning and put the other bird in its place when it chirruped at her, rolled and tapped her with one outstretched foot in a very un-birdlike way. Then it dived toward the riverbank, fluttered to a halt—and transformed into a slim, angular faery with blond hair falling into his eyes.

Ivy's heart swelled with incredulous delight. So she and Molly had been right to use their blood on him, back in Gillian's workshop—though why it had worked she couldn't imagine. She plunged through the air and landed beside him in her own shape. "Richard! I thought you'd been trapped forever!"

"So did I, for a while," he replied. "But it seems that all the magic I put into healing you made us kinfolk of a sort after all. There's a precedent, but I won't embarrass you with the details." He gave his sly smile. "So you got my message, then?"

"What? Oh." He must mean the dream-message he'd sent her while he was trapped. She didn't have the heart to tell him how misleading his broken words and scattered memories had been, or how little difference they'd made in the end. "Yes. I'm sorry it took us so long to set you free."

"I didn't think anyone could." He was serious now, his gray eyes sober as she'd ever seen them. "It appears I owe you my life. Again."

"I don't think so," said Ivy, blushing a little. "I never repaid you properly for saving me from Mica, and you only got trapped in the Claybane because you were trying to find Cicely for me. If anything I'm in your debt, not the other way around."

"Tell me the rest of your story, then, and we'll call it even." He motioned to the grassy bank beside him, inviting her to sit. "I had part of it from Molly, but she told me you'd gone back to the Delve. What brings you here?"

She sat cross-legged by the river's edge and told him everything, her restless fingers tearing at the long grass until her hands were sticky with sap. She told Richard how she'd stopped Gillian and rescued the piskeys, how she'd gone with Cicely into exile, and all that had happened since.

"But I don't know what to do," she finished. "I can't keep living with my mum—there's not enough room, and Cicely needs her more than I do. And I can't return to the Delve, not while Betony's in control."

With an expert flick of the wrist Richard sent a stone skipping across the water; it bounced three times before it sank. "Why not try the other half of your ancestry?" he said. "There must be a faery wyld somewhere that would take you, if you made yourself useful."

Ivy had considered that, but the thought of walking into a group of strange faeries and asking to join them, especially now that she knew what her piskey ancestors had done to their kind, made her uneasy. "If I did, would you come with me?"

"Not an option." He picked up another stone, turning it slowly in his fingers. "You see, I'm a fugitive at the moment."

Ivy was startled. "What for?"

"Murder. Or actually, two." The pebble changed to a silver dagger; he stabbed it point-down into the grass. "Last spring I killed the Empress and her would-be successor in front of about five hundred other faeries. And I've been running ever since."

"*You* killed the Empress? How? I mean—why?" No, that

wasn't the right question either; the answers were obvious already. "What happened?"

"Ask Marigold. She saw me do it. And she was glad."

Were you? Ivy almost asked, but she knew the answer to that question as well. If he'd had any joy in killing the Empress, it hadn't lasted long. *Is there a murderer here? No. I am...*

"Are you afraid of me?" asked Richard. He spoke lightly, as though he were indifferent to the answer. Only a slight twitch in his cheek said otherwise.

Ivy considered this. "No."

"You might want to think a little longer about that," he said. "The Claybane worked on me, remember... and whoever my parents were, I very much doubt either one of them was a piskey. I'm no good with horses, but I admit to being quite interested in treasure, and I seem to have a way of influencing air currents, not to mention probabilities..."

That startled a laugh out of Ivy. "You mean that after all this, you really *are* a spriggan?"

"Part spriggan, anyway. I don't see what else I could be." He pulled the dagger out of the ground, flipped it back into a pebble, and let it fall. "I always knew I wasn't quite like other faeries, but I never knew why. Now I wonder where I came from, and if there's anything—or anyone—left to go back to."

"We could try and find out," said Ivy.

Richard gave her a sidelong look. "Are you offering to come with me?"

Ivy picked a few more blades of grass and let them flutter away on the breeze. Finally she said, "I want to help my people. But I don't know how, yet. I need to learn. I need to travel. I need to find something that will make Aunt Betony listen to me—or convince the others that they ought to listen even if she won't." She turned back to him. "So yes, I would like to come. If that's all right."

One corner of his mouth turned up. "If it's what you

want, I know better than to try and stop you. But it won't be comfortable. Or safe. And I can't tell you where we'll be going."

"That's all right. I don't have anywhere particular in mind." She gave him a tentative smile and added, "And you can teach me more about birds on the way."

He rose slowly, dusting off his trousers, and gazed down at her a moment. Then he said, "We can start with the house martin. That's the bird-shape I take most often. And it's also my name. Martin."

"Good," said Ivy, taking the hand he offered and letting him pull her to her feet. "Richard didn't really suit you, anyway."

THE STORY CONTINUES
IN THE FLIGHT AND FLAME TRILOGY
BOOK 2: *NOMAD*

ACKNOWLEDGMENTS

Thanks to Steve Laube and the team at Enclave Publishing for giving Ivy another chance to fly, and to my agent Josh Adams for helping us work out all the details to make that happen.

Swift would not be half the book it is without the loyal support, shrewd insights, and generous assistance of Pete Anderson, Erin Bow, Deva Fagan, Meg Burden, Brittany Harrison, Saundra Mitchell, and Kate Johnson. I'm also grateful for Brittany Landgrebe, who suggested the title on Twitter and started the whole idea percolating; Lesley Livingston, who helped me find the perfect Shakespearean soliloquy for "Richard" to introduce himself; Thu Ya Win, whose photos and insights were invaluable in helping me get to know the city of Truro even before I'd had the chance to see it for myself; and Michelle Minniss, who graciously read over the manuscript to make sure I'd got various Cornish details right.

Finally, thanks to all the faithful readers and reviewers who've e-mailed, tweeted and contacted me on Facebook to let me know they've enjoyed my other books and have been looking forward to this one. Here it is, and I hope you found it worth the wait!

About the Author

Born in Uganda to missionary parents, R.J. (Rebecca Joan) Anderson is a women's Bible teacher, a wife and mother of three, and a bestselling fantasy author for older children and teens. Her debut novel *Knife* has sold more than 120,000 copies worldwide, while her other books have been shortlisted for the Nebula Award, the Christy Award, and the Sunburst Award for Excellence in Canadian Science Fiction. Rebecca lives with her family in Stratford, Ontario, Canada.

FORGET EVERYTHING
YOU THINK YOU KNOW ABOUT
FAERIES...

DISCOVER THE SECRETS OF MARTIN'S PAST
AND THE BATTLE AGAINST THE EVIL FAERY EMPRESS IN

Knife

Rebel

Arrow

Available Now!

www.enclavepublishing.com